A Mute Gospel

The People and Culture of the Medieval English Common Fields

SHERRI OLSON

Mainstream historiography has traditionally found the roots of peasant action, and much of the meaning of that action, in legal status difference between lords and peasants, and among peasants themselves. In the last several decades, this older class conflict model has lost some ground to an interpretation of status that still emphasizes difference but focuses on questions of gender, sexuality, and "alterity." Other students of medieval rural society have shifted interest away from questions of status, and focused instead on peasant economic influence and self-determination. Such evolving models of peasants' economic and political agency have not only extended our understanding of the complexity of rural life, they have made the issue of villager identity as significant a research objective as the identity of members of the elite, merchants, city-dwellers, and saints. The goal of this study is to gain a more balanced view of medieval society by considering how peasants thought about themselves and their world as revealed in English manorial court rolls and other records of estate administration.

STUDIES AND TEXTS 162

A Mute Gospel

The People and Culture of the Medieval English Common Fields

SHERRI OLSON

PONTIFICAL INSTITUTE OF MEDIAEVAL STUDIES

Library and Archives Canada Cataloguing in Publication

Olson, Sherri, 1954–
A mute gospel : the people and culture of the medieval English common fields / Sherri Olson.

(Studies and texts, 0082–5328 ; 162)
Includes bibliographical references and index.

ISBN 978–0–88844–162–1

1. Peasantry – England – History. 2. Manorial courts – England. 3. Court records – England. 4. Commons – England – History. 5. Community life – England – History. 6. Village communities – England – History. 7. England – Social life and customs – Medieval period, 1066–1485. 8. Great Britain – History – Medieval period, 1066–1485. I. Pontifical Institute of Mediaeval Studies II. Title. III. Series: Studies and texts (Pontifical Institute of Mediaeval Studies) 162

HD1534.O48 2009 305.5'63309420902 C2008-907971-X

59 Queen's Park Crescent East
Toronto, Ontario, Canada M5S 2C4

www.pims.ca

MANUFACTURED IN CANADA

For Arthur, Aidan, and Josiah

and in memory of my mother
Mary Louise Woodcox Olson
1927–2004

and of my teacher, Father J. Ambrose Raftis, CSB,
1922–2008

All things with which we deal, preach to us. What is a farm but a mute gospel? The chaff and the wheat, weeds and plants, blight, rain, insects, sun, – it is a sacred emblem from the first furrow of spring to the last stack which the snow of winter overtakes in the fields.

RALPH WALDO EMERSON, *Nature* (1836)

Fields have eyes and woods have ears.

Proverb, dated to 1225

Table of Contents

Acknowledgments

Portions of Chapter Five were given at a conference on English Court Rolls at the University of Copenhagen and the University of Aarhus, Denmark, in March 1997, and at the International Congress on Medieval Studies at Kalamazoo in May 1997. Portions of other chapters were presented subsequently at conferences at SUNY Binghamton, Barnard College, Fordham University, the University of Leeds, the Annual Conference of the Centre for Medieval Studies at the University of Toronto, sessions of the International Congress on Medieval Studies at Kalamazoo, and the New England Historical Association's Fall Meeting. My thanks to the people who heard these papers and gave me valuable commentary and criticism. I would also like to thank the two anonymous readers for the Pontifical Institute of Mediaeval Studies' Publications Department for their careful reading of the manuscript. It is my pleasure gratefully to acknowledge Arthur Smith, John Sexton (who also compiled the index) and Erin Heidkamp who gave so generously of their time to read the entire manuscript, and make excellent suggestions on revisions (most of which I followed) and corrections. Of course, the mistakes that remain are mine alone.

I wish to thank the University of Connecticut Humanities Institute for a Faculty Residential Fellowship for the academic year 2004–2005, which allowed me to complete most of the research and much of the writing of this book. I am also grateful to the History Department, the Medieval Studies Program, the Office of the Dean of the College of Liberal Arts and Sciences, the Office of the Provost, and the Humanities Institute, all of the University of Connecticut, for their financial contributions towards the publication costs of this book.

I would like to pay special respects to Father J. Ambrose Raftis, who passed away 20 April 2008. He was an unfailing source of inspiration, from the first seminar I took with him in Toronto in the fall of 1980 up to the present as I have re-read some of his scholarship while working on the present book. I like to think of *A Mute Gospel* as a study that has tried to follow up on some of the questions he raised more than forty years ago in *Tenure and Mobility* (1964), and I hope that he would have allowed me that indulgence.

INTRODUCTION

Peasant Culture and the Village Court: Medieval England's "Invisible World"

The student of history who works with English manorial court rolls can, like any other historian, create a "usable past": an interpretation of a historical period or topic that is informed by the desire to understand, perhaps even improve, the present. As William Bouwsma explains it:

> [H]istory is not the private preserve of professional historians, just as divinity, law, and medicine do not "belong" to clergymen, lawyers, and physicians. Like other professional groups, historians are properly the servants of a public that needs historical perspective to understand itself and its values, and perhaps also to acknowledge its limitations and its guilt. Historians have an obligation, I believe, to meet public needs of this kind.[1]

We may consider the notion of a usable past further by looking at a fairly commonplace entry, taken from the court roll for the village of Upwood, dated 6 December 1333, which records that Agnes, the

1 William J. Bouwsma, *A Usable Past: Essays in European Cultural History* (Berkeley, 1990), 1. Indeed, Bouwsma speaks of History as a "public utility ... much like water and electricity." Similarly, for a focus on revitalizing local government and local control, see J.A. Raftis, *A Small Town in Late Mediaeval England: Godmanchester, 1278–1400* (Toronto, 1982). In his study of artisan autobiography of the early modern period, James S. Amelang remarks that in "recovering their present, we recover our past. We also take a small step toward a more democratic history, and toward a more democratic culture." *The Flight of Icarus: Artisan Autobiography in Early Modern Europe* (Stanford, 1998), 9. A recent example of this kind of history is also found in Judith Bennett, *History Matters: Patriarchy and the Challenge of Feminism* (Philadelphia, 2006).

widow of Stephen le Write, comes into the court and publicly affirms her right to hold, for the remainder of her life, the tenement she had held with her husband, according to the custom of the manor, and that she takes the oath to perform all services and render all dues faithfully (*venit ... et clamat dictam terram esse suam ad terminum vite sue secundum consuetudinem manerii ... . Et facit fidelitatem* [*servitii*]).[2] This entry might be read for the light it sheds on the transmission of land within the family, on widow's rights and peasant marriage, on the incidents of customary tenure, or on the court's sphere of authority and the power of localism, among other possibilities. Evidence of a fourteenth-century countrywoman taking an oath in a public forum regarding her own future conduct, thus assuming to some degree a legal identity in her own right and by her own words, might also serve the writing of a "usable past" by historians of gender. In the present book, this entry is approached within a cultural history framework as evidence for the complex agency of the individual in a society founded mostly on "collective habits and responsibilities," to use Susan Reynolds's phrase.[3]

Mainstream historiography has traditionally found the roots of peasant action, and much of the meaning of that action, in legal status differences between lords and peasants and among peasants themselves. In the last several decades, this older class conflict model has lost some ground to an interpretation of status that still emphasizes difference but focuses on questions of gender, sexuality, "alterity," in addition to legal status.[4] Other students of medieval rural society have shifted interest away from questions of status and focused instead on

2 See citation and translation in J.A. Raftis, *Tenure and Mobility* (Toronto, 1964), 38, 218. (For an example where the full extension of the phrase regarding the oath *Et facit fidelitatem servitii* can be found, see pages 35 and 216). The issue of women's activity in the court is addressed below, in Chapters One and Two.

3 Susan Reynolds, *Kingdoms and Communities in Western Europe, 900–1300* (2nd ed., Oxford; New York, 1997), 122. For a useful discussion of rural collective activity, see especially Chapter Five, "Villagers and Rural Neighbourhoods."

4 A good recent review of developments in the historiography of medieval English peasants may be found in Phillipp Schofield, *Peasant and Community in Medieval England, 1200–1500* (New York, 2003), especially the chapters dealing with markets and politics (Chapters Seven and Eight).

peasant economic influence and self-determination. Thus, it has been shown that peasant initiative drove the demand for land in the countryside; peasant economic production was significantly influenced by urban commodity markets and stimulated rural industries; and much of the work of government, particularly in its day-to-day aspects, was done by villagers.[5] Such evolving models of peasants' economic and political agency have not only extended our understanding of the complexity of rural life, they have made the issue of villager identity as significant a research objective as the identities of the elite, merchants, city-dwellers, and saints.

Ellington and Upwood, the villages whose documents will be investigated in this study, are highly representative of the kinds of farming communities that underlay the medieval economy and sustained most of Europe's pre-modern population. More than half a century ago, R.W. Southern noted the powers of endurance of medieval village life, observing that "there was probably remarkably little difference between the life of the peasant in the thirteenth century and in the village before it was transformed by modern mechanisms." Medieval civilization bears the impress of the village, which "communicated to society at large in all its activities the rhythm and standards of workmanship of a peasant community ... village life is the basis of every activity, and scholars and artists carry into the world of the spirit the qualities learnt in the stubborn struggle with the land."[6] Indeed the omnipresence of such communities, in time

5 See J.A. Raftis, *Peasant Economic Development within the English Manorial System* (Montreal, 1996); James Masschaele, *Peasants, Merchants, and Markets: Inland Trade in Medieval England, 1150–1350* (New York, 1997); Christopher Dyer, *Making a Living in the Middle Ages: The People of Britain, 850–1520* (New Haven, 2002), especially pp. 163–178; Susan Reynolds, *Kingdoms and Communities*; Rosamond Faith, *The English Peasantry and the Growth of Lordship* (London, 1997); and Sherri Olson, *A Chronicle of All That Happens: Voices from the Village Court in Medieval England* (Toronto, 1996).

6 Richard Southern, *The Making of the Middle Ages* (1953; repr., New Haven, 1992), 74–76. For other studies that have drawn particular attention to the role of peasants in the formation of medieval civilization, see works cited in note 5 above. Note in particular James Masschaele's discussion of the formation of markets in England in *Peasants, Merchants, and Markets*, where he points out that the shape these commercial

and place, enhances the value (perhaps even the "usable-ness") of the present inquiry and others like it, since they may add to our understanding of the farming village in its universal history: as Edward Muir has pointed out, whether our ancestors originally came from Asia, Africa, or Europe, they "shared a common experience of living and working in farming villages. Until very recently that was the common lot of most of humankind."[7] A study of the interiority of "ordinary people," in this case, medieval peasants, and of their power, collectively and as individuals, to construct and influence their world, may contribute to the writing of a usable past.

Objectives

The purpose of this introduction is to lay out a threefold argument: first, that current interest in the study of mentality can be pursued for medieval rural society, even though in proportion to their numbers countrymen and women have been relatively neglected in mainstream historiography; second, that highly diverse materials survive for the study of peasant mentality, including (among others) medieval proverb collections, homiletic material, and the records of estate administration, in which last category pride of place must be reserved for the court roll; and, third, that the collective framework of village society was a formative influence on peasant personality and fostered a sense of power. A general model of peasant mentality will be outlined here, with in-depth treatment of selected aspects of that mentality to be covered in the chapters that follow.

Reconstruction of an Invisible World

The present book takes inspiration from Albert J. Raboteau's book *Slave Religion: The "Invisible World" of the Antebellum South,* a study of "black religion under slavery," a topic once overlooked or

---

patterns took by the thirteenth century survived intact down to the era of the Industrial Revolution.

7 Edward Muir, introduction to *The Renaissance in the Fields: Family Memoirs of a Fifteenth-Century Tuscan Peasant*, ed. Duccio Balestracci, trans. Paolo Squatriti and Betsy Merideth (University Park, PA, 1999), x.

derided in the mainstream historiography of slavery.[8] According to Raboteau, while prejudice was an overwhelming factor in historians' neglect of slave religion, another reason was "the assumption that sources for a study of slave religion simply [did] not exist."[9] The world of slave beliefs and experience was unknown because it was thought to be both unknowable and unworthy of being known, hence "invisible." Until quite recently, a similar state of affairs has existed for the mainstream historiography of the Middle Ages: the "world of belief and experience" of medieval peasants, typically seen as a "subaltern" class, was to a considerable extent an "invisible world."

Seeking to recover and understand medieval peasant mentality may not impress all historians as meriting significant scholarly attention. In some quarters, the general idea that rural communities were locked into a kind of "eternal present,"[10] a *longue durée* more potent than any that obtained in urban settings, seems to obviate the need for research. As Duccio Balestracci has put it, there has long been a common assumption that "once outside the city gates, society lost all its complexity and nuance."[11] Notions of a "timeless agriculture," and

8 Albert J. Raboteau, *Slave Religion: The "Invisible Institution" in the Antebellum South* (1978; updated ed., New York, 2004), ix–x.

9 Raboteau, *Slave Religion*, ix–x. In an afterword (pp. 323–334) written for the 2004 edition, Raboteau reiterates the importance of the "written and oral narratives of ex-slaves as historical evidence," texts that made possible a "more detailed and nuanced account of slave culture and religion than previously thought possible" and that have "elucidated the agency of the slaves and the distinctiveness of their culture – 'the world the slaves made.'" Indeed, emphasizing the link between culture and agency, he notes that "the vitality and creativity of slave culture ... constituted a central premise in the discussion of slave agency." Quotations at pp. 326, 330.

10 The phrase is Mark Gregory Pegg's. See his remarks along these lines in *The Corruption of Angels: The Great Inquisition of 1245–1246* (Princeton, 2001), 16–17.

11 Balestracci, *The Renaissance in the Fields*, xviii. For an example of how this view of the countryside surfaces in studies devoted to a quite different topic, see C.H. Lawrence's important survey of medieval monasticism, specifically Chapter Thirteen, which deals with the friars and the social context that produced them. There he states that "the closely regulated and enclosed society of the rural manor exerted on the individual an almost irresistible pressure to conform, whereas town living, with its

more recently (as will be discussed below) the belief that a lack of subjective sources denies us access to peasant interiority, necessarily place the majority of pre-modern peoples (indeed, the majority of all people) in the realm of "unknowable." It might be said, then, that an assumption of "invisibility" has surrounded the medieval peasant, deriving from a number of sources.[12]

Yet an interest in peasant mentality is perhaps best seen as an inevitable progression in the scholarship in this field. The central questions of the present book were clearly asked, for another rural population, twenty-five years ago by David Sabean in his book *Power in the Blood: Popular Culture and Village Discourse in Early Modern Germany*. Sabean pointed to a need for further research "on how villagers actually formulated their ideas, conducted themselves, and interacted with their fellows."[13] Such an inquiry is implicit – indeed, has been a major focus – in the work of other early modern historians who have focused on the non-elite majority, such as Natalie Zemon Davis, Carlo Ginzburg, and Robert Darnton. Medievalists, of course, have been interested in questions of mentality as well: Warren Ault, in a study of village bylaws based on English court rolls, concluded with the hope that the evidence he had presented would "throw some light on that most obscure of medieval subjects – how the village community carried on its life."[14] George Homans, working from the premise that

relative freedom from customary constraints, its political turbulence and the constant stimulus of economic competition, fostered a more critical mentality and provided readier opportunities for the communication of new ideas." *Medieval Monasticism: Forms of Religious Life in Western Europe in the Middle Ages* (3rd ed., Harlow; New York, 2001), 239–240.

12 A new kind of "invisibility" has emerged in the lack of attention paid to farmers and farming. As Peter A. Coclanis points out in "Agriculture as History," *Historically Speaking* 4.2 (November 2002): 3–4, "[w]ith farmers constituting such a small proportion of the U.S. labor force, and with the cultural turn in the humanities two decades ago, agriculture and agriculturalists now seem so elemental, so *material* in the eyes of many as to disqualify these subjects from the lists of those deemed worthy of serious ... scholarship. It's hard to make hogs or harrows transgressive, I guess."

13 David Warren Sabean, *Power in the Blood: Popular Culture and Village Discourse in Early Modern Germany* (Cambridge, 1984), 199.

14 Warren Ault, "Manor Court and Parish Church in Fifteenth-Century England," *Speculum* 42 (1967): 53–67, at 67. Ault's published scholar-

villagers mostly governed themselves, averred that "the rules ... the means ... are matters of which scholars are still ignorant. One hint is ... the bylaw and another ... the reeve ... [but] they do not come near to revealing the whole constitution of village self-government."[15] In the conclusion to *Tenure and Mobility*, J.A. Raftis asked, "what type of man was the villager whose life we have been studying?"[16]

More recently, in a collection of essays on medieval agriculture, Del Sweeney has asked: what were the "realities of medieval peasant life? What did peasants themselves believe about the world in which they lived?" Even for the ninth and tenth centuries, a period far less well documented than the thirteenth through fifteenth centuries, Paul Dutton states: "what could be more important for our proper appreciation of an age like the Carolingian, in which the countryside and agricultural concerns dominated, than to acknowledge the centrality and, indeed, intelligibility of popular thought?" By "popular thought," he means, "[w]hat farmers thought, how they imagined their world to work, and what strategies they consciously adopted to confront a capricious natural world."[17] As indicated by the title, David Stone's recent book *Decision-Making in Medieval Agriculture* also focuses on reconstructing "what we can about the mental world of medieval farmers." Stone points out that "[o]n most demesnes the day-to-day decisions about marketing, sown acreage, livestock numbers, and the intensity of cultivation were left to local unfree reeves to make and hired bailiffs to supervise, checked only from time to time by stewards and other centrally based estate officials."[18] The present study aims to delve further into that "mental world."

---

ship using court roll evidence had begun more than forty years earlier, with *Private Jurisdiction in England* (New Haven, 1923).

15 Note that Homans's book was first published in 1941. See his *English Villagers of the Thirteenth Century* (1941; repr., New York, 1975), 331. Homans was speaking of a village at farm (that is, leased to its tenants) in this passage, but it could be said of practically any medieval village, to a greater or lesser extent.

16 Raftis, *Tenure and Mobility*, 209.

17 Del Sweeney, introduction to *Agriculture in the Middle Ages: Technology, Practice, and Representation* (Philadelphia, 1995), 1; for Dutton's comment, see Paul Edward Dutton, "Thunder and Hail over the Carolingian Countryside," in Sweeney, *Agriculture in the Middle Ages*, 111–137, at 111.

18 David Stone, *Decision-Making in Medieval Agriculture* (Oxford, 2005), 5, 13.

The question has been raised, however, whether the evidence exists to permit such detailed study of the links between peasant thought and behavior. It has been argued, for example, that because we do not possess peasant "letters, diaries, and other intimate personal records" we can never know how they felt about marriage and family.[19] It is true, to revert to the American history analogy cited earlier, that the work of recovering the once "invisible world" of slave religion has had incomparable sources in slave biographies and interviews with people who lived under slavery. Through the study of the personal testimonies of individual men and women, a vast dimension of historical experience in the American past that most scholars knew little about was made visible. As Raboteau observes, "elucidat[ing] the agency of the slaves and the distinctiveness of their culture" has done more than simply "reveal" hitherto unknown chapters in American history – it has transformed it.[20]

19 Judith Bennett, "Medieval Peasant Marriage," in *Pathways to Medieval Peasants,* ed. J.A. Raftis (Toronto, 1981). In *Women in the Medieval English Countryside: Gender and Household in Brigstock Before the Plague* (New York, 1987), 126, she makes the same point more forcefully, that no "personal diaries, no observers' reports, no letters survive to illuminate the private satisfactions of rural ale-wives." Paul Freedman, *Images of the Medieval Peasant* (Stanford, 1999), 8, also remarks that "peasant diaries and memoirs are in short supply." As the title of his book indicates, Freedman uses a vast range of texts to "discern repeated themes in the discourse" about peasants, producing a history of "elite regard" of peasants, rather than a history of how peasants thought about themselves. It is the latter question with which the present book is concerned.

20 For a sampling of such materials, see *God Struck Me Dead: Religious Conversion Experiences and Autobiographies of Ex-Slaves*, ed. Clifton H. Johnson (Philadelphia, 1969); *Lay My Burden Down: A Folk History of Slavery*, ed. B.A. Botkin (Chicago, 1945); *The Book of Negro Folklore*, ed. Langston Hughes and Arna Bontemps (1958; repr., New York, 1983); *Slave Testimony: Two Centuries of Letters, Speeches, Interviews, and Autobiographies*, ed. John W. Blassingame (Baton Rouge, 1977); *Weevils in the Wheat: Interviews with Virginia Ex-Slaves*, ed. Charles L. Perdue, Jr, Thomas E. Barden, and Robert K. Phillips (Charlottesville, 1976). For quotations in Raboteau, see his afterword to the 2004 edition of *Slave Religion*, pp. 326 and 334. In spite of the abundance of ex-slave accounts, Blassingame points out that "only three of the sixteen state studies of plantation slavery published between 1902 and 1974 draw even moderately on slave testimony." He notes that while the many and

While medievalists cannot interview their subjects, they have found sources and devised methodologies for uncovering the mentality of "ordinary" people. Handbooks for confessors, saints' lives, sermon literature, and inquisition records are plentiful for the medieval period, and all had complex links with the world of lay popular beliefs, assumptions, and ideas. This scholarship has played an important part in revising historians' understanding of medieval society in the direction of heterogeneity of outlook and experience, and in terms of what might be called a diffusion of cultural "power."[21] The conventional view of a top-down flow in the creation of medieval culture, from elites to commoners, with certain heretics and visionaries occasionally ruffling the waters, has given way to a prevailing view of a mobile society with enormous generative and regenerative powers that emanated from many sources, many people.

The medieval world revealed here looks like it could well be the precursor of the rich cultural world of early modern Europe, an era that historians have long thought to be much better served than the medieval period by evidence for the study of *mentalité*.[22] The history of emotion, personality, identity – and human interaction – that has been written for the few and the many, town and country, clerics and

---

varying accounts of "white eyewitnesses" were routinely used, the prevailing feeling about ex-slave narratives was that they were "issued with so much abolitionist editing that as a class their authenticity is doubtful" (quoting Ulrich B. Phillips). See *Slave Testimony*, xvii.

21 This now comprises a vast number of studies, by scholars such as Aron Gurevich, Jean-Claude Schmitt, Carlo Ginzburg, Donald Weinstein, Rudolph Bell, and others. For some recent examples of use of hagiographical materials, see Sharon Farmer, *Surviving Poverty in Medieval Paris: Gender, Ideology and the Daily Lives of the Poor* (Ithaca, 2002), and Robert Bartlett, *The Hanged Man: A Story of Miracle, Memory, and Colonialism in the Middle Ages* (Princeton, 2004); for inquisition records see note 26 below; for use of the records of common law courts to recover the lives of the many, see *Voices From the Bench: The Narratives of Lesser Folk in Medieval Trials*, ed. Michael Goodich (New York, 2006).

22 The cultural life of everyman and everywoman that has been revealed by early modern historians such as David Sabean, Edward Muir, Robert Muchembled, Natalie Zemon Davis, James Amelang, Carlo Ginzburg, Guido Ruggiero, Peter Burke, Martin Ingram, and others had its medieval counterpart – indeed, its medieval preparation.

laity in the sixteenth, seventeenth, and eighteenth centuries has of course also been pursued by medievalists, though chiefly for the literate elite and urban populations.[23] It is a fundamental argument of this book that such inquiry can be pursued for the farming majority of medieval Europe, that the veil of "invisibility" can be partly lifted, using materials that differ from the confessors' manuals or inquisition records typically employed by medieval cultural historians. These valuable sources are the minutes of village or "manorial" courts which survive for hundreds of English villages from the end of the thirteenth century.

Court Rolls as a Source of Data

In spite of a long tradition of scholarly interest in local tribunals and their records (going back to F.W. Maitland's *Select Pleas in Seignorial and Other Courts*, published in 1889), and of the current importance of the study of mentalities across the historical discipline, there are no monographs that employ the exceptional court roll data that exist for medieval England to uncover the cultural history of villagers – in short, to make their mental world more "visible" and "knowable." The cat massacres, monstrous births, and exorcisms that have been emerging from the studies of early modernists did not spring into existence *ex nihilo*, nor do their roots lie buried in an imperfect premodern record trail, only partly illumined by literature or confessors'

23 Thus, a recent study of what the author terms a "culture of enmity" in medieval England discusses questions of internalization, personality formation, and emotion in medieval Europeans, especially villagers and townspeople, ordinary churchgoers, litigants, etc. See Paul R. Hyams, *Rancor and Reconciliation in Medieval England* (Ithaca, 2003), especially Chapter Two, "Social Emotions in a Culture of Vengeance," 43–59. Hyams uses the records of the common law courts (beginning with the hundred courts), confessors' manuals, biblical glosses, Church canons, and other pastoral writings, as well as entertainment literature. According to Hyams (p. 44), the "rarity of direct anecdotal evidence" means that the historian must "mostly deduce the secular countermodel from the behavior patterns the Church targeted." Carlo Ginzburg, *The Cheese and the Worms: The Cosmos of a Sixteenth-Century Miller*, trans. John Tedeschi and Anne Tedeschi (1980; repr., New York, 1982), xx, has characterized the extension of the "historic concept of 'individual' in the direction of the lower classes" as a "worthwhile objective."

manuals. Much of the world of medieval popular culture can be retrieved by studying the minutes of village courts, an unparalleled serial record of behavior at ground level.[24]

The present study is founded primarily upon a close analysis of court rolls for the villages of Upwood and Ellington, both located in Huntingdonshire.[25] Our period of investigation, 1280–1460, begins when these two court roll series begin and ends when these records become less communicative than they had been earlier. This qualitative change in the evidence has its own story to tell, for it is linked to the weakening of the medieval tradition of local jurisdiction and a corresponding increase in state power beginning in the later fifteenth century.

English court rolls are among the premier ethnographic materials that have come down to us from the Middle Ages, alongside – indeed complementing – inquisition records that are more familiar to most medieval and early modern historians.[26] The villages of Ellington and Upwood, which belonged to the estates of Ramsey Abbey for more than half a millennium, have been studied in an earlier book by the

24 Not all would agree. Richard M. Smith avers that court rolls cannot compare with inquisition records, that "no English village could be studied in the same way as the now celebrated Montaillou." See Smith, " 'Modernization' and the Corporate Medieval Village Community in England," in *Explorations in Historical Geography: Interpretative Essays*, ed. Alan R.H. Baker and Derek Gregory (Cambridge, 1984), 140–179, at 171.

25 It is worth pointing out that the wealth of detail, varieties of people and action, and amount of business found in our two representative court roll series is replicated in others. For a recent list of court rolls in print, some in translation, see the bibliography in Phillipp Schofield, *Peasant and Community in Medieval England, 1200–1500* (New York, 2003).

26 There is a long history of scholarly interest in inquisition records. Among cultural historians, the work of Carlo Ginzburg has been most influential. See his *The Cheese and the Worms,* as well as *The Night Battles: Witchcraft and Agrarian Cults in the Sixteenth and Seventeenth Centuries*, trans. John Tedeschi and Anne Tedeschi (New York, 1985). Medieval historians who have used inquisition materials include James B. Given, *Inquisition and Medieval Society: Power, Discipline and Resistance in Languedoc* (Ithaca, 1997); John H. Arnold, *Inquisition and Power: Catharism and the Confessing Subject in Medieval Languedoc* (Philadelphia, 2001); and Pegg, *The Corruption of Angels.*

present author.[27] What is presented here is a specialized investigation of village cultural history, growing out of that earlier study that explored village self-regulation and local government.[28] Although court rolls are abundant[29] and have been studied since the nineteenth century, there is much in them that remains to be explored, particularly in light of the calls to reassess sources for their use in cultural history studies.[30] The present book uses these, and other, related sources that derive mostly from the lordship of Ramsey Abbey, in the light of the cultural history approaches that have been driving so much historical research for the current generation of scholars.[31] Case

27 Olson, *A Chronicle of All That Happens*. The records for these two villages are not as consecutive or voluminous as the series that survive for other places, such as the manor of Hales in Worcestershire, or Wakefield in Yorkshire. See Zvi Razi, *Life, Marriage and Death in a Medieval Parish: Economy, Society and Demography in Halesowen, 1270–1400* (Cambridge, 1980); and see Helen M. Jewell, "Women at the Courts of the Manor of Wakefield, 1348–50," *Northern History* 26 (1990): 59–81, for an example of article literature based on the Yorkshire collection.

28 If writing two books based on the same court roll series for two villages seems excessive, the reader is referred, by way of analogy, to F.W. Maitland's comment in the preface to his 1891 edition of medieval formularies for seigneurial courts (*The Court Baron, Being Precedents For Use in Seignorial and Other Local Courts* ... , ed. F.W. Maitland and W.P. Baildon [London, 1891], vii), that "from one of these books I was led on to another, and so to a third, and to a fourth; for, having once opened this new vein of materials, one could not easily stop working it until it had been somewhat fully explored."

29 See the bibliography of court roll sources in *Medieval Society and the Manor Court*, ed. Zvi Razi and Richard Smith (Oxford, 1996), 569–637.

30 This reassessment may not be viewed as necessary by scholars who argue that such records were weapons in the arsenal of adversarial lords, not instruments facilitating self-government. For an example of such a traditional view, see Peter Franklin, "Politics in Manorial Court Rolls: The Tactics, Social Composition, and Aims of a pre-1381 Peasant Movement," in Razi and Smith, *Medieval Society and the Manor Court*, 162–198. Indeed, Franklin argues that, as records wielded for the purpose of seigneurial control, the court rolls may even misrepresent events and conceal information.

31 While historians' ideas about the value of court roll evidence have been expanding in recent years, these records, unlike other types of legal records, have not made a significant contribution to recent cultural history

studies such as the present one, informed by an interest in cultural history, enable the historian to look at village society from the vantage point of local affiliations, which mattered more than others to most people in this period. Indeed, Ramsey Abbey had one of the most extensive franchises (grants of rights of jurisdiction) of any monastic house or secular lordship in the country: the abbot was a kind of king in his lands – and he mostly left his tenants to govern themselves. How they did so can be uncovered by studying court rolls, among other records of behavior.

Court rolls are documents of practice that capture people in their ordinary, everyday mode, not just at moments of crisis (such as being on trial for heresy). Nor do they directly promote the study of religious belief (as does sermon literature, for example), which is often apprehended as the only aspect of medieval popular mentality that we can uncover, and is sometimes seen as determinative (peasant mentality often being equated with religious belief). Rather, court rolls and to a lesser extent other records of estate administration, such as deeds of land transfer, account rolls, custumals (records that list the customary rents and services owed to a lord by his tenants), terriers (topographical surveys of tenant and demesne lands), and even formulary ("how to") books for holding a manor court (all of which are employed in the present study), bear the imprint of the forces of lordship and collective action that shaped village society. The quality of villagers' participation in the "manorial" court in particular enhances the value of these records as "insider" documents for, as Eric Kerridge has pointed out, village government was "fundamentally democratic, all matters being decided by a consensus or a clear majority of all the heads of houses of husbandry, their tenants and subtenants, whether men or women."[32]

---

scholarship. For example, Aron Gurevich has pointed out that studies of European witch hunts have shifted away from "learned treatises on demonology to analysis of the innumerable legal cases available, which conceal real human destinies and tragedies." He argues that this shift has not only shed "fresh light ... on aspects of the problem" but has "revealed new aspects of popular culture during the period" (*Historical Anthropology of the Middle Ages*, ed. Jana Howlett [Chicago, 1992], 17).

32 He notes that this form of local government had its origins in Anglo-Saxon times, and was "already well-established in the thirteenth century." See Kerridge, *The Common Fields of England* (Manchester, 1992), 87.

Village courts had extensive powers of public jurisdiction, and their records are among the earliest and fullest witnesses to that standard feature of medieval politics and society, "the rights of public jurisdiction in private hands."[33] These local courts enforced royal statutes regarding ale and bread production, regulated the various dues and services owed to the lord by customary tenants (that is, villagers holding customary land, to which was attached the obligation to work on the lord's demesne land in the village), and oversaw a multitude of local business having to do with the control of violence, settlement of disputes, debt adjudication between villagers, and the like. Thus, the record of a single court session could include entries concerning stray animals, the election and swearing in of officials, work defaults on the lord's demesne, proclamations of agricultural bylaws, retirement arrangements for elderly parents, disputes over land, cases of slander, the raising of the hue and cry,[34] the fining of brewers, and trespass of many sorts. Moreover, since the entries refer to the actors involved by their first and last names, it is possible to reconstruct the patterns of behavior of real individuals – not peasant "types" – over time, within their community, and in relation to other people. (The court rolls for Upwood and Ellington alone preserve the names of nearly three thousand people between 1280 and 1460). The minutes of local courts may not reveal a peasant "self" as a diary or memoir might do; however, as detailed, serial records of behaviors for numerous people acting many roles, behaviors that were reported in a court whose procedures were shaped by its suitors, the court rolls merit a close reading by the historian interested in rural mentality.

A sampling of routine entries from Upwood's court rolls for the 1280s and 1290s reveals the deep specificity and multi-layered quality of these documents: in 1294 Philipp de Sywell was fined for unjust detention of two bushels of barley, two bushels of wheat, and two bushels of peas from Philipp reeve – and he is to pay off this debt "at

33 Ault, *Private Jurisdiction in England.* For a full discussion of the court roll, see Olson, *A Chronicle*, especially pp. 6–27.

34 The hue and cry was a local policing practice whereby anyone witnessing a crime was to call for help, and all who could hear were supposed to go to the scene. People who raised the hue and cry "unjustly" (*iniuste*) were cited and fined.

the new grain" (*Ideo satisfaciet ei ad nouum granum*).[35] This entry at once reveals that villagers contracted debts (in this case, a debt in kind) with each other, and that repayment schedules could be monitored in the court and according to village notions of time. Another entry, one that also conveys something of the variability of "village time" (here, linked to the court itself), occurs in 1280 in two cases where it is noted that the head of a "tithing" or local policing group must have one of his members before the Steward at his next coming (*ad proximum adventum suum, ad proximum adventum Senescalli*). Sacred time, of course, also figures in village calculations and hence in the court rolls, as in a 1297 notice that Thomas Frere "while he was beadle" didn't care to collect the sheaves of cornbote, a grain payment (*non colligere curauit garbas de cornbote*), until the feast of St Clement (23 November), though the cornbote ought to have been collected at the feast of St Michael (29 September).[36] In another early roll (1295), Thomas Aspelon was cited for breaking the stile at the top of the town next to John de Clervaus, allowing animals to graze on the lord's grain (*fregit schala ad capud ville ... propter cuius defectus bestie pascebant bladum domini*). In that same year, several fathers and mothers were fined for "receiving" their sons "outside tithing" (allowing their sons to remain in the village without being sworn into a "tithing," as was required for all males over the age of twelve): Alice Bygge received her sons Simon and Thomas, Agnes Brun received her son Hugh, Robert Bonseriaunt received his son John, and Walter ad Pirum his son Robert. Debt arrangements between villagers, obligations attached to officeholding, the regulation of farming, and even parental behavior: these entries, like the citation concerning Agnes le Write's coming into court to take the oath for a tenement for which

35 All citations from the court rolls in the text will indicate the year, thus referring the reader to the Manuscript Sources in the Bibliography. Also note that names of persons, places, things, etc., will not be standardized, but will always be given as they are spelled at the particular point in the original. Such variability is integral to the court roll as a document of practice embedded in time, and thus is important for several lines of inquiry pursued in the present study.

36 For an excellent discussion of the villager's sense of time see Eamon Duffy, *The Stripping of the Altars: Traditional Religion in England, c.1400–c.1580* (New Haven, 1992), Chapter One, "Seasons and Signs," especially pp. 37–52.

she alone now bears primary responsibility, suggest the range of "knowable" daily village experience. Further, a single entry is never really single because it connects at different points across that spectrum of local experience, as the following pages will repeatedly show.

While historians have emphasized the village court as an arena for the formulation and enforcement of local law, it is apprehended here more broadly as a village assembly, or an "assembly of cultivators," as Joan Thirsk has called it, and thus as an "all-purpose" forum similar to the better-known popular assemblies of other periods (for example, classical Athens) that embraced an array of legal, political, social – and cultural – powers.[37] The authority of such local assemblies was grounded both in the right to participate (citizenship in the classical city-state, tenure of land in the medieval village), and in the collective powers of the group so assembled. As J.A. Raftis observed years ago, "custom gave a stature, if not a legal status, to the villager's way of life"; indeed, the conditions of his life conferred a kind of "citizenship."[38] Given the spectrum of business handled by the court, whose suitors are consistently identified by first name and surname, the court rolls possess a kind of ethnographic power of a quality very different from inquisition records, sermon literature, and other sources more typically employed to study medieval popular culture.

Moreover, since these courts usually met several times a year (some as frequently as every three weeks), the minutes of their sessions form a serial type of record attached to specific villages, over generations, even centuries, that allows us to focus on change over time. This point is quite important for the village historian's research strategy, since the ideas and values of the non-literate majority may surface most clearly in the evidence when they change; the "invisible" becomes more perceptible to us in its continuous development.

37 Thirsk's terminology has not been readily adopted by other historians. See the reprint of her 1964 article "The Common Fields" in *The Rural Economy of England* (London, 1984), 36. It is noteworthy that medievalists are turning their attention to assemblies at the present time, as in the recent collection of essays edited by P.S. Barnwell and M. Mostert, *Political Assemblies in the Earlier Middle Ages* (Turnhout; Cheltenham, 2003), which clearly conceives of large collective gatherings more broadly than the older, "proto-democratic" bent of scholars had allowed. But note that none of the essays concerns rural villagers and their courts.

38 Raftis, *Tenure and Mobility*, 11, 205.

Maitland observed this quality as well, describing the court rolls as a document that displays the manor "in motion" while the manorial extent (a valuation or survey) "displays the manor at rest."[39] These are the qualities that make the court roll so valuable to the village historian who desires to "venture afresh into the territory of *mentalités*."[40]

It is worth pointing out that some of the contrasts frequently instanced between medieval and early modern sources have perhaps been over-emphasized. For example, while court rolls do not equal the detailed depositional material studied by Sabean, nor the first-person pardon petitions used by Natalie Zemon Davis in *Fiction in the Archives*,[41] they do possess narrative properties, because, as we will see, storytelling was essential to the functioning of the court. Moreover, while it is true that one of the strengths of the court roll lies in the materials it provides for investigating collective culture over time, that history comes to us couched in terms of individuals and their actions as reported in the court. The historian need not wait until the sixteenth century to have access to substantive evidence of the individual, nor to raise questions about identity, internalization, and agency for the rural majority.

What sort of work did the court perform and how did it do so? How do the court rolls, as records of individual actions, provide evidence of collective culture and its impact on village society? The present book rests upon the village "case study" method, benefiting from a tradition of village and regional research that has been used regularly by medieval historians since the mid-twentieth century. Analyzing the records of only two villages may not enable us to say something about all of Europe's medieval peasants in their millions, especially given our growing appreciation of the pronounced localism of medieval society.[42] But village studies to date have revealed communities – and

39 F.W. Maitland, *Select Pleas in Manorial and Other Seignorial Courts: Reigns of Henry III and Edward I* (London, 1889), xi.

40 As urged by Paul R. Hyams, "What Did Edwardian Villagers Understand by Law?" in Razi and Smith, *Medieval Society and the Manor Court*, 88.

41 Natalie Zemon Davis, *Fiction in the Archives: Pardon Tales and Their Tellers in Sixteenth-Century France* (Stanford, 1987).

42 Phillipp Schofield has recently emphasized the importance of acknowledging diversity in peasant economies, societies, and customs in *Peasant and Community in Medieval England, 1200–1500*.

court roll series – that are broadly similar.[43] In the view of this writer, the single village study is the best foundation upon which to base conclusions about peasant behavior and behavioral change, especially for English evidence, because of the serial nature of the court rolls and the continuous record of behavior that they provide for individual communities.[44] In addition, every case study provides the historian with a new opportunity to reassess the various categories of medieval

43 Thus, John L. Fisher's *A Medieval Farming Glossary of Latin and English Words* (London, 1968) is useful for the entire country, though it is based mostly on records from the county of Essex. Merely reading through the published court rolls for villages, fair towns, and boroughs, in fact, reveals societies more striking for their similarities than their dissimilarities. For some published series, see *The Court Rolls of Walsham le Willows, 1303–1350*, ed. R. Lock (Woodbridge, 1998); Maitland, *Select Pleas* vol. 2; *Select Cases in Manorial Courts, 1250–1550*, ed. L.R. Poos and L. Bonfield (London, 1998); *The Court Rolls of Ramsey, Hepmangrove and Bury*, ed. and trans. Edwin B. DeWindt (Toronto, 1990). For discussions of borough and fair town court rolls, see G.H. Martin, *The Early Court Rolls of the Borough of Ipswich* (Leicester, 1954); Ellen Wedemeyer Moore, *The Fairs of Medieval England: An Introductory Study* (Toronto, 1985). For further village study bibliography, see Schofield, *Peasant and Community*, 262–263. Studies of medieval German village assemblies and French villages (neither of which has records comparable to English court rolls in terms of the latter's early date, detail, and wide availability) convey the same impression of broad similarities across medieval peasant societies. See for example Gadi Algazi, "Lords Ask, Peasants Answer: Making Traditions in Late-Medieval Village Assemblies," in *Between History and Histories: the Making of Silences and Commemorations*, ed. Gerald Sider and Gavin Smith (Toronto, 1997), 199–229; and Monique Bourin, *Villages médiévaux en Bas-Languedoc: Genèse d'une sociabilité, Xe–XIVe siècles* (Paris, 1987), especially volume 2: *La démocratie au village*.

44 Some historians who have used court roll evidence prefer sampling across a large number of villages; while this approach allows the scholar to use a greater amount of material, it does not take advantage of the unique strength of these records as consecutive and local sources. For an example of the sampling method, see Marjorie K. McIntosh, *Controlling Misbehavior in England, 1370–1600* (Cambridge, 1998). The same author has also employed the single village study; see *Autonomy and Community: The Royal Manor of Havering, 1200–1500* (Cambridge, 1986), and *A Community Transformed: The Manor and Liberty of Havering, 1500–1620* (Cambridge, 1991).

sources and how they may be used in cultural history research, as Aron Gurevich has called for.[45] In the same vein, Jean-Claude Schmitt has pointed out that "it is not so much the documents that are lacking as the conceptual instruments necessary to understand them."[46]

Methodology: Defining "Culture"

Sabean's study of early modern village Germany emphasizes a "processual notion of culture." He argues that scholarly focus should be on the process, "not the thing produced." Culture is a "series of arguments among people about the common things of their everyday lives. What they share are the material and symbolic things which connect them, not the attitudes, positions, perceptions, strategies, or goals."[47] As an investigative approach, an emphasis on "process" favors court roll evidence because the sharing of resources within the community compelled villagers to continually rethink or rework local "policy," an activity that appears overtly in court proceedings. An emphasis on process also leaves analytical room for the diversity of ideas that historians increasingly see as characteristic of medieval societies.[48]

45 See note 31 above.

46 Jean-Claude Schmitt, *The Holy Greyhound: Guinefort, Healer of Children since the Thirteenth Century*, trans. Martin Thom (Cambridge; Paris, 1983), 171. Similarly, anthropologists Sidney Mintz and Richard Price have spoken of the "poverty of our conceptual tools" for the study of African-American culture. See their discussion of this point in *The Birth of African-American Culture: An Anthropological Perspective* (Boston, 1992), 9–12.

47 Sabean, *Power in the Blood*, 94–95.

48 In the present book, therefore, peasant cultural history will not be pursued in order to uncover the "vulnerable underbelly of the hegemonic discourse" of medieval society (to use Adam Kuper's felicitous phrasing, in *Culture: The Anthropologists' Account* [Cambridge, MA, 1999], 232), but rather to demonstrate that court rolls are witnesses that have preserved discoverable "cultural" activity, as well as the political, economic, and social activity that has been the traditional focus of historiography. It should be noted that, unlike court rolls, most inquisition records are not serial accounts. For example, Pegg's recent study is synchronic, based on the extraordinarily rich inquisition records for a single year, 1245–1246. In *Night Battles*, Ginzburg traces the *benandanti* from the early sixteenth to nearly the mid-seventeenth centuries, but he focuses on a

An investigation that centers on individual behaviors and diverse ideas may successfully avoid the tendency to reify culture, or to treat it as a whole or as a single system, and thus to fall into the trap wherein "culture shifts from something to be described, interpreted, even perhaps explained, and is treated instead as a source of explanation in itself," as Adam Kuper has warned.[49] According to Kuper,

> to understand culture, we must first deconstruct it. Religious beliefs, rituals, knowledge, moral values, the arts, rhetorical genres, and so on should be separated out from each other rather than bound together into a single bundle labeled culture, or collective consciousness, or superstructure, or discourse. Separating out these elements, one is led on to explore the changing configurations in which language, knowledge, techniques, political ideologies, rituals, commodities, and so on are related to each other ... if the elements of a culture are disaggregated, it is usually not difficult to show that the parts are separately tied to specific administrative arrangements, economic pressures, biological constraints, and so forth.[50]

Kuper's observations provide a technique, the "disaggregation" of "elements of culture," that works well with court rolls; records that proceed entry by entry, listing individuals involved in numerous activities, decade after decade. "Separating out these elements" of village culture will enable us to examine how they are "related to each other" in the community, where individual and group "arguments" were grounded on the common material and symbolic things of everyday life (to paraphrase Sabean). We may think of this common material framework as composed of land, animals, houses, implements – and people,[51] what Mary Patricia Hogan has aptly called "the labyrinth of

---

cult or series of related cults over time, rather than the broad cultural traditions for a people or group as is attempted here.

49 Kuper, *Culture*, xi.

50 Kuper, *Culture*, 245–246. Kuper quotes Eric Wolf, who defines culture as a "series of processes that construct, reconstruct, and dismantle cultural materials, in response to identifiable determinants."

51 Recurrent reference to work, interactions with others, and memorable events that are identified specifically with land, houses, and the like is observable in the autobiography of a modern peasant, Pedro Martínez. For example, Martínez often remembered receiving important news or the occurrence of important events when he was standing outside his home

houses, inhabitants, and their efforts."[52] The notion of a labyrinth is analytically useful in the present study: it suggests both structure and people thinking about that structure, and gives rise to the image of villagers making their way through a maze of possibilities in an environment that offers both opportunity and restraint. Further, the sense of intricacy and inter-relationship of parts suggested by a labyrinth accords well with the great economic facts of common field agriculture and the varied practices of collective farming.

Among the elements that can be "disaggregated" in court roll evidence are those that display a time-sensitivity, particularly to demographic change, strong enough to register in the village court's arena of collective jurisdiction. Much of the analysis in the present book is driven by the abundance of names in the court rolls, a fertile source of information that has been under-used, given its potential. Thus, one of the most striking examples of response to demographic change can be found by examining the names given to people and to the land. As we shall see in Chapter Five, the village practice of using local topographical elements to formulate new surnames (for example, John Abovestreet, Agnes Atwater, and Henry Bythebrook) in the late thirteenth and early fourteenth centuries gave way after plague and continuing population loss to the practice of giving one's family name to

---

making rope. See *Pedro Martínez: A Mexican Peasant and His Family*, ed. Oscar Lewis (New York, 1964), 107, 145.

52 See Hogan, "The Labor of Their Days: Work in the Medieval Village," *Studies in Medieval and Renaissance History*, n.s. 8 (1986): 75–186, at 80. The labyrinthine character of peasant living and working conditions is well attested. Christopher Dyer, "English Peasant Buildings in the Later Middle Ages," Chapter Eight in *Everyday Life in Medieval England* (1994; repr., London, 2000), 153, notes that "[p]easant messuages contained not just a house but a group of buildings. The long-house was a localized type, and over most of the country animals were either housed separately, or kept in yards. Of other buildings, barns were most common, followed by kitchens and bakehouses, and a variety of other structures." According to Raftis, *Tenure and Mobility*, 91, the "key to the village economy proper seems to lie in very small, variable, and perhaps often irregular and enclosed units. How little we know about the existence of these small units from ordinary sources is most easily seen by an effort to reconstruct the village, buildings, lots, and gardens, from a manorial survey ... furthermore, the small unit was the focus for the most active land market among villagers!"

the land, evident in local place names like Vernonsgate, Taylorslane, and Walkelynwood. This response, set in the post-plague era of high mortality and increased mobility, reflects a connection between landscape and memory, a change in the notions that underlay tenure, and a new incarnation of a traditional desire for stability. The evidence of metronymic surnames (for example, "Mariott," derived from the female given name Mariota, and "Deneys" from Dionysia), together with several high profile cases of women holding land as heads of household, open up a window into the tensions surrounding the transmission of land (Chapter Two). While female succession to land was fully sanctioned by customary rules of inheritance, rules that sought first and foremost to safeguard the family claim to land, it clearly also raised tension in a setting where male inheritance was preferred. Thus, the phenomenon of "woman as landholder" was a real event, illustrated in 1333 by Agnes le Write, that both activated and contributed to a village stock of ideas about women, to a village tradition of "thinking with women." Other elements of culture that invite analysis are the evidence for landed trespass in the village, an activity informed by notions of tenure, space, and even personal identity (Chapter Four), and villagers' use of a wide range of documents, including the court roll, which demonstrates their pragmatic Latin literacy (Chapter Three). Indeed, the procedures of the manorial court itself may be "deconstructed" as providing a setting for performance and for the ritual of self-government (Chapter One). In all these cases, analysis of specific court roll entries permits us to address the types of questions, central in cultural history scholarship, that explore the world of thought and agency within the labyrinth of the rural medieval village.

This "disaggregative" approach allows the historian to proceed with ambitious aims indeed, since a focus on process implies a focus on discernible activity (in which court rolls abound), and action is deeply linked to human personality. Sociologist Margaret Archer has argued for a "primacy of practice" in "being human," that "our continuous sense of self, or self-consciousness, emerges from our practical activity in the world."[53] Clifford Geertz has argued, along these same lines, that "meaning is use ... [meaning] arises from

53 Margaret S. Archer, *Being Human: The Problem of Agency* (Cambridge, 2000), 3; see especially Part 2, "The Primacy of Practice."

use."[54] Historians have always inferred thought from action, and all people are practical philosophers in the sense that thought and action are linked: people think about their actions and their actions influence their thought. The close connection between thought and action that characterized the working lives of pre-modern farmers living in largely autonomous communities is a historical phenomenon that favors the historian working with medieval court rolls, if we accept that thought may be inferred from the visible institutions and symbols that were brought to bear in the village court. While we cannot enter their family circle and ask about gender roles or marriage,[55] we can infer something from the procedures of the local court, the ways villagers are named, or the rich particularity of their everyday material culture.

The Evidence of Things

Inferring thought from the thing produced is standard practice for scholars in the humanities, but it is not usually applied to those who work with their hands, in spite of the connection between thought and concrete, even mundane, material objects that has long been emphasized in traditional intellectual history. Josef Pieper has observed that:

> [to] philosophize means to withdraw – not from the things of everyday life – but from the currently accepted meaning attached to them, or to question the value placed upon them. This does not, of course, take place by virtue of some decision to differentiate our attitude from that of others and to see things "differently," but because, quite suddenly, things themselves assume a different aspect. Really the situation is this: the deeper aspects of reality are apprehended in the ordinary things of everyday life and not in a sphere cut off and segregated from it ... it is in the things we come across in the experience of everyday life that the unusual emerges, and we no longer take them for granted – and that situation cor-

54 Clifford Geertz, *Local Knowledge: Further Essays in Interpretive Anthropology* (New York, 1983), 118.

55 As John Boswell has noted, the interior life of the family is among the most reclusive, less likely to leave evidence than any other interpersonal activity. *The Kindness of Strangers: The Abandonment of Children in Western Europe from Late Antiquity to the Renaissance* (1988; repr., Chicago, 1998), 4–5.

> responds with the inner experience which has always been regarded as the beginning of philosophy: the act of "marvelling."[56]

The view offered here is that peasants' way of life and work fostered the act of "marvelling" at the deeper aspects of reality present in "ordinary things," and thus that an examination of common items mentioned in court rolls and other administrative records can illuminate how peasants understood reality.

Before we examine data from court rolls, we may contextualize our discussion of medieval peasants' relationship to "the ordinary things of everyday life" by looking briefly at the evidence of objects in their milieu. To begin with, peasants routinely "thought with things," activating and contributing to a village stock of ideas about the objects surrounding them. Reasoning through objects survives in proverbial wisdom, aphorisms, familiar phrases, common symbols, and analogies; and insofar as proverbs represent the "wisdom of many,"[57] most of these traditional sayings originated in peasant culture, and thus drew heavily upon agrarian imagery. In fact, a large and important group of such sayings in the "worldwide distribution of proverbs"[58] derives specifically from "traditional wisdom and folklore, and country proverbs that relate to husbandry, the seasons, and the weather."[59] Such turns of phrase as "to walk on tenterhooks," "great as a goose egg," "to vanish (or spring up, fade, or wither) like hay," and "heavy as a millstone" appealed to common experience and knowledge, though the individual's visualization or interpretation of the activity could vary a great deal: as Natalie Davis has suggested, "to the villager, his common proverbs – wide-ranging in metaphor and tone, inconsistent with each other and flexible – were available for many different circumstances and for recommending different courses of action."[60] A

56 Josef Pieper, *Leisure, the Basis of Culture*, trans. Alexander Dru (1952; repr., New York, 1963), 98–99.

57 See the volume *The Wisdom of Many: Essays on the Proverb*, ed. Wolfgang Mieder and Alan Dundes (New York, 1981).

58 Betsy Bowden, "A Modest Proposal, Relating Four Millennia of Proverb Collections to Chemistry within the Human Brain," *Journal of American Folklore* 109 (1996): 440–449, at 441.

59 *The Concise Oxford Dictionary of Proverbs*, ed. J.A. Simpson (Oxford, 1982), ix.

60 See her essay entitled "Proverbial Wisdom and Popular Errors," in *Society and Culture in Early Modern France* (Stanford, 1975), 227–267,

major category of proverbs, one that includes "many of the more colorful examples," uses "specific observations from everyday experience to make a point which is general," such as "you can lead a horse to water but you can't make him drink," "don't put all your eggs in one basket," "to go gleaning before the cart has carried," "a greased cart goes more easily," "everyone feeds the fat swine for the lard," "as [numerous] as Risoms [corn stalks] in a rank field," and "to put one's hand to the plow."[61]

That peasants were surrounded by a vast array of objects is made clear in testamentary evidence, even for people of modest means,[62] and is given graphic representation in the well-known village church paintings known as "Christ of the Trades" or the "Sunday Christ," showing Christ surrounded by "a very large number of tools and other objects signifying the different types of agricultural work, or ... the

---

especially the discussion on pp. 230–244 (quotation at p. 243). Davis has also argued for using proverbs "to hear the voice of the people therein," and notes that "their metaphors drew upon subjects familiar to countryfolk – oxen, horses, dogs, grains, fallow fields."

61 The sayings that employ plow imagery are particularly numerous and specific in their details: "the father to the bough, the son to the plow," "no man holds the plow so well that he does not balk [leave a ridge unplowed] at times," "three oxen in one plow never draw well," "to plow with an ox and an ass together," "a plowman should go no farther than his plow," "to set the sullow [plow] before the oxen," "he is soon weary that plows with a wolf," etc. The proverbs given here can be found in *Proverbs, Sentences, and Proverbial Phrases; from English Writings mainly before 1500*, ed. Bartlett Whiting and Helen W. Whiting (Cambridge, MA, 1968); the collection edited by Simpson cited in note 59 above; and *Cassell's Dictionary of Proverbs*, ed. David Pickering (1997; rev. ed., London; New York, 2001). This topic is too vast to be developed further here; for current literature see the journal *Proverbium: Yearbook of International Proverb Scholarship*, ed. Wolfgang Mieder. Herman Braet, in " 'A Thing Most Brutish': The Image of the Rustic in Old French Literature" (Sweeney, *Agriculture in the Middle Ages*, 201 n17), draws attention to collections of proverbs and sayings specifically attributed to "the *villain*." For examples of plantation proverbs see Hughes and Bontemps, *Book of Negro Folklore*, 118–121: "De noise of de wheels don't measure de load in de wagon," "Dar's a fam'ly coolness 'twix' de mule an' de single-tree."

62 See Christopher Dyer, *Standards of Living in the Later Middle Ages: Social Change in England, c. 1200–1520* (Cambridge, 1989), Chapter Six, "Peasants as Consumers," especially pp. 169–177.

work itself."[63] These and other sources point to a well-developed material culture, where tools and objects were ubiquitous, were often highly specialized, were usually of local manufacture, and required constant attention in the form of upkeep, repair, and storage. Given that many implements and parts of implements lasted across generations (particularly large ones such as wagons, plows, and plow parts, which are common heritable items in testaments), a person might even develop a strong connection with a particular tool (since "an old cart, well used, may last out a new one abused"). What Natalie Davis has called "the concrete particularity and order in popular culture" may have derived in part from an intense familiarity embedded in a quotidian reality of work, the implements of work, and problem-solving.

With these considerations in mind, the evidence suggests that when medieval farmers "thought with things," they had at their disposal a wide array of diverse workaday objects that were mostly instrumental (as distinguished from ornamental or merely functional). Many of the traditional sayings, some still familiar and vivid, clearly show the tendency to pass readily from a world of objects to a world of ideas that bravely wrestles with the existential realities of decision-making, problem-solving, and moral choice in the life of the individual, as well as in social relationships: "a rotten apple injures its neighbor" (1340); "a short horse is soon curried" (1350); "a bad workman blames his tools" (thirteenth century); "strike while the iron is hot" (thirteenth century); and "one beats the bush, another takes the bird" (1300).[64]

63 For a discussion of this artistic tradition, see Gerhard Jaritz, "The Material Culture of the Peasantry in the Late Middle Ages: 'Image' and 'Reality'," in Sweeney, *Agriculture in the Middle Ages*, 163-188, at 178, and see accompanying illustration. Like the study of proverbial wisdom, this topic is too vast to be handled in the present book. For a recent study of parish church wall painting in connection with *Piers Plowman*, see C. David Benson, "*Piers Plowman* and Parish Wall Paintings," *Yearbook of Langland Studies* 11 (1997): 1–38; the image of Christ surrounded by tools is discussed in note 3 on pp. 1–2. The church of All Saints in Ellington today shows "very faint traces of wall painting, probably a Doom [Judgment Day], above the chancel arch, but most of it has been destroyed." See *The Victoria History of the County of Huntingdon*, ed. W.W. Page et al. (London, 1926–1936), 3: 48.

64 For an interesting, brief introduction to the proposal that aphorisms are good for the brain, see Bowden's article, cited in note 58 above. Hyams,

Thus, a great number and variety of implements may be added to the land, people, and tasks in the "labyrinth of houses, inhabitants, and their efforts" that villagers navigated every day. Yet, as will be discussed more fully below, the basic conditions of village life extended even further the range and complexity of items that could be employed in the "marvelling" that leads to philosophy: agrarian material culture was not only abundant and varied, it also exhibited the property of extreme divisibility, even malleability, a fact that is illustrated in the well-known peasant knack for turning a single item to many uses. As Christopher Dyer has pointed out, "[i]n the peasant's world, in which production and consumption were intermeshed, the same object would have a variety of functions."[65] The routine divisibility of things is strikingly illustrated in arrangements concerning the central machine of farming, the plow. As Nellie Neilson describes it, a plow team or plow could be held "piecemeal, or jointly, by groups of peasants; plowshares might be held by one group, one ox by another group, a second, or even a fraction of an ox, by yet another." Further, it was customary to regard strips in the open fields as held individually by the peasants only during that period of the year when the crops were growing and being reaped. Thereafter they relapsed into

---

Rancor and Reconciliation, 48 n66, makes a brief reference to analogies between legal maxims, proverbial sayings, and parish priests teaching the Ten Commandments to parishioners. This important point deserves further study. A still-common saying perfectly illustrates the popular readiness with which connections are made between the most common material objects and well-known truths: "if wishes were horses then beggars would ride, if watches were turnips I would wear one by my side, if ifs and ands were pots and pans there'd be no work for tinkers." For other and earlier versions of the same, see *English Proverbs and Proverbial Phrases*, ed. W. Carew Hazlitt (London, 1869), 225: "If wishes were butter cakes, beggars might bite; if wishes would bide, beggars would ride; if wishes were thrushes, beggars would eat birds."

65 Dyer, *Standards of Living*, 171; and see Masschaele, *Peasants, Merchants and Markets*, 14–15, where he notes that "one measure of the panoply of specialized skills in existence" in the village is the "ingenuity with which laborers used things we would consider useless." For example, the butchering of one cow could give employment to at least twenty-five different artisans. Further, "the same artisans who achieved such levels of specialization also frequently occupied themselves with more than one trade."

common use, even for the short period of the gleaning.[66] Thus, over a single agricultural year the same piece of land varied in possession, from severalty to commons and back again.

The variety of items, their propinquity, their malleability, and the farmer's view of them as tools to accomplish essential, life-sustaining work, encouraged people to understand and employ them in varying ways: that is, everything with which they dealt entered into their mental world and became "grist for their mill." "Our world," according to James Deetz, "is the product of our thoughts."[67] Our thoughts in turn are shaped by the world in which we live and the objects that surround us. What is a farm but a mute gospel?

Analogous Voices and Texts

The active way in which thought and object are linked interiorly in the thinking of a historical person deserves further consideration here. Again, evidence for this phenomenon is preserved in a variety of sources, including a textual genre familiar to medievalists, though by no means confined to the Middle Ages, that of spiritual autobiography. A particularly striking modern example has survived in a book written by Rebecca Cox Jackson, a nineteenth-century visionary and Shaker eldress. Jackson, a free black woman whose life was passed in labor, and who acquired literacy in middle age, continually "thought with" and was inspired by objects of ordinary workaday reality. Describing how God had enabled her to "manifest" the love of "friend and foe, saint and sinner" alike in her conduct, she wrote: "And sometimes when praying and in speaking I would manifest this in meeting, when the effects that followed, were as if I had opened a bottle of cayenne pepper among the people."[68] After a period of fasting and praying, she had a vision of how "a light and trifling spirit would rob my soul of all the grace of God. Like a tub filled with water having a leak in it,

66 Nellie Neilson, *Medieval Agrarian Economy* (New York, 1936), 9, 12.

67 James Deetz, *In Small Things Forgotten: An Archaeology of Early American Life* (rev. ed., New York, 1996), 35. Deetz provides a broad definition of material culture that is useful for our present purposes: "that sector of our physical environment that we modify through culturally determined behavior."

68 *Gifts of Power: The Writings of Rebecca Jackson, Black Visionary, Shaker Eldress*, ed. Jean McMahon Humez (Amherst, 1981), 87.

though small, it would let all the water out before you are aware of it."[69] She clearly underscores the relationship between her innermost state and the most ordinary objects that lie to hand, declaring that "there was nothing in my nature contrary to the work of God but was showed to me and in a way so simple I could not misunderstand"; elsewhere she refers to God teaching her in "dreams and visions and revelation and gifts."[70] Her accounts of her dreams similarly demonstrate a process of reasoning with the material objects of everyday life, as in her "Dream of the Cakes" and "The Dream of Washing Quilts." In these highly detailed accounts, hot griddles, batter spoons, washtubs, and clean bed quilts are the vehicles by which her "visions and revelations" are given to her, and by which she is instructed.[71]

69 Ibid., 88.

70 Ibid., 88, 96. For a clear case in which agrarian symbolism of the most ordinary kind shows its tremendous emotive and psychological powers, see Liana Vardi, "Imagining the Harvest in Early Modern Europe," *American Historical Review* 101 (1996): 1356–1397.

71 Humez, *Gifts of Power*, 99–102. Jackson carefully recorded the most minute and concrete practical details surrounding her actions in the visions she received. For example, she comments in the "Dream of Baking Cakes" that in her dream she proceeded just as she does when really baking cakes: "I don't think I put on more than a spoonful [of batter] each time – it is my manner in baking any kind of batter cakes to try the griddle with batter enough to make a cake the size of a half a dollar, so that if it sticks, then there is not much batter wasted." (p. 100). In the "Dream of Washing Quilts" she is "squatting down, washing three bed quilts and singing as I was awashing," and though she is perched dangerously over a pool of water "[y]et I did not feel to move till I had done my washing. So I sat still singing until I was done" (p. 100). The powerful ordinariness of bed quilts is revealed by their use in the "story quilt" tradition and as signals along the Underground Railroad. Joan of Arc's visions and voices came to her in the ordinary objects she met with in her daily perambulations about the village. Jacob Boehme, a German cobbler, had a conversion experience in 1600 when he saw a flash of light in a pewter dish (a different kind of "flash in the pan").

That the things people think with are historically resonant – and therefore revealing to the historian – is also exemplified in the *Meditations* written by the emperor and Stoic philosopher Marcus Aurelius in the decade or so before his death in A.D. 180. In ruminating upon the "grace and fascination that there is even in the incidentals of Nature's processes," the emperor instances phenomena that would not occur to

Jackson's visionary life was clearly linked with agency and power: this is apparent in her forty-year career as a preacher and founder of the first black Shaker community in Philadelphia. Indeed, there is a close connection between her inner world of imagery, belief, and reasoning, her life of manual labor, and her mission. Along these same lines, it is worth noting that accounts of the working lives of pre-modern and early modern countrywomen emphasize the multitude of tasks they regularly performed, the skill that these required, and the "satisfaction of doing productive work" that they might have enjoyed.[72]

One is struck, indeed, by the similarity between Jackson's linking of object and revelation and the imagery of household chores found in *The Doctrine of the Herte*, a devotional text for cloistered (probably Franciscan) women: "Knowleche of the synnes by the mouth in confession is nothing ellis but puttyng out filthes of the hous of our hert by the dore of the mouth with the brome of the tonge."[73] The *Fasciculus Morum*, a fourteenth-century treatise on the seven deadly sins, makes abundant use of such imagery: for example, a section dealing with "what things hinder almsgiving" directs the hearer to sow the seed of good deeds by properly preparing the soil, and uses the imagery of the "plowshare of confession." The "spiritual plow and all that goes with it" (a phrasing highly reminiscent of the language of wills and of estate administrative records) names the coulter, share, oxen, stubbles, bad weeds, marl, seeds, hoe, harrow, harvest of sheaves, and, finally, the "barn of good conscience where the crop is threshed

---

most modern thinkers: the cracks that appear in a loaf of bread "though not intended in the baking," figs "at their ripest," olives "on the verge of falling," "the drooping head of a cornstalk, the wrinkling skin when a lion scowls, the drip of foam from a wild boar's jaws." See *Meditations*, trans. Maxwell Staniforth (Harmondsworth, 1964), 53. These points deserve further development than can be attempted here.

72 G.E. Fussell and K.R. Fussell, *The English Countrywoman: A Farmhouse Social History, A.D. 1500–1900* (London, 1953), 42.

73 I am indebted for knowledge of this text to a paper given by Dr Denis Renevey, of the University of Lausanne, at the International Medieval Congress (University of Leeds) in July 2001. Dr Renevey is currently working on an edition of *The Doctrine of the Herte*, and I thank him for permission to cite his translation here.

in frequent penitential exercises."[74] Thus, thought and object have frequently been linked by those who, like medieval peasants, spent their lives working and who were surrounded by the instruments and the products of their labor.

Understanding Court Roll Data as Evidence of Peasant Thought

In our discussion of the links between thought and objects, we have so far glanced at historical analogies and also at "texts" that might properly be styled "documents of ideas": proverbs and church wall paintings may be viewed as sources that preserve evidence regarding the thought and behavior of those who made and used them. Such primary materials created by the "many" (rural and urban) dovetail with the prescriptive literature, sermons, and confessors' manuals that have been widely studied by historians of popular culture, as discussed earlier, since the latter texts targeted the "many" and were profoundly shaped by them.

Fortunately, a closer view of specific medieval rural communities is possible; chiefly through study of the many different types of estate administrative records,[75] all of which have something to tell us about the tenants who held land of and worked for their lords – in the present case, the abbot of Ramsey. Account rolls record the lord's receipts and expenses manor by manor, and thus are weighted toward revealing seigneurial interests. In association with those interests, however, the rolls record both payments to rural artisans for the making of tools and utensils for the monastic community and cultivation of the demesne, as well as the purchase of a truly astounding range and variety of goods, most of them manufactured locally by tenants and servants of Ramsey Abbey lands. Upwood's account roll of c. 1298 is a good representative record of the kinds of routine entries made under "Expenses" that reveal local manufacturing and its products: for example, under the heading *Caruce* (plows), note is made of either monthly or annual wages paid to a smith (*faber*) for making plowshares and horseshoes (*ferura equorum*), and to a *carpentarius carucarum* (a carpenter who makes plows); under *Carte* (carts), pay-

74 *Fasciculus Morum: A Fourteenth-Century Preacher's Handbook*, ed. and trans. Siegfried Wenzel (University Park, PA, 1989), 549–551.

75 These records are discussed in more detail in Chapter Three below.

ments are recorded for the purchase of pieces of iron for binding wheels (*ad rotas ligandas*), for one hundred cart nails (*C. de cartenayl*), canvas halters (*3d in capistris factis de canabo*), and 20d in wages for one man for making harness for fifteen days (*Et in stipendio unius hominis pro hernes' fact'*).[76] Small miscellaneous purchases were also noted under such headings as *Res minute*, *Minute emptiones*, *Cetera minuta*: a sampling of the items found there in Upwood's early fourteenth-century account rolls includes saddles, horse collars (*colar'*), axes, *stratnayls*, kippecord (a piece of harness), sacks, baskets (*sporte*), seedlips (*salopus*, *saticulum*, the sower's seed basket), a cider-press (*pressurium*), platters (*platellis*), sieves, windlasses, towels (*manutergium*), boots, a doorlock (*cerura ad hostium*), a lock for the door of the hay barn (*i sera ... ad hostium Grangie feni*), and bolters (*taratantar'*) for sifting flour.

It will be instantly seen that these sorts of items would also be found among the "*principalia* of peasant households,"[77] indeed were frequently made there, both for the manorial lord and for the peasants' own use. Data found in the 1290 lay subsidy on movable goods, levied by the king and based on a household's movable wealth, confirms this picture: not only grain and livestock, but also carts of varying quality, pots and vessels, fishing nets, boats, and other items appear, adding to our sense that the villager was normally surrounded by "things."[78] Taken together, the evidence suggests that villagers' long-term, complex relationship with the manorial lord extended their material culture. This culture may be viewed more closely through court roll data.[79]

76 In court rolls and related documents, pence are regularly abbreviated as "d" and shillings as "s"; both denominations were in common use in the village, as shown by villagers' ability to pay court fines and fees.

77 Hogan, "The Labor of their Days," 98.

78 For a study of lay subsidy data for this region of England, see *Early Huntingdonshire Lay Subsidy Rolls*, ed. J.A. Raftis and M.P. Hogan (Toronto, 1976).

79 The very language of the record can reveal a community of material interests between lord and villager, as in Upwood's 1311 court where it was noted that the woodland of a neighboring lord, John de Deen, "has encroached on" (*se extendet super*) a rod of land held by William le Neweman and a forera (headland) of William le Couper "to the disinheritance of the lord and of his tenants" (*ad exhereditationem domini et tenentium suorum*).

Like account rolls, court rolls contain numerous references to "things" (although not in the systematic and exhaustive enumeration found in the former). More usefully, they give us a glimpse of the arrangements that villagers routinely made to share goods, land, labor, and expertise, and thus to "build resilience into the material life of household and village."[80] Again, a few examples of this vast area of routine court roll data must suffice here.

The use of goods in ongoing working arrangements is exemplified in two entries in Ellington's 1294 roll: William Bok acknowledges himself bound to William Aldyth for two posts valued by the jurors to be worth 8d (*recognouit se teneri Willelmo Aldyth in duobus postis appreciatis per Iuratos ad viiid*). In the same court Aldyth acknowledged that he had been bound to Bok for a pair of harness traces, a draft animal, and line measuring twelve feet in length called "bryggestere" (*recognouit se detinuisse Willelmo Bok vnum par' tractuum. i bestam et vnum lignum quod dicitur bryggestere Longitudine xii pedes*). Because he had not returned these to Bok at the time agreed upon, Aldyth was fined for damages and for an "unjust withholding" (*pro iniusta detencione*). Another routine type of entry that records "things" and the arrangements in which they figure is the citation of alewives who were to bring their gallon, pottle (that is, half-gallon), and quart measures to court to be checked: for example, it is noted in Ellington's 1294 court that Joan Pylecok brought her gallon and pottle measures (*tulit g.p.*); Alice Twyt did not (*non tulit*; and she also sold watered-down ale, *debilem cervisiam*); and the wife of Simon de Elyngton brought all her measures (*nihil deliquid*, "nothing lacking"). Other citations include a debt involving a rotten cask (*de quadam tina putrida*), a broken agreement (*conventio*) concerning sheep not salved, the illegal taking of doves with nooses (*cum laqueis*, Upwood, 1353, 1435), unjust detention of a belt (*zona*, Upwood, 1350), a debtor attached *per vaserea et alia utensilia* (his possessions seized, Upwood 1443), theft of a bronze pot, the discovery of eight horse collars ornamented with silver and left behind by a suspected felon (*unam ollam eneam, viii coliara de ~~argert~~ argentat'*, Upwood 1450), and the charge that a priest who had apparently left the village took some of

80 Raftis and Hogan, *Early Huntingdonshire Lay Subsidy Rolls*, 18–19.

the parish church plate with him (Upwood 1439).[81] These examples of working arrangements, obligations, and debts reveal something of villagers' attitudes towards and ideas about objects, and the legal arrangements that enforced these attitudes.

The standard injunction found in the court rolls in connection with the personal suretyship system and distraint, that "more should be taken until" (*plus capere donec*) satisfaction is made, also evinces the commonality of tools and again, most importantly for the present discussion, the readiness with which they could be entered as counters in a variety of institutional arrangements. A local official might be ordered to "attach" a personal possession, that is, to seize and hold it, until a person charged with a delict had answered the charge or made satisfaction (this is also called distraining the person, found in citations where an official is ordered to distrain someone: *Et preceptum est quod distringatur*). Such "attached" items found in our two court roll series include a wide variety of articles, such as knives, sacks, gloves, sickles, hoods, tunics, axes, bills, hatchets, bee hives, and, in Upwood's rolls in the 1290s, bird decoys (*pro uno volatu habendo*). Thus, in 1301 William de Rauele was attached by a knife to answer for having taken greenwood out of the lord's wood at Rokesgroue (*attachiatus fuit per unum billum ad respondendum de hoc quod asportauit virgas extra Rokesgroue*). Because William was unwilling or unable to clear himself of the charge of stealing greenwood, it was ordered that his knife be kept and that more should be taken until he made satisfaction (*et non iustificat se Ideo teneatur et plus capiatur donec etc.*). The range of objects includes implements, grain, animals, even the person's body: William de Stowe, who did not appear in Ellington's 1290 court as ordered to answer charges of beating

81 Colin Platt has made the point that the office of churchwardens, and somewhat later their accounts, first appear in the fourteenth and fifteenth centuries, at the moment when parishioners' contributions to the church fabric had generated a critical mass of property that they were anxious to safeguard. See his *The Parish Churches of Medieval England* (London, 1981). Upwood's 1439 court roll contains a reference to two churchwardens, styled as *custodes bonorum et catallorum ecclesie,* "keepers of the goods and chattels of the church," who bring a charge "against William Petry, priest in a plea of detention of two chalices" (*versus Willelmum Petry preest in placito detentionis duorum calicium*).

another villager, was to be attached "by the body" (*per corpus*).[82] In a 1320 Upwood case a "Byl" was taken on Grigory, the servant of a local lord, John de Deen, and "more" was "to be taken" until he cleared himself of the charge of damage in the lord's wood (*plus capere donec justificit se de dampno facto in bosco domini*). Axes taken on outsiders trespassing in the lord's wood (Ellington 1306) are to be kept (*retinere*) and more taken until they answer for the trespass (*et plus capere donec iustisiteuerunt se ad respondendum*). As these examples show, objects and people alike could be reconceived as symbols of obligation. Indeed, objects could even be equated with people. The first entry recorded in the earliest surviving court roll for Ellington (1278) records an incident where a father and son patch up a broken retirement agreement in court, the father hands over the tenement to his son, and then makes arrangements to leave the village with his chattels (*recedere extra villam cum suis catallis*). In this case the chattels assume an almost symbolic quality, as it is their removal which marks the father's permanent departure from the village.

With the idea that goods could be apprehended in multiple ways we return to the metaphor of the labyrinth. A useful conceptualization of structure and process in village life is provided by viewing both the village and the messuage (a house and its yard) as a labyrinth through which services, implements, land, and labor readily flow because of their inherent liquidity or interchangeability. The value of this model is supported by the minutiae of court roll data. In Upwood's 1311 court, Nicholas son of Adam acknowledged that he violated what seems to be a joint landholding arrangement with John son of Robert Atewodestrate by withholding half of the crop of one-half acre of wheat (*fregit conventionem ... de vestura dimidie acre frumenti de qua medietatem ei detinuit*). In an agreement entered into the 1422 record (an enigmatic agreement, because few details are provided), the jurors say that William Cary will have one-third part of all the movable goods of John Byg except his six plow animals and plow with appurtenances (*tertium partem omnium mobilium Iohannis Byg exceptis sex animalibus caruce sue caruca cum toto apparatu*) because John will maintain William's tenement (*eo quod sustentabit et manutenebit tenementum suum*); and the Steward assigned (*assignauit*) four men to make division of the said

82 The varieties of pledging are discussed fully in Olson, *A Chronicle*, 46–55.

goods (*pro bonis mobilibus predictis diuidendis*). Evidence of a vibrant local land market characterized by a flow of small parcels, usually for short-term lease, survives in entries recording the purchase or sub-lease of land between villagers. Thus, in Ellington's 1311 court, John Pylcok purchased one half acre of land (*perquisit dimidiam acram terre*) from William Walkelyn in Sybethorp, and Richard de Coten' and Laurence Peuerel are his pledges that he show his charter at the next Court. In 1306 William Aldyth leased two rods of customary land to a freeman, Thomas le Skynner, and the land was to be taken into the lord's hand.[83] A study of agrarian bylaws preserved in court rolls has turned up the imaginative provision that money collected from the fines for keeping unrung pigs[84] would be given to the local poor.

Other entries that reveal inter-villager associations and transactions involving labor, money, land, and animals include references to villagers borrowing money from each other, receiving salaries from each other, fathers receiving salaries earned by their children, and debts involving the care of animals (Upwood 1428, 1429, 1430): in the Upwood court of 25 June 1429, Richard Baker impleaded (prosecuted) Richard Newman in a plea of debt for payment of his salary for five and one half years (*pro solutione pro salario suo pro v annis et dimidia*). One entry in the 1430 roll involves a charge of debt of 2s 4d, apparently involving a loan of money and ale, against the bailiff of Upwood from ten years earlier (*x annis elapsis ex mutuo et per cervisiam*). Mutual dependence for labor in the less populous villages of the 1440s and 1450s is clearly visible in injunctions published at that time that no workers in the village (the 1448 roll specifies carpenters and tailors) are to serve outside the vill if the lord or a tenant has need of their services (*ad servicium eorum Necessitatem*

83 For a fuller discussion of peasant land transactions, see Raftis, *Tenure and Mobility*, especially Chapter Three, "Conveyance Among Customary Tenants," 63–92. On page 77 Raftis notes that the court was "sensitive to the loss of villeinage to outsiders or freemen," and that "such violations were strictly corrected by taking the land into the lord's hands."

84 Pigs' noses were ringed to keep them from destructive digging and feeding. Warren Ault, *Open-Field Husbandry and the Village Community: A Study of Agrarian By-laws in Medieval England* (Philadelphia, 1965), 29. This essay provides abundant evidence of peasant ingenuity in managing shares in land, labor, and implements.

habent), under a penalty of 6s 8d to be paid to the lord, and another 6s 8d to be paid to the church, a provision discussed in more detail below, and yet another example of a creative use being made of the fines generated in court.

A variety of textual sources, then, and especially court rolls, provides a detailed picture of behaviors that arose from the flow of resources, labor, time, and people within the labyrinth of the village. Such a picture, which differs so dramatically from the old conceptualization of the "immobility" of village life, may, if read carefully, reveal what anthropologists Sidney Mintz and Richard Price have called the "unconscious 'grammatical' principles, which may underlie and shape behavioral response." To this end they call for the study of "cognitive orientations, on the one hand, basic assumptions about social relations (what values motivate individuals, how one deals with others in social situations, and matters of interpersonal style), and on the other, basic assumptions and expectations about the way the world functions phenomenologically (for instance, beliefs about causality, and how particular causes are revealed)."[85]

For the villager, such "orientations" might include what could be called "instrumentality," that is, reasoning through ("thinking with") implements, objects, and work, which includes elements of analogizing and symbolic thinking, as clearly expressed in proverbial wisdom. Robert Darnton's question "what things were good to think with?"[86] may be answered in many different ways for the medieval peasant. As suggested above, peasants had the habit of "thinking with" things, "thinking with" women (for example, women help to define office-holding because they cannot take part in it), and (in our villages, which belonged to a monastic lordship) even "thinking with" monks. Such a mode of cogitation must have leaned heavily on the village reality of the partibility and interchangeability of goods, labor, and land: a villager could be pledged by another man or his own body, be ordered to "be at

85 Sidney W. Mintz and Richard Price, *The Birth of African-American Culture: An Anthropological Perspective* (Boston, 1992), 9–10. The discussion in this chapter, "The Encounter Model" (pp. 7–22), is extremely valuable.

86 Robert Darnton, *The Great Cat Massacre and Other Episodes in French Cultural History* (New York, 1985), 4.

his law six-handed,"[87] be distrained by an axe, lease out a small portion of his tenement for a money payment, care for another villager's animals for a salary, share the aftermath of a hay crop, or hold shares in a total plowing machine where one man owns the draft animals, another owns the traces, and still others own various plow parts. Lordship itself provided a powerful mirror of such arrangements in the institution of commutation: "Just as the lord might commute certain work-units to a money payment and hire wage labour in its stead, so the villager might hire others to perform his servile obligations."[88] Peasants' (and lords') "unconscious grammatical principles," their assumptions and expectations about the world and their place in it, were influenced by the mobility and interchangeability evinced by everything around them.

The Medieval Village Construction of the Individual

While court rolls provide material for investigating the connections between work, agency, and sense of self, other estate administrative records make that connection in a wholly explicit manner: George Homans cites a 1209 manorial custumal for the royal villeins of Cirencester which refers to the villeins who "have their own free power, and live by their own labor, and are made *sulfodes*." According to Homans, in village families, the non-inheriting children who left home to make their own living (as opposed to those who stayed at home and were supported by their parents) were "called by a special name ... *selfodes* or *sulfodes*. The derivation of this word is unknown – it may have come from such form [sic] as *selfhood*."[89] Margaret

87 "To be at one's law six-handed" (also referred to as oath-helping, conjuration, or compurgation) means that the accused must show up at the next court with five other men who will swear with him that his story is true or that he is a trustworthy person. The same practice has been found for Carolingian Europe, half a millennium earlier: see Pierre Riché, *Daily Life in the World of Charlemagne* (Philadelphia, 1988), 260.

88 Raftis, *Tenure and Mobility*, 15–16.

89 See George Homans, *English Villagers of the Thirteenth Century* (1941; repr., New York, 1975), 209–210. Interestingly, according to the *Oxford English Dictionary*, s.v. "selfhood," the earliest use of this word was in a 1649 English translation of Boehme's letters (from the original German selbheit, ichheit, meinheit, eigenheit).

Archer has defined "selfhood" as "a continuous sense of self," and argues that the "embodied practices of human beings in the world [are] more important than their social relations for the emergence of selfhood ... and for the development of its properties and powers, meaning reflexivity [that is, reflection, evaluation], which only exists *in potentia* for every neonate."[90] While the emergence of selfhood, reflection, and the effects of reflection are not issues typically raised in connection with the peasant portion of humanity,[91] historians have not hesitated to make other types of pronouncements about peasant personality, describing it as essentially conformist, passive, even undifferentiated, especially in connection with the demands of common field agriculture.[92] The data of the court roll, a source which is preeminently a record of peasant behavior, open up new approaches to exploring the medieval villager's personality along the lines of choice and action.[93] What kind of individual personality was fostered in village society, a "small world" that was governed locally by farmers whose dominant economic mode was collective agriculture? What would the interior values of such a person be, and how were these values inculcated in individual men and women?

In order to answer these questions, we turn to another example of village life comparable to that of the medieval English peasant: Sabean's study of the village of Neckarhausen in early modern Germany, cited above. As the kings of early modern Europe harnessed the reservoirs of power which had been built up in communities like Upwood and Ellington from the time of their foundation in the earlier

90 Archer, *Being Human*, 121.

91 Steven Feierman takes a somewhat different approach to peasant thought in *Peasant Intellectuals: Anthropology and History in Tanzania* (Madison, WI, 1990), a study of the history and transmission of political ideas in some modern-day Nigerian peasant communities.

92 This is certainly the prevailing view of peasant personality in *Peasants and Peasant Societies*, ed. Teodor Shanin (2nd ed., Oxford, 1987), and in Jack M. Potter, et al., *Peasant Society: A Reader* (Boston, 1967); and see Oscar Lewis's description of Pedro Martínez in *Pedro Martínez: A Mexican Peasant and His Family*, especially pp. xxxv–xl.

93 Perhaps historians have too often made a mistake to which Pedro Martínez made rueful reference in his autobiography: that when city-dwellers look at peasants, they often "mistake what is outside for what is inside."

Middle Ages, the "formative age of European history,"[94] a new understanding of personality and the individual was imposed upon pre-existing peasant culture. Investigation of these changes will lead us to the earlier peasant self-concept, which will provide a useful model for understanding medieval English villagers' mentality and for interpreting court roll data.

Sabean argues for an "early modern construction of the individual" in which the state waged a "massive attack" on peasant culture "aimed at creating an image of the individual as a productive member of a house and cutting many of the ties which bound house inhabitants to their fellows," an attack in which "the officials of the sacral state also played a central role," creating an ideology that "arose in a framework of professional pastoral care."[95] From the sixteenth century on, the newly-powerful state tried to foster the notion of a "consistent personality, one that does not bend and change shape within shared experience, a unique individual."[96] Emerging in the early mod-

94 David Herlihy, *The Black Death and the Transformation of the West* (Cambridge, MA, 1997). According to Robert Muchembled, in late medieval France "real power was fragmented, since neither the Church nor the monarchy had the means to impose an efficacious centralization. France was a mosaic of small *pays*, of villages and towns that possessed a certain independence, even if all belonged within the same political and religious whole. The popular masses, under these conditions, enjoyed a relative cultural autonomy. Autonomy was even necessary to hold together every community, urban or rural, to provide a coherent explanation of the world, and to arm men against life's hardships." Thus, the mass of people "were not as totally subservient or as alienated as their distant descendants would be in the age of the Sun King." See Muchembled, *Popular Culture and Elite Culture in France, 1400–1750*, trans. Lydia Cochrane (Baton Rouge, 1985), 14–15. It is significant that much of the "explosion of documentation" in the early modern era is associated with the records of the state.

95 Sabean, *Power in the Blood*, 205. As noted earlier, the early modern state expanded its fiscal and military demands and made new claims to superior jurisdiction and legislation. Eamon Duffy's study of the English Church and the destruction of traditional religion, *Stripping of the Altars*, may be read as confirmation of this point.

96 Sabean, *Power in the Blood*, 209–210. As a result, according to Sabean, the "only model available was that of contamination," leading to the witch craze of the seventeenth century. Sabean understands the craze phenomenon as part of the "dialectic between state and population," one

ern period was "an ever developing and ever more precise notion of the individual as an integrated whole, detachable from the matrix of social relations, and definable in terms of a discrete set of needs," a result of the growth of state power so striking that "[i]n general, we will find villagers resisting in one way or other a notion of the unique, integrated, more-or-less consistent individual."

According to Sabean, before the state imposed the concept of the individual as a unique, integrated, and consistent self, villagers understood "inner psychological states as undetachable parts of *social* experience" (emphasis added). In "village and small town experience, ... the individual was grasped in community and communication modeled partly on the spoken word. In some way, sharing words with another was to commit oneself to him, to participate in a set of relationships." Hence the consequences of individual action in village society were broadly felt: a person was not "divorceable from his fellows and his sin could have disastrous consequences for his neighbors."[97] This was a social understanding rooted in the cooperative and collective mechanisms that were characteristic of most medieval societies, including urban centers, where guilds and communes are the most obvious examples of "solidarities."[98] These observations are valuable for considering the view of medieval English village person-

---

of whose effects was to "disseminate a notion of the person as detachable from the matrix of local relations." This definition has much in common with Geertz's description of the "modern Western notion of the person" as a "bounded, unique, more or less integrated motivational and cognitive universe ... organized into a distinctive whole and set contrastively both against other such wholes and against its social and natural background." Geertz, *Local Knowledge*, 59.

97 Sabean, *Power in the Blood*, 209–210.

98 The medieval university may also be viewed as a new urban solidarity drawing on older collective powers in the social order that derived ultimately from collective agriculture: groups of scholars, both students and masters, together created a powerful new institution in the growing towns and cities of twelfth-century Europe. Use of the term "solidarities" follows the work of Susan Reynolds, who has written extensively on the "collective activities of medieval lay people and the solidarities that underlay them" in both town and country. See *Ideas and Solidarities of the Medieval Laity* (Aldershot, 1995), vii, and Chapter Five in her *Kingdoms and Communities in Western Europe, 900–1300* (2nd ed., Oxford; New York, 1997) for a discussion of solidarity in villages and rural neighborhoods.

ality being advanced here, particularly the notion of a prevailing personality type that does "bend and change shape within shared experience" – the common field experience.[99]

Sabean's notion of a socially embedded human personality in the pre-modern era (and under state attack in the early modern period) and Archer's thesis of the "primacy of practice" add up to a picture of the medieval villager's mentality that is consonant with court roll evidence: we may think of the villager as a person who was not "detachable from the matrix of local relations," whose internal states were part of social experience, and whose sense of self was centered on agency, on labor, on getting work done. This working model of the villager's personality expands our reading of court roll evidence – indeed, the variables we are working with provide a rich field for inquiry: small-scale agriculturalists engaged in some form of collective agriculture who attended frequent and regular court sessions, situated in a political context in which the "State" was relatively weak and distant, and where real self-regulation, local and immediate, hinged on a vigorous "climate of debate" whose end-product is preserved in medieval court rolls. Court rolls have a particular value here because they preserve evidence of a working legal system whose laws "do not just regulate behavior, they construe it"; thus they possess an "imaginative, or constructive, or interpretive power, a power rooted in the collective resources of culture rather than in the separate capacities of individuals."[100]

Court rolls preserve evidence of numerous such collective mechanisms in the English village, in particular the tithing or frankpledge groups, the suretyship or pledge system (where a pledge must act as a guarantor for another person's behavior), group pledging, compurgation or oath-helping (also referred to as "being at one's law," defined earlier), and the hue and cry; even the jurors presenting the cases in court may be seen as a cooperative or collective phenomenon. Other fragments of evidence reveal the operations of common field agriculture itself, for example, in terms of trespass upon each other's strips in the open fields. Local cooperative mechanisms could be either

99 As we have seen, most historians who have raised the issue of the impact of collective ideas and practices on peasant personality have emphasized passivity and conformity and argued that common field farming discouraged entrepreneurship and, hence, individualism.

100 Geertz, *Local Knowledge*, 215.

comprehensive (in the sense of village-wide), or could bring smaller groups together in a variety of activities that fluctuated with time and purpose: thus solidarities existed that might follow the fluid lines of family relationship, neighborhood, landholding, and work activity that kept alive not only notions of cooperation but also participation. These kinds of formations are thus another expression of the collective cultural life of the village.

The present book focuses primarily on cooperative and inclusive practices, phenomena that are observable in court roll and other evidence, but that have been less frequently studied by students of medieval rural society. The rituals of the village court, the collective naming of persons, places, and things, were traditions that left their mark upon the individual's life and personality, corresponding to Sabean's view that the villager's "inner psychological states" were "undetachable from social experience."

A "construction of the individual" based on undetachability from village life with its fluid collective practices, in a setting where people were accustomed to (indeed depended on) the mobility and interchangeability of their surroundings as discussed above, may provide a key to understanding one aspect of English peasant society that has been viewed by most historians as an obstacle to analysis, that is, that one villager could be known by a number of different names (we return to this point more fully in Chapter Three). Judging from the evidence of court rolls (whose texts preserve the very language people used to refer to each other in everyday interactions), one person could be known by his or her parentage, place of origin, residential location in the village, occupation, official status, personal idiosyncrasies, and so on. Galfridus son of Eda, Galfridus of Coten', Galfridus Edessone, Galfridus Edithsone, Galfridus Reeve (*Galfridus filius Ede, Galfridus de Coten', Galfridus Edessone, Galfridus Edithsone, Galfridus Prepositus*) are all names that refer to the same man in late thirteenth- and early fourteenth-century Ellington. Presumably, medieval farmers did not find such multiplicity of names confusing or inefficient – quite the contrary, we must assume that such a system of naming fit in well with other aspects of normal village life, indeed was generated and sustained by them.[101] Instead of being an

101 One person having many names, and thus perhaps many personae, is a practice with analogues in other cultures. The phenomenon of recycling per-

obstacle to analysis, this naming system may itself be evidence of a flexible concept of the individual.

Multi-dimensional Village Storytelling

Thus far, our "disaggregation" of court roll data has emphasized its quality as a record of behavior; however, court rolls also preserve evidence of the medieval tradition of storytelling, just as inquisition trials, canonization proceedings, and other deposition-type texts do. As discussed earlier, these records are more familiar than court rolls are to the historian interested in peasant culture. The inquisition records used by Le Roy Ladurie, Ginzburg, Sabean, and more recently Pegg, Bartlett, and Arnold, the pardon tales in letters of remission studied by Davis, the records of complaint from twelfth-century Catalonia used by Bisson, the stories embedded in medieval chronicles used by Schmitt, the tales found in macaronic sermon literature studied by Siegfried Wenzel,[102] and testimonies recorded in village

---

sonalities which surface variously has been described in a recent study of Asian philosophy as part of a healthy existential mode. See Joel Kupperman, *Learning from Asian Philosophy* (New York, 1999), Part Two, "The Fluidity of Self." It is interesting to compare our depiction of the peasant experience of the social order with the modern personality construct of "thick-boundaried" and "thin-boundaried" people, the latter being those who "are flexible or fluid in their identities ... do not separate themselves from the natural world, but see themselves as continuous with nature, including animals and other humans." See Jerome Kroll and Bernard S. Bachrach, *The Mystic Mind: The Psychology of Medieval Mystics and Ascetics* (New York, 2005), Chapter Three, "Mysticism and Altered States of Consciousness," especially pp. 55–59. Note that this discussion anchors the construct in personal psychology, of which our sources give no direct evidence, rather than life experience. We would have to consider the latter as important here if we wish to entertain the idea of "thin-boundariedness" for medieval peasants.

102 See the works by Arnold, Bartlett, Davis, Goodich, Pegg, Sabean, and Schmitt cited earlier; see Emmanuel Le Roy Ladurie, *Montaillou: The Promised Land of Error*, trans. Barbara Bray (New York, 1978); Thomas N. Bisson, *Tormented Voices: Power, Crisis, and Humanity in Rural Catalonia, 1140–1200* (Cambridge, MA, 1998); Siegfried Wenzel, *Macaronic Sermons: Bilingualism and Preaching in Late-Medieval England* (Ann Arbor, 1994).

court rolls, all point to a pervasive storytelling tradition in medieval and early modern society where peasants figured as principal narrators (a topic we return to in the next chapter). What are the storytelling properties of the records of estate administration, and what kind of evidence do they provide?

Historians have drawn attention to the richness and longevity of the storytelling tradition. Medieval literature and sermons were frequently based on stories drawn from oral tradition. According to Robert Darnton in an essay entitled "Peasants Tell Tales," the sermons that were collected in preachers' manuals and other texts throughout the medieval period "refer to the same stories as those taken down in peasant cottages by folklorists in the nineteenth century." With respect to modes of transmission over time, Darnton notes a sixteenth-century account of the French *veillée*, "an evening fireside gathering, where men repaired tools and women sewed while listening to stories that would be recorded by folklorists three hundred years later and that were already centuries old."[103] The *veillée*, or "working bee," is a good example of the intimate connection between work and storytelling, each helping the other move forward.

The desire for entertainment and for outlets of expression may easily be instanced as part of the impetus that lay behind village storytelling, but what else might aid our analysis? When "peasants told tales," what else was happening? The work of psychologist Bruno Bettelheim, who has studied children's reception of fairy tales, can be

103 Darnton, *Great Cat Massacre*, 17. For a more extensive account of the *veillée* of the early modern period, and an excellent description of the larger social and economic context within which it flourished, see Olwen Hufton, *The Prospect Before Her: A History of Women in Western Europe*, vol. 1: *1500–1800* (New York, 1996), especially Chapters Three and Four, and pages 128–129. Sabean, *Power in the Blood*, 203–204, refers to the *Spinnstube*, the "spinning bee" of early modern German peasant life, "a winter evening gathering of unmarried women, which combined work and relaxation." (The *Spinnstube* was also one of the village institutions which the state, in its interest in controlling marriage and property descent, and with an eye on the "peasant farm as an object of taxation," was attempting to control by ordinance in the sixteenth and seventeenth centuries). For a more recent study of the numerous connections between medieval tales and the classic fairy tales of the nineteenth century, see Jan M. Ziolkowski, *Fairy Tales from Before Fairy Tales: The Medieval Latin Past of Wonderful Lies* (Ann Arbor, 2007).

useful because it can be applied more broadly to the ways in which stories and storytelling work in diverse settings for narrators and auditors of any age. According to Bettelheim, hearing stories enables people to more readily ponder and understand their own life experiences, because fantastic stories centering on other, fictional, yet ordinary people create safe objects within a removed context, "facilitating projections and identifications," so that problems and anxieties can be brought out into the open and confronted emotionally and psychologically. When people *tell* their stories, they make their experience more valuable still by subjecting it to the gaze of others. Public narration prompts the narrator to heighten and extend the meaning of his or her experiences, contributing perhaps to self realization, self awareness.[104]

In the village court session, officials, complainants, and defendants, too, stepped forward to make presentments, to tell their story.[105] In addition, and taking a larger view (as will be shown in Chapter One), the participation of villagers in the court proceedings amounted to a collective remembering and reworking of recent local history, that is, whatever was locally justiciable that had occurred since the "last Court" (*ultima Curia*). The past was subject to the same process of negotiation

104 See Bruno Bettelheim, *The Uses of Enchantment: The Meaning and Importance of Fairy Tales* (New York, 1977), especially the Introduction and Part One, pages 3–150. Quotation at p. 40. Certainly, telling one's story is the basis for much modern therapy; isn't public storytelling the key to AA's success? Joan Didion has remarked that "we tell ourselves stories in order to live," *The White Album* (New York, 1979), 1. Poet and novelist Janet Frame's comments on her childhood reaction to fairy tales accords with Bettelheim's description of the effect of these stories: "All the stories had a similar measure of delight ... none of [the characters] were more nor less than we were for all the list of extraordinary gifts, miracles, transformations, cruelties, and the many long years of wandering and searching, full of hope and expectation. Grimm's Fairy Tales was everybody's story seen in a special way." Quoted in Michael King, *Wrestling with the Angel: A Life of Janet Frame* (Washington, DC, 2000), 28.

105 In his discussion of the leet court or view of frankpledge, Maitland wrote: "Twice a year the villagers, bond and free, had to report themselves and tell tales one of another, while no tale went outside the manor to the ears of jealous neighbours or rapacious officials." Frederick Pollock and F.W. Maitland, *The History of English Law before the Time of Edward I* (2nd ed. 1898; repr., Cambridge, 1968) 1: 581.

as the business of the present. The village court, like the *veillée*, was a reunion where work and tale-telling came together.[106] In other words, for the purposes of studying the belief and action of the vast medieval majority, court rolls may be said to bear comparison with other types of records that are seen as containing "folk" narratives.

The Common Field Village and Analogous Communities

As we shall investigate in detail in the chapters that follow, peasant institutions and ideas necessarily developed around a powerful center: common field farming that was organized in the village on the basis of the tenement – the family holding.[107] This "smallholders' regime" of common-property rights formed the economic and cultural base of thousands of medieval villages, wherever a common field

106 In reading Ronald Blythe's interviews with elderly English village residents in the mid-twentieth century, one is struck by their effortless use of the language of epic in relating their everyday life experiences; see *Akenfield: Portrait of an English Village* (New York, 1969). As Blythe puts it, "Suffolk farm-workers use the incomparable English of the Book of Common Prayer and the King James Bible with naturalness and ease" (p. 62). According to one of his interviewees (a schoolmaster originally from Norfolk who described himself as a foreigner), the villagers "hate to forget a scrap of the past. It is all hoarded up and, if they live long enough, some of the ordinary things that have happened to them this week will end up as epics. Experiences have to turn into tales, and this process takes a long time" (p. 177). The penchant for storytelling may also derive from that the fact that (as one forty-five year old farm-worker observed), "Every bad thing gets to sound pleasant enough when time has passed" (p. 95).

107 Mintz and Price, *Birth of African-American Culture*, 24, use the image of concentricity to refer to the formative power exerted by a single, dominant institution or fact: "In the special context of early New World slavery, only certain types of institutions could be developed by the slaves ... we may conceive of the institutions created by the slaves as taking the form of a series of concentric circles." As we will see, in the present study this notion will be developed somewhat differently – the model provided by Mintz and Price is suggestive (indeed they themselves state that the word "concentric" is not particularly apt), but customary tenants were of course not slaves, even though the fact of constraint and limitation is important for medieval villagers, as we will see.

agricultural regime was practiced. (One estimate puts the percentage of English population living in common field townships at approximately two-thirds by the fourteenth century).[108] In a common field village, continuous management was required so that all residents could carry out farming operations in close quarters. For medieval common field farmers, the arenas for such constant management were assemblies such as the village court.

According to Eric Kerridge, smallholders in this system had "considerable flexibility in the choice of common field crop rotations, but all inside the rigid framework of fixed field-courses ... [m]aximum regulation of field-courses, maximum freedom in cropping, was ever the rule in common fields."[109] The machinery of regulation, run by villagers, made use of the common ideas, rituals, and symbols within the village labyrinth, giving rise to a society of great "complexity and nuance."

The powers unleashed by the primacy of labor within a context of self-regulation have been explored in other historical epochs. In her study of the peasant-citizen of classical Athenian democracy, Ellen Meiksins Wood asserts that the "independence of the labouring poor" was the very key to the world's first democratic regime, and the source of its "distinctive character."[110] According to Wood, Athenian democracy, in its "disposition of property rights as in its political institutions ... was uniquely determined by the logic of the smallholders' regime" with its "unparalleled climate of debate in juries and assemblies."[111] Further, many of the "most cherished ideals of Athenian culture, and even some of the most exalted notions of Greek philosophy, may owe their origins to the experience and aspirations of the Attic peasantry," especially the ideals of autonomy and self-sufficiency.[112] Crucial to these developments were the "practices of public deliberation and law-making" which

108 See Bruce M.S. Campbell and Ricardo A. Godoy, "Commonfield Agriculture: The Andes and Medieval England Compared," in *Making the Commons Work: Theory, Practice, and Policy*, ed. Daniel W. Bromley (San Francisco, 1992), 99–127, at 102.

109 Kerridge, *The Common Fields of England*, 71.

110 Ellen Meiksins Wood, *Peasant-Citizen and Slave: The Foundations of Athenian Democracy* (London, 1988), 81–82.

111 See Wood, *Peasant-Citizen and Slave*, 119–120, for a discussion of the "logic of the smallholders' regime." Quotation at p. 168.

112 Ibid., 126, 127.

> brought to fruition the flux of social values set in train by the evolution of the polis, and the felt need for a discourse [that is, philosophy] to deal with the grounds of ethical and political principles which could no longer be taken for granted. Even the form of this discourse owed much to the procedures of democracy, the dialectic of the law court, the lawyer's rhetorical principle that there are "two sides" to every question, and the worship of "holy persuasion," the essence of the polis which ... replaced both the tribal law of blood vengeance and the dominance of aristocratic jurisdiction.[113]

According to Wood, "[w]ith productive capabilities hardly superior to many impoverished peasant societies, Athens sustained an intellectual and artistic life whose fruits are with us still."[114]

The independence and self-regulation of the small-scale polis, whose economy and society were based on local agriculture, bear comparison with similar features in the village settlements of medieval Europe, where most day-to-day governance occurred at the local level, and where the weakness of the supra-regional state was at least as notable as its strength. (Indeed, as noted above, a substantial increase in the power of the state is seen as one of the great divides between the medieval and early modern periods).[115] The Athenian peasant-citizen "like other peasants" was "subject to the pressures of poverty and marginal property ... was not the undisputed master of the ... countryside but ... coexisted with landlords and the threats their superior wealth represented," yet he was fairly "free of juridical disabilities or political subjection." Wood's observation that the peasant-citizen "had the strength, as it were, to turn his weakness into law" may apply as well to the medieval peasant.[116]

113 Ibid., 171.

114 Ibid., 162.

115 A clear illustration of the tension between local and state power that connects with our earlier discussion of proverbial wisdom, may be found in Davis, *Society and Culture*, 242. She quotes one learned seventeenth-century editor and compiler of French local customs who described the purpose of his cutting and rearranging of proverbs as a step toward "the conformity, reason and equity of a SINGLE LAW ... under the authority of His Majesty."

116 Wood, *Peasant-Citizen and Slave*, 120. One might say that the village community, the "basic constituent unit of the polis," had a concentric function in

Taken together, historians' ideas about the power of medieval lordship and the limitations imposed by collective agriculture, as well as a modern sensibility biased in favor of "individualism" (and a rather narrow notion of individualism at that), have tended to emphasize the constraints of village life and their effect on peasant personality.[117] The goal of this study is to contribute to a more balanced view of medieval society by considering how peasants thought about themselves and their world. So far we have seen that their lives and even their identities were not static or passive, and we have considered some of the origins and attributes of that complexity. The system in which they lived did (like all systems) impose constraints and limitations, but it will be argued here that those "constraints" clearly marked out a theater of action whose very limits endowed villagers with power and a consciousness of that power. Indeed, the juxtaposition of constraint and power epitomizes common field agriculture, as we have seen above.

Freedom within structure – even within constraint – is one of the cornerstones of the "logic of the smallholders' regime." The cultural

---

Athenian political and social life, just it had in the civilization of the Middle Ages. In both places, the "logic of the smallholders' regime" was dispositive.

117 For a recent example of this pervasive view, see Hyams, *Rancor and Reconciliation*, 248: "Villagers knew the reasons behind violent acts that enlivened the dullness of rural life far better than we can." Similarly, Joel T. Rosenthal, in *Telling Tales: Sources and Narration in Late Medieval England* (University Park, PA, 2003), describes villagers enjoying a rare feeling of importance when testifying before the king's official in Proof of Age proceedings: "... these undistinguished peasants and artisans were, at least for the moment, elevated and dignified by virtue of their moment in the sun. The ephemeral mantle of status and credibility fell upon those summoned to participate in the king's affairs" (p. 2). The weakness of this stereotypical view is that it imposes meaning from the outside. Further, many historians have assumed that the "contempt for labor" *topos* in the classical and medieval literary traditions had a depressive effect but, as Wood points out, this is an aristocratic view which, in the case of Athens, has been "made to represent the ethos of the Athenian people as a whole, ascribed even to the labourers who were the prime targets of anti-democratic attitudes. The tendency to generalize from these aristocratic attitudes has traveled freely across ideological boundaries and has ... played an important role in both conservative and Marxist histories" (*Peasant-Citizen and Slave*, 138).

history approach outlined here suggests that, however much it may strike modern sensibilities as paradoxical, power and a sense of freedom developed out of the customary control of mostly modest-sized tenements within boundaries set by a collective framework. Boundaries impose limits, but they also mark out an arena within which thought and activity take root and develop: the African-American experience under slavery would be an extreme example of such culture and constraint. Culture offers to the individual "a horizon of latent possibilities – a flexible and invisible cage in which he can exercise his own conditional liberty."[118] Perhaps the medieval villager, like the Athenian peasant-citizen, "was uniquely well situated to impose his logic of self-preservation on the whole community," indeed, "to turn his weakness into law." The following chapters will explore aspects of that traditional freedom, and how these were expressed in the village and in the minds of the villagers themselves.

118 Ginzburg, *Cheese and the Worms*, xxi.

CHAPTER ONE

Performance, Ritual, and Storytelling: Drama with a Purpose

The century and a half covered in the present study embraced the closing of the era of late medieval economic and demographic expansion, the famines and epidemics of the fourteenth and fifteenth centuries, and the varying course of reconstruction and retrenchment that characterized the first half of the fifteenth century. The jurors who stepped forward each year to take their oath and make their presentment of "all that had happened" since the previous court, and all the other villagers who came as suitors, complainants, and respondents to that assembly, may be viewed as steady witnesses to those turbulent times in the village. Much of the "complexity and nuance" of the European countryside in our period derived from the ebb and flow of village life in an era of demographic loss and economic change.[1]

1 Ellen Meiksins Wood draws attention to the moment-by-moment quality of historical change in her analysis of the origins of the Greek concepts of freedom and autonomy. She argues that in the period after the reforms of Solon in the late sixth century B.C., it was the "status of the 'multitude' ... in relation to their erstwhile lords" that gave the concept of freedom in the fifth century its "distinctive emphasis on individual autonomy and masterlessness, the quality which for Aeschylus distinguished Athens so radically from states with *subjects* and no *citizens*." Freedom "derives its meaning from an opposition not to chattel slavery but to the formerly dependent condition of the peasantry." Indeed, she asserts that what historians see as the "height of 'classical' culture may in fact derive its distinctive characteristics from its transitional character ... at *an unrepeatable moment* [emphasis mine] in the development of this society as it passed from the oral tradition to literacy." See *Peasant-Citizen and Slave: The Foundations of Athenian Democracy* (London, 1988), especially Chapter Four (pp. 126–172); quotations at pp. 132–133 and 168–

In the present chapter, we examine how the demands of village life gave rise to one aspect of what Charles Phythian-Adams has called "a whole, vigorous and variegated popular culture, the matrix of everyday life"[2] – ritual. We may imagine the imperatives of common field farming and self-regulation running like electrical currents through the meetings of the local court, charging the work of those assemblies, and requiring villagers to summon up their cultural reserves and construct a purposeful drama to do that work. Indeed, it was the necessity of getting such work done that helped ensure the vitality of these local courts, until the encroachment of the state in the early modern period.[3] Such an interpretation invites the historian to focus on the performance and ritual aspects of the court and accords well with the notion of the "primacy of practice," that is, that self-consciousness emerges from our practical activity in the world.[4] An examination of the ritual aspects of the court will provide a clearer understanding of the part it played in the lives of medieval villagers.

The court roll, as suggested earlier, was the product of a changing and diverse community. Alongside its obvious judicial and regulatory functions, the court was also a forum for public announcements, a place to record agreements, acknowledge debts, and resolve disputes.

---

169. For a recent synthesis of Black Death scholarship that vividly reasserts the plague's impact as a "turning point in History," see Ole J. Benedictow, *The Black Death, 1346–1353: The Complete History* (Woodbridge, 2004). The significance of post-plague developments in Upwood and Ellington will be discussed in Chapters Four and Five below.

2 Charles Phythian-Adams, "Ceremony and the Citizen: The Communal Year at Coventry, 1450–1550," in *Crisis and Order in English Towns, 1500–1700*, ed. Peter Clark and Paul Slack (Toronto, 1972), 57.

3 Edwin B. DeWindt has contrasted the liveliness and longevity of the village court with the contemporaneous baronial or honor courts whose more restricted area of jurisdiction and body of suitors caused those assemblies to wane long before their village counterparts did. See *Land and People in Holywell-cum-Needingworth* (Toronto, 1976).

4 As George Homans observed, "one of the most important functions of courts ... is giving ceremonial representation to many of the vital myths of a society." See *English Villagers of the Thirteenth Century* (1941; repr., New York, 1975), 341. Medieval and early modern historians are increasingly aware of the ritual and theatrical dimensions of court: see, for example, *The Court as a Stage: England and the Low Countries in the Later Middle Ages*, ed. Steven Gunn and Antheun Janse (Woodbridge, 2006).

It had competence to oversee a broad range of matters: offer vacant tenements for possession, proclaim stray animals, select and swear in officials, publicize bylaws that governed agricultural operations and the management of animals (especially the kind that might get loose and trample grain), cite cases of the hue and cry that had been raised since the previous court and evaluate their legitimacy, call upon the head or chief man of each tithing group to verify that all males over the age of twelve were properly sworn into the group, and hear local cases of blood-letting and slander and settle them by determining guilt, assessing and charging fines and damages, and assigning personal pledges to ensure that these obligations were met. Such an all-purpose forum drew the vast majority of adult villagers, men and women, into the court year after year in connection with a great variety of business. This lively meeting gave rise to a document teeming with people and activity, oriented around cases that concerned individuals, families, groups of varying size and composition, and *tota communitas*, the entire community.

Further, this treasure trove of historical detail is attached to the actions of named men and women who emerge over the course of the proceedings as real people.[5] Information and knowledge of precedent were needed to act upon the cases that came before the court, and that information gathering depended heavily upon the public recitation of "facts" by jurors and other officials, as well as complainants, victims, witnesses, and suitors to the court. In short, the routine participation of many people to establish fact was central to the operation of the court. The objective of the present chapter is to explore the ways in which power was created and used in the court session, as men and women would advance, speak, and retire from center stage in a living drama of public debate and decision-making. In such public recitations, a feeling of inclusion was fostered in all participants, recent history was canvassed collectively, and local custom, a hybrid of both seigneurial and village making, was discovered, cited, and affirmed.

5 Note the difference between this assertion and that of Larry R. Poos, who has argued that "what is given in the documents are names and not persons," in "Peasant 'Biographies' from Medieval England," in *Medieval Lives and the Historian: Studies in Medieval Prosopography*, ed. Neithard Bulst and Jean-Philippe Genet (Kalamazoo, 1986), 201–214, at 208.

When the court was called upon to help keep the peace,[6] its character as a performance arena possessing a ceremonious quality must have been particularly activated, in order to create an environment that favored the processes of negotiation and resolution-seeking. Explicit examples of such activity occur throughout the court rolls, as in Ellington's 1391 record where an audience of several local troublemakers with the lord as peace-maker is staged, probably in the court with the steward serving as the lord's agent: "It is ordered by the lord that Agnes Reynold and Thomas Foot and Elena his wife, both before him, conduct themselves rightly towards the other [Agnes]" (*Preceptum est per dominum quod Agnes Reynold et Thomas Foot et Elena uxor eius uterque coram bene se habeant versus alteram*). Disputes might be settled or an issue brought forward at the request or "at the instance" (*ad instanciam*) of a third party, as in a 1278 Ellington case where friends intervene to settle a quarrel between a father and son, and a 1306 case where the rector intervenes to ask the abbot's permission (*ex speciali gratia*) to send a boy from a local family outside the village to study. Villagers also paid to have court recognition of their settlement of debts and other points of conflict between them, as in a 1306 Ellington entry which exemplifies both this and a case of "instancing": a licence of agreement is recorded for Agnes Gyngyl and pledged by Ranulph Grym, and the fee is excused at the instance of Ranulph (*Et condonatur ad instanciam eiusdem Ranulphi*). While the exact procedure is not specified in these cases, it must have involved the "instancer" coming forward to claim the court's attention and make his request. Clearly, peace-keeping, public reconciliation, and negotiation were indispensable mechanisms in a common field regime; and while the village court was not the only forum where such issues could be joined, it was the only one to be minuted.[7]

6 See Paul R. Hyams, *Rancor and Reconciliation in Medieval England* (Ithaca, 2003), especially 196–208, for a discussion of the peace-keeping role of the court and the local clergy. Interestingly, the latter sometimes also had a special location for their activities as mediators: Hyams cites G.H. Cook, *The English Mediaeval Parish Church* (2nd ed., London, 1955), who notes in one church a room over the porch used by the priest for peace-keeping. See *Rancor and Reconciliation*, 203 n84.

7 Warren Ault has argued that there must have been "non-manorial meetings of the villagers" to regulate open field and common field husbandry in villages of divided lordship, and when demesne acres were farmed to

To begin an exploration of village culture via court records with a focus on performance and ritual is a useful approach because these aspects of the court emphasize its instrumentality. The court with its officials and suitors, its cases and precedents, and its imperative need to find solutions, constituted a framework within which action could be effectively taken as in the *ad instanciam* ritual described above. The assumption of offices, oath-taking, answering to charges, providing sureties, and other routine business were the primary instruments of that court, and may be viewed as clear examples of "culture as process," particularly since the court met fairly regularly, year after year, with broad jurisdictional and governing powers.

Clifford Geertz has argued that we can learn something about how people define themselves as persons by "analyzing the symbolic forms – words, images, institutions, behaviors – in terms of which ... people actually represented themselves to themselves and one another."[8] In the court, by their words and actions, people conveyed information and expressed their views about themselves, each other, and their common experiences, indeed, "grasped [one another] in community and communication modeled partly on the spoken word," as Sabean explained it.[9] The actions and routine procedures that carried forward the business of the court were thus interior as well as public experiences that linked agency and personality; their preservation in the court rolls provides material for an investigation of villager mentality, perhaps even village "common sense," that is, a "historically constructed cultural system" which Geertz defines as "what the mind filled with presuppositions ... concludes."[10]

Medieval people from all walks of life recognized and relied upon the court to protect customary rights and define space, and to function as a long-standing, permanent placeholder, as a setting for negotiation, and as a reminder of the claims of lordship: thus, when lords

---

the tenants. See *Open-Field Husbandry and the Village Community: A Study of Agrarian By-Laws in Medieval England* (Philadelphia, 1965), 51; and see same for proof that even such non-manorial meetings could generate documents.

8 Clifford Geertz, *Local Knowledge* (New York, 1983), 58.

9 David Warren Sabean, *Power in the Blood: Popular Culture and Village Discourse in Early Modern Germany* (Cambridge, 1984), 209–210.

10 Geertz, *Local Knowledge*, 76, 84, 93.

leased out their manors as a total economic concern, they frequently retained the jurisdiction of the court and its profits, even though the latter were usually fairly modest. Indeed, according to P.D.A. Harvey, by the later Middle Ages the existence of such a court "served to define the manor itself." One of the meanings of the word "manor" by the fifteenth century was "a piece of landed property with tenants over whom the landlord exercised rights of jurisdiction in a private court," thus "the word moved from the vocabulary of estate management to become a technical legal term, a position it retained from the sixteenth century to the twentieth."[11] The plasticity of meaning attached to the court suggests that its rituals were of greater moment to the majority of Europeans in their everyday life than were the large-scale displays of royal and ecclesiastical power that have long attracted most of the scholarly attention.

Medieval Rituals

Medieval civilization, like all civilizations, lived by ritual. Countless events that ranged across the spectrum of social, cultural, and political life were accompanied by ritual, apparent in the coronations, courts, and parliaments of kings, in the liturgies of the Church, and in the public entries, guild processions, and festivals of town and city. The articulation of ritual continued before smaller audiences as well, where its purposeful character might be more intimately apprehend-

11 Harvey, *Manorial Records* (London, 1984), 2. Maria Bertram's feelings of self-importance are considerably increased as the carriage brings her up to Sotherton Court, the "ancient manorial residence of the family, with all its rights of Court-Leet and Court-Baron," in Chapter Eight of Jane Austen's *Mansfield Park* (published in 1814). Also see Gadi Algazi, "Lords Ask, Peasants Answer: Making Traditions in Late-Medieval Village Assemblies," in *Between History and Histories: The Making of Silences and Commemorations*, ed. Gerald Sider and Gavin Smith (Toronto, 1997), 199–229, where he notes that possession of the court recitations was often used as proof of a lord's jurisdiction. For a recent early modern study emphasizing the Tudor propensity for drawing on the powers of the ancient parish, see Robert Palmer's study showing how Henry VIII used the parish to police the clergy and carry out the reformation of the English church, *Selling the Church: The English Parish in Law, Commerce, and Religion, 1350–1550* (Chapel Hill, 2002).

ed. In this vast and varied category, we might place the ritual burial of lepers, marking their separation from society when the priest with a spade cast earth on the leper's feet, saying "Be dead to the world, but live again with God."[12] Homage and fealty were sworn between men by clasping hands and swearing oaths. The transfer of land was frequently effected by placing a clump of earth on the charter that recorded the details of the transaction.[13] A striking example of the "concrete particularity" that might inform medieval rituals is found in the practice of the Cluniac house of Marcigny (Autun), where the office of abbess was held by the Blessed Virgin, "as a sign of which an abbatial stall was always kept empty for her in choir."[14] Stephen White has shown that the process of proposing and avoiding judicial ordeals in late eleventh-century France was "stylized, even ritualized."[15] The English ritual for a person abjuring the realm (that is, taking an oath to leave forever, a penalty that could be applied to felons) included truly dramatic elements: the abjuror, after making his way to the nearest possible port, was to seek speedy passage and if he could not find it immediately, he was to "walk into the sea up to his

12 "Ceremony for the exclusion of a leper," cited by John Shinners in *Medieval Popular Religion, 1000–1500: A Reader* (Peterborough, ON, 1997), 280.

13 For examples of the "transfer of a sod of earth from the estate granted" or the "placing of the sod or of the charter on an altar or gospel-book" in Anglo-Saxon England, see Susan Kelly, "Anglo-Saxon Lay Society and the Written Word," in *The Uses of Literacy in Early Mediaeval Europe*, ed. Rosamond McKitterick (1990; repr., Cambridge, 1995), 44. Thus, the same altar where the bread and wine were transformed into the body and blood of Christ could work other transformations as well. According to Heinrich Fichtenau, *Living in the Tenth Century: Mentalities and Social Orders*, trans. Patrick J. Geary (Chicago, 1991), 46, in such a conveyance of property, the "twig [or] clod of earth served as a small portion of the property being exchanged ... what counted was the gesture of its transferal to the other person, not the specific piece of wood used. ... [W]hat was important was the object's capacity to make invisible occurrences visible and understandable."

14 Cited in C.H. Lawrence, *Medieval Monasticism: Forms of Religious Life in Western Europe in the Middle Ages* (3rd ed., New York, 2001), 220.

15 Stephen D. White, "Proposing the Ordeal and Avoiding It: Strategy and Power in Western French Litigation, 1050–1100," in *Cultures of Power: Lordship, Status, and Process in Twelfth-Century Europe*, ed. Thomas N. Bisson (Philadelphia, 1995), 89–123, especially 107–110.

knees every day as a token of his desire to cross it." These rituals, according to R.F. Hunnisett, were "sufficiently colourful and entertaining to ensure a good attendance" – and, we might add, to fix the event in people's memories.[16]

Such efficacious ritual, or purposeful drama, takes place within a "performance arena," a setting that is created by the presence of "performer and spectator" and their agreement, their "mutual awareness" of the fact that "theatre is being performed." According to Jacqueline Martin and Willmar Sauter, this would include the "set of conventions that clearly indicate the 'theatre,' be it a red curtain, a knocking on the stage floor ... the masked face of the performer ... or simply the gathering in a specific ... building."[17] Ritual is also inherently purposeful, and not only in the obvious cases where it restates accepted "truths," reaffirms norms, makes public an important change, or maintains boundaries around groups or communities: as anthropologist John MacAloon notes "performance is constitutive of social experience"; it is not something "merely additive or instrumental."[18] As we shall see, medieval village courts were an "arena" where a performance was enacted that was constitutive, as well as instrumental.

Scholars have long understood the importance of "public performance" in strengthening the power and claims to power of state, church, and city in medieval civilization.[19] Indeed, the late medieval and Renaissance periods are rich in state ceremonials such as coronations, funerals, and royal entries, in large part because this was the

16 See R.F. Hunnisett, *The Medieval Coroner* (Cambridge, 1961), 37–54, for a full description of this ceremony; quotations at 45–46, 42.

17 Jacqueline Martin and Willmar Sauter, *Understanding Theatre: Performance Analysis in Theory and Practice* (Stockholm, 1995), 9–10.

18 *Rite, Drama, Festival, Spectacle: Rehearsals toward a Theory of Cultural Performance*, ed. John J. MacAloon (Philadelphia, 1984), 2.

19 János Bak describes coronations as "symbolic and ritual acts that served both to legitimate and to present monarchic rule," and sees the coronation *ordines* as the "liturgical scripts which guided the actors of the rites." *Coronations: Medieval and Early Modern Monarchic Ritual*, ed. János M. Bak (Berkeley, 1990), 1. Gordon Kipling describes late medieval civic triumphs as pageants that "lie on the frontier between drama and ritual." He cites Geertz's notion of "metaphysical theatre," that is, "theatre to present an ontology and, by presenting it, to make it happen – make it actual." Kipling, *Enter the King: Theatre, Liturgy, and Ritual in the Medieval Civic Triumph* (Oxford, 1998), 19, 47.

era in which the modern European state came into being.[20] The articulation of ritual and the exercise of power are natural concomitants in medieval society; but the use of ritual to embody ideas – indeed, even the ability to formulate ideas – has been largely seen as the proper activity of leisured, prosperous, mostly city-based elites, as discussed earlier. If countryfolk had rituals, it was assumed that these were "invisible," leaving little trace of themselves in the evidence, or that they survived only in fragmentary and inferior late forms. This assumption is incorrect, for rituals are preserved in court rolls, among other documents.

"How to Hold a Manor Court"

The performance dimensions of the village court are clearly visible in another genre of document that, like court and account rolls, also first appears in the later thirteenth century, the period when the first court records begin to survive for English villages.[21] These are the formal treatises, or books of precedents, in French and in Latin and sometimes both, on how to hold a manor court. Such manuals include *La Court de Baron*, *Modus Tenendi Curias*, and *De Placitis et Curiis Tenendis*. In these texts and others like them, "stewards, clerks, pleaders would learn their duties": stewards would learn "how to preside, clerks how to enrol, pleaders how to count and defend [that is, how to charge someone with a wrong and how to deny a wrong]," in the words of F.W. Maitland, who edited four such treatises dating between c. 1270 and 1342.[22]

20 Ralph E. Giesey, "Inaugural Aspects of French Royal Ceremonials," in Bak, *Coronations*, 36.

21 See Figure 1.1, "Distribution of starting dates of manorial court roll series deposited in the PRO and other archival respositories," in Zvi Razi and Richard M. Smith, "The Origins of the English Manorial Court Rolls as a Written Record: A Puzzle," in *Medieval Society and the Manor Court*, ed. Razi and Smith (Oxford, 1996), 42. Similar manuals appeared at the same time, such as *Fleta*, *Seneschausy*, and Walter of Henley's *Husbandry*; see *Walter of Henley and Other Treatises on Estate Management and Accounting*, ed. D. Oschinsky (Oxford, 1971).

22 *The Court Baron, Being Precedents For Use in Seignorial and Other Local Courts, Together with Select Pleas From the Bishop of Ely's Court of Littleport*, ed. F.W. Maitland and W.P. Baildon (London, 1891). To

These texts include instructions for court "personnel," including model dialogue and what might even be called "stage directions." Thus, in the *Modus Tenendi Curias* of c. 1342, the formula to be followed by the steward in swearing in the jurors is provided (with the matter to be enrolled given in Latin, and instructions and actual words to be spoken given in French): "and the beadle shall hold a book in his hand and the steward shall say: Hold up your hands. You shall loyally inquire among yourselves and loyally present all the articles of which you shall be charged on behalf of the King and the lord of this court to the best of your knowledge, so help you God in the day of judgment," and then the articles of presentment (that is, the matters which the jurors must bring before the court) are listed: defaults of suit of court, tithing groups, hue and cry, bloodshed, etc.[23]

The treatise entitled *La Court de Baron*, which can be dated to the final quarter of the thirteenth century, illustrates how specific charges are to be made (examples are given for charges of hue levied,[24] for breach of assize of bread and beer, for selling fish against the franchise of the vill, etc.), and how the steward shall speak when he holds the courts (*e le office du seneschal coment il deit parler la ou il tent les curz*). It also promises to teach a young man, possibly a steward-in-training, "how he shall speak" (*E si put un junes hom aprendre coment il parlera*).[25] Under the charge of "fruit carried off from the garden of the lord,"[26] we find a story, stage directions, and some model dialogue, all together – and not without an element of humor and human interest as well.

> "Sir steward, the bailiff Robert by name, who is here, complaineth of William of the Street, who is there, that against the peace of the lord he sent Thomas his son on such a day at such an hour in the

---

these one might add the *Novae narrationes*, a late thirteenth-century formulary designed to "guide lawyers in the art of counting on writs, telling the plaintiff's stereotyped tale in proper fashion." *Novae narrationes*, ed. E. Shanks and S.F.C. Milsom (London, 1963).

23 Maitland and Baildon, *Court Baron*, 93.

24 To "levy the hue" means to raise the hue and cry, and "charges of hue levied" means checking into any hues raised to make sure they were raised justly.

25 Maitland and Baildon, *Court Baron*, 20.

26 Ibid., 36–37.

year that now is, over the walls newly built and erected and commanded him to carry off of every manner of fruit at his will; and when the bailiff heard the fruit being knocked down, he ... at once entered the lord's garden and found the boy right high on a costard tree ... he made him come down and ... asked him by whose commandment and whose sending he entered the lord's garden over walls well closed on all sides, and the boy answered and said that William his father, who is present there, bade him enter the garden and urged him on to the trees with the best fruit; so the bailiff suffered the boy to carry off all that he had taken," etc.

"William (saith the steward), at least thou canst not deny that he is thy mainpast," etc.

"Sir for the deed of my son and the trespass I am ready to do thy will."

"But how wilt thou acquit thyself of the sending and bidding?"

"In such wise, sir, as this court shall award that acquit myself I ought."

"I tell thee then that this court awardeth that thou be at thy law six-handed at the next court."

"That will I, sir."

The image of a father sitting on the garden wall, urging his son on to the best fruit trees, is reminiscent of stories from the Upwood court rolls (1295, 1297) involving two youthful offenders who stole chickens, leeks, and cheeses from John Arnold and John Gleu, and whose father may have supplied a role model: "And [the jurors] say that the children of Hugh Barun found John Arnold's chickens in their father's Court and took and ate them. And they dug up leeks in the Court of the said John and carried them off and sold them." (*Et dicunt quod pueri Hugonis Barun invenerunt gallinas Iohannis Arnold in Curia patris eorum et illas ceperunt and manducauerunt. Et porectos in Curia dicti Iohannis fodierunt et asportauerunt et apud vendiderunt*). In 1297: "And they say that Richard and Rose children of Hugh Barun came to John Gleu's house and took ten small cheeses and carried them off. Therefore they are to be attached by the body." (*Et dicunt quod Ricardus et Roysia filii Hugonis Barun venerunt ad domum Iohannis Gleu et ceperunt .x. parvos caseos et asportauerunt. Ideo attachientur per corpora*). In the same court it is also noted that Hugh Baroun was placed in the stocks (*in compediis*) for breaking the lord's park (that is, entering without permission) seven times. (Although recourse to the stocks is rarely noted in the court rolls, placing a person in the stocks would be another ritual and spectacle charged with drama). Other cases involving parents and their children in such activities include Agnes le Reues, who cut oak trees with the help of her sons in the second quarter of the fourteenth century, and Emma Webster, who was fined in 1430 for cutting and carrying hedges, "aided by her children" (*per pueros suos*).

Thus, the formulary books do indeed read like the text of a procedural template that gave order both to the actual meeting of the court and to the court roll which it produced. The vitality of the manuscript tradition (which survived into the print tradition in the sixteenth century) may be inferred from the fact that these treatises were frequently bound in manuscripts that included a heterogeneous collection of highly practical documents, such as precedents for bonds and wills, manorial accounts, articles for the view of frankpledge, etc. In short, the village court had its *ordines* literature, just as did coronations and royal entries.[27]

The Opening Rituals of the Village Court

What was the "set of conventions" that signaled a performance was about to begin in medieval Ellington, Upwood, and thousands of other villages throughout England and Europe?[28] The performers,

27 See Maitland's introduction to *Court Baron*, 3–18: thus, a 1269 formulary is bound with precedents for conveyances, leases, bonds and wills, and manorial accounts (p. 12); a 1307 treatise is bound with various precedents, forms for "inbreviating [stating] and ordaining the duty of the reeve and the steward," accounting methods, articles for the view of frankpledge, and the like (pp. 14–15). Maitland emphasized the practical nature of such treatises (p. 3): they "may teach some things that we should hardly learn from real court rolls, just as the student of modern English land law is likely to learn much from a good book of conveyancing precedents that he would hardly, if ever, discover in any chance assortment of real instruments."

28 Though they did not make the "shift from oral to written procedures" as English village courts did, similar legal institutions existed on the continent as is clear from many sources, not least of which is the abundant practice of inquest upon which medieval government, local and pan-regional, secular and ecclesiastical, was predicated. See Razi and

audience, and ritual of the court session, the gathering in a specific place that was typically the same from year to year, the particular disposition of the various participants – all these are elements that together created the "agreement between performer and spectator" that "theatre was being performed." Not only was a performance at hand, but a theatre was created; not one in which the "playfulness," the willingness-to-be-amused, or the "suspension of disbelief" of the audience was engaged or required in order to make the drama work and create an "imaginary world," but rather, one in which the thoughtfulness and corroboration of the audience were required for the court to fulfill its responsibility which was, fundamentally, the rendering of authoritative decisions.

Moreover, the theatre created was a compelling one, both because of the real judicial and legal powers of the court, and because of the nature of the regular "audience" of a village court. Since suit of court (that is, attendance) was one of the conditions of tenure for customary tenements in the village, each court session threw a wide net over the community and included not just all the participants involved in the "central ritual," officials, complainants, and the like, but also numerous other people with no immediate personal issue to be joined in the court that day. In fact, as we shall see, absence from the court engendered its own small ritual, since an absent suitor was required to "essoin" or excuse himself from attendance by sending a proxy who would step forward at a specific moment in the court session to formally declare his principal's non-attendance.

As has been demonstrated for other rural court settings, the English village court followed its own local ritual, beginning with the sitting of the court in a traditional spot (under a tree, or in the manor hall, rectory, or church), with the steward often presiding, the clerk taking the minutes, and the formal pronouncement that the court was in session.[29] The jurors were then sworn in and charged to "tell the

---

Smith, "The Origins of the English Manorial Court Rolls," 36 n1, for a discussion of village courts elsewhere in Europe.

29 For rare information on the actual location of a series of Ellington courts, see BL 39736, a composite account roll for the "view" or audit held in the rectory of Ellington, 1285–1289. Gadi Algazi, in "Lords Ask, Peasants Answer," 199–229, describes a similar ritual for west German village assemblies: "The lord summoned the assembly on traditional dates,

truth" (*ad dicendam veritatem*, as it is given in Upwood's roll of 1428). These opening formalities, which established a framework for the *déroulement* of ritual, had the effect of creating the "mutual awareness" that a performance was about to occur.

It is noteworthy that for most of its history, first place in the order of business, once the court was in session, was given to those procedures whose effect was to establish the body of suitors who were to attend court that day: clustered just after the list of jurors' names, at the start of the roll, year after year, there appeared a variety of entries all concerned with who should appear, did appear, or did not appear on that day. First, the essoins or "excused absences" are recorded at the start of the session (when no one is absent, the entry *Esson' nullus* is sometimes given).[30] Second, payment of the *capitagium* (also called *chevagium*, that is, chevage) was often among the first items recorded after the juror list. This was a traditional payment that, by the late thirteenth century in Ramsey's rolls, referred to a standardized group head tax paid so that young men who did not hold any land could be excused from attending court. Because these landless men were often absent, notice of the chevage payment at this early point in the session illustrates the recognized importance of defining the body of suitors as an assembly of tenants with a stake in the village. Third, notices

---

often three times a year. On the evening prior to the assembly he arrived at the village and received food and lodging from the peasants. The assembly was ceremoniously opened the following morning, a privileged space was marked off from its surroundings, and a special peace was proclaimed. The peasant jurors ... formed a circle in the middle, along with the chairman of the court, usually the lord or his local representative. After the presence of the peasants obliged to appear in court had been verified the laws were related by the peasant jurors, a practice known in German as *Weisung*" (p. 199). Information regarding the actual placement of persons (the jurors and the lord's representative in the middle) is lacking in all the English court rolls known to the present writer, hence these are extremely valuable details.

30 Usually essoins occurred just after the jurors' names, but they could also be placed before them, as in the fifteenth-century rolls where the word *Essoin' nullus* appears right after the heading stating the type, time, and place of the court meeting (see for example Ellington's court of 19 October 1453).

of people who had been "called" to be jurors but had refused to come, as in Upwood in the 1290s,[31] are also placed near the start of the roll. Finally, beginning in the 1370s in Ellington and the 1390s in Upwood, the rolls usually list in or near first place the names of the people who are outside the manor with or without the lord's permission (*extra feodum domini sine licencia*). In short, it was an enduring convention of the court that its first order of business was to establish clearly the body of suitors, a convention that must have mirrored – indeed may have derived from – the procedure in the more purely agricultural "extra-manorial" meetings where all local farmers had to be present in order to make enforceable decisions about field management, crop rotation, when to begin the harvest, when to open the fields to common grazing, and the like.

The ritual swearing in of the jurors was not an empty ceremony, since it could be and was challenged. A concern for correct oath-taking ritual is apparent in the entries mentioned above, in which men were fined if they had been called to serve as jurors and had refused to swear or were "unwilling to swear" (*noluit facere sacramentum*) as was Hugh of Backenho in Ellington in 1294, since unwillingness to swear was equivalent to refusing the office. Others "swore badly" (*male facit sacramentum*), as did Hugh again, along with William Twyt and William in le Mersh, who were cited and fined 6d each in the court of 1292. The importance of the oath is apparent also in connection with other offices. Ale-tasters, whose task was to make sure that the ale brewed and sold locally was of good quality and was sold at the fixed price using accurate measures, were regularly cited as making their presentments on oath, as in Upwood's court of 18 October 1322 where it is noted that *Willelmus Heryng et Stephanus Aubyn et Iohannes Alkok tastatores ceruisie de Upwode dicunt per sacramentum suum quod* ("say on their oath that"). When William Denby and Thomas Burgeys were elected constables in Ellington's autumn court in 1400, the scribe used the verb *presto* (to perform, display, exhibit) to describe their taking of the oath: *presti-*

31 This complicated series of episodes is described fully, within a larger discussion of the *capitagium*, by J.A. Raftis, *Peasant Economic Development within the English Manorial System* (Montreal, 1996), 35–40; and see below, Chapter Four.

terunt sacramentum.[32] Thus, in its opening rituals, court procedure clearly emphasized the establishment of two groups of "actors" in the assembly: the officials whose presentments provided most of the material for the court's work, and all other suitors and attendees whose presence seems – at first glance – to be less essential.

Studies of ritual in other cultures shed light on how participation in the village court might have been understood. Bruce Kapferer has analyzed Sri Lankan exorcisms which, like the medieval village court or peasant-citizen assemblies in Athens, are purposeful gatherings where essential work is done to establish right order. He argues that "all those who gather at a rite can be regarded as participants in it,"[33] whether as the focus of the ritual, as performers, or as spectators. This analysis suggests that the village court drew power from the care with which it assembled "all those who gathered at the rite" for the purpose of a public deliberation.

Once all participants are gathered, the ritual can begin, and we may turn to an exploration of process. According to Kapferer, rituals are "reflexive"; they have the power to "comment upon the everyday," a power that depends heavily upon the "ability of the participants in ritual to assume the role of audience, that is to be distanced from their own actions and the actions of others." Ritual performance gets work done by "objectifying aspects of the everyday world people live and act in,"[34] allowing individuals to gain "deeper insight" into their world and

32 The court rolls do not record oaths taken by the lord's officials, such as bailiffs, woodwards, and haywards, but they certainly made formal presentments in court.

33 Bruce Kapferer, "The Ritual Process and the Problem of Reflexivity in Sinhalese Demon Exorcisms," in MacAloon, *Rite, Drama, Festival, Spectacle*, 179–207.

34 Kapferer, "The Ritual Process," 186–189. Kapferer's "minimal definition of performance" is "the enactment of ritual roles and behaviors in a particular setting" (p. 187). Henry Rey-Flaud has observed that in a "theater of the Middle Ages the spectator is active. It is [the spectator] who creates space and time at each moment of the action." Cited by Jane B. Dozer-Rabedeau (who disagrees with this observation), in "*Rusticus*: Folk Hero of Thirteenth-Century Picard Drama," in *Agriculture in the Middle Ages: Technology, Practice, and Representation*, ed. Del Sweeney (Philadelphia, 1995), 205–226, at 207. For a discussion of the Mass that also raises the issue of spectators and participants see Eamon Duffy, *The*

their place in it, because they "can experience the [cultural and social] world of their construction and then stand back and reflect upon its various meanings."[35] The public deliberation in court necessarily "commented upon the everyday." Happily, estate administrative records provide the evidence for a deeper look into the inclusive and constitutive qualities of the ritual performance enacted in the village court.

The Performance Arena

Close examination of the court rolls reveals a language of performance, of appearance and retirement from a "performance arena" upon which collective attention is centered: *Et dicunt quod, Et presentant quod, Compertum est quod, venit et dicit quod, et contradicebat, sepius vocatus et non venit, venit et recognouit, presens venit dedicit* ("they say," "they present," "they show," "it is found that," "he comes and says," "he contradicted," "he is often called and doesn't come," "he comes and acknowledges that," "being present he comes and declares"). Suitors to the court, individual men and women, were continually cited, and called forward in the court – to serve, to swear, to bring, to show, to present, to deny, to affirm, to come and speak, to pledge, and to be pledged. In enacting these numerous and varied roles, the villagers themselves become instruments for the enactment of the central rite in the judicial "performance arena."

At first glance, understanding the court as a performance arena may seem most valid analytically for such apparent rituals as swearing in officials, having a proxy step forward to declare a principal's absence, and the like. But the staging of ritual and the heightened

---

Stripping of the Altars: Traditional Religion in England, c.1400–c.1580 (New Haven, 1992), 109–116.

35 Kapferer, "The Ritual Process," 204–205. Such analysis reveals the limitations of modernist assumptions that inform the conventional exercise of trying to determine "whose court" the village court really was, whether the lord's, "elite" villagers' (such as jurors), or the whole community's. The discussion of reflexivity is reminiscent of Josef Pieper's observation, discussed earlier, that to "philosophize means to withdraw – not from the things of everyday life – but from the currently accepted meaning attached to them ... it is in the things we come across in the experience of everyday life that the unusual emerges." *Leisure, the Basis of Culture*, trans. Alexander Dru (1952; repr., New York, 1963), 98–99.

sense of moment that accompanied it also occurred at many other points in the proceedings, thanks to the power of analogizing that formed part of the villager's mental framework. The affirming power of ritual was also engaged when a villager came forward to answer or bring a charge, show a charter, acknowledge a debt, find or be assigned a pledge, make a presentment as an official, provide information, or request information from the court. Indeed, this continual movement of individuals, as they advanced to and retired from the center of staged action in connection with varied business, may have been as central to the progress of the ritual as the swearing in of officials or the making of presentments.

Thus, in Ellington's 1294 court Richard Messor impleaded (made a formal complaint, raised an action against) William le Hoppere regarding unjust detention of grain, and "William being present comes and acknowledged all the aforesaid debt" (*Et Willelmus presens venit et recognouit totum debitum predictum*). In 1299 Galfridus Geroud undoubtedly would have stepped forward when he "shows his charter" that he held of the lord in chief (*Et dictus Galfridus ostendit cartam suam ad tenendum de domino in capite*). William Othestede was asked to declare, to state publicly, a fact regarding 3s he owed to Edward Hawet; he was fined 3d in Upwood's 1391 court because he could not declare (*non potest dedicere*) [when] he had detained the money. In the 1428 record, "Agnes Persey comes now into the Court and claims to hold of the lord one acre of land" (*Agnes Persey venit hic in Curiam et clamat tenere de domino vnam acram terre*). When the ale-tasters made their presentments, each brewer "comes and brings" her brewing vessels to be measured (*venit et tulit*), that is, she steps forth from the body of suitors with her pots in hand.[36]

A suitor to the court may come forward and play a number of different roles even in a single session, as in the case of William de Wenyngton of Upwood. William was a juror in the court of 28 November 1334, and in that same session also acted as pledge for his wife who was a brewer, pledged her again in a case of a hue and cry raised upon her, was fined 6d for trespass with his horses in the meadow, and was cited in connection with a hue and cry that had been raised upon him and that was judged "unjust" in court that day. The multi-

36 Such examples could be multiplied, and merit further discussion than space permits here.

ple officeholding of some men in the fifteenth-century court rolls would be another example of people playing many roles.[37] The weaving in and out of the court's business by a single individual is even more pronounced if the pattern of participation is studied over a period of several years.

Jurors, specially-empanelled jurors, reeves, ale-tasters, haywards, bailiffs as well as pledges, trespassers, and ale-wives, those seeking a formal inquest of the court into a dispute over tenure or trespass, those with information to share, those with an accusation to make and the people whom they accused, those required to reply to a charge, all these might variously come forward in a single session. A typical roll for one court session in Upwood or Ellington easily cites more than one hundred people for dozens of different activities. While the records convey an impression of a lively meeting, governed mostly by traditional practice, even informed by a script provided by the manuals for holding a manor court, it is also true that an element of unpredictability, of the sort to be met with in any live performance, is equally palpable.

The court roll then is a textual embodiment of a central ritual intimately connected with an audience whose component parts were constantly in flux.[38] The ritual action took the form of individuals stepping literally onto "center stage," that is, into an open space in the center of the body of suitors, alongside the jurors, steward (if present), and scribe assembled there (if we may safely generalize from the placement of people in late medieval German village assemblies noted

37 See discussion of multiple officeholding in Sherri Olson, *A Chronicle of All That Happens: Voices from the Village Court in Medieval England* (Toronto, 1996), 195–201.

38 We might equally say that the emphases of the court varied continually; the business handled, and thus the suitors called, changed from one court session to another. A session including the view of frankpledge would necessitate calling the tithing groups and noting absences; courts held in the autumn soon after harvest might include work defaults. Further variation is, of course, apparent from a diachronic view of the court rolls: for example, the suretyship system and the hue and cry, so prominent in the early rolls, were practically defunct institutions by the early fifteenth century, as discussed fully in Olson, *A Chronicle*, 97–99, 102–103, 176–178, 194–195. As we will see more fully below in Chapter Four, trespass is a common item of business but its nature and incidence change constantly.

by Gadi Algazi).[39] Thus, anyone cited in the court would have moved forward through the ranks of his or her fellow villagers to take up a position in the circle at the center: "being present he comes and says," "she comes and brings."[40]

Virtually every type of entry in a court roll suggests not only a body of suitors whose composition is changing by the movement of individuals into or out of that circle, but also the collective ties that bind that individual to the people from whose midst he or she has just emerged. A woman who has raised a public hue and cry since the previous court session must answer for it, if it is found to have been raised "unjustly" (*iniuste*); a head juror makes the presentments for all the "xii men"; at times the obligation to make inquest is placed on the entire community (the vill) which renders its decision in the same court.[41] Upwood's 1295 court roll provides two examples of such a collective responsibility to gather information, deliberate, and reach a decision which must be delivered in court: William son of John de Raveley placed himself upon an inquisition of his peers and the customary tenants regarding whether he owed plow service; Juliana widow of Adam son of John gave 6d in the same court for the jurors' verdict in a land dispute over a portion of one virgate of land formerly her husband's (*pro consideratione Curie habenda super portione unius virgate terre quondam mariti sui*), and the *xii Iurati* gave their verdict in the same session. In the 4 December 1294 court roll, it is noted that Richard Hering gives the lord 12d for having the verdict of the twelve jurors concerning an encroachment allegedly made by Thomas Aspelon at Rycroftwell (*dat domino xii d pro consideratione habenda de duodecim Iuratis inter ipsum et Thomam Aspelon*).

39 See note 29 above.

40 Such a positioning of suitors to the court also restores some of the force behind the language found in the formulary books, where the steward calls out for someone to show himself or step forward. See for example in the treatise *La Court de Baron*: "Where art thou, William the Lorimer?" "Sir, see me here" (*Ou estes vus William le Lorimer. Sire veez moy ci*). Maitland and Baildon, *Court Baron*, 50.

41 *La Court de Baron* records a precedent for such a collective inquest, one regarding the sale of "stinking rotten fish" (*pessoun puaunt e purri e en totes maneres corumpu*). See Maitland and Baildon, *Court Baron*, 50–51.

Compurgation or oath-helping, *facere legem*, "to be at one's law," was another important ritual that depended for its working upon the ties of personal interdependence and village collective culture. As we have seen, to "make one's law" a person charged with an offence must find a certain number of men to step forward and swear to his probity and trustworthiness, as in Ellington's court of 19 January 1294 where Richard le Beumeys impleaded Richard Hayward (*Messor*) that the latter had unjustly detained five out of ten sheep which Beumeys had given him to keep in his fold by an agreement made between them (*per conuencionem*): "And Richard Hayward being present sufficiently made his law that he did not break the agreement" (*Et Ricardus Messor presens sufficienter fecit legem quod non fregit conuencionem*). Hayward would have stepped forward and named his compurgators; those men in turn would have stepped forward to swear, and then retired from center stage. Indeed, we may say that swearing in groups of men to perform various tasks, an activity which abounds in the court rolls,[42] is not only one of the central activities of the court and essential to its operation, but also constitutes a type of group ritual which is activated by – because it mirrors – all villagers' power to assume a role by swearing an oath.

This point is supported by the terminology used for the jurors, that is, the men who held the most prominent and stable of village

42 *Compertum est per inquisicionem* abounds in the select court rolls for Littleport edited by Maitland, usually of unspecified villagers. But see the court for 1324 (Maitland and Baildon, *Court Baron*, 139) for an example where the men are named: "Hugh Belde and Henry Fisher are sworn to survey the lord's stock and to present from court to court the sales and purchases and the [deaths by] murrain among the same when occasion for presentment shall arise, and also any deficiency in the wainage." And "John Manimester, John Lovering, and John Fox the elder are sworn to survey and to present from court to court trespassers in the fen, for instance by mowing and digging, and also trespasses in the warren touching the birds and beasts of the warren etc." Such cases also indicate how swearing men into service could be an *ad hoc* procedure (here perhaps arising from a recent visitation of murrain, or a sudden increase in poaching), and how various were the tasks they could be sworn to perform. (Also see the Upwood case of 1422, cited above in the Introduction, where the steward assigned to four men the task of making a division of the movable goods of John Bygg).

offices.[43] Jurors were consistently referred to in the court roll and related texts in ways that emphasized their oneness with their fellows, their lack of exceptionality. This is evident in the words *iurati, iuratores, preiurati* ("those who have sworn"), and similarly in phrases such as the *xii men* (when the record is in English),[44] and in the French of the procedural treatises, *les doyseners*, where the emphasis is clearly upon the oath taken, the role assumed, not the person. The main "players" stand not just for themselves but for everybody. By means of a ritual, that is, the taking of an oath, jurors like Thomas Wodeward, Walter Bythebrok, or Richard Thatcher, as well as ale-tasters like John Pappeworth or Robert le Neuman, temporarily assumed a distinctive responsibility or relationship to the rest of the community.

The demands of self-government prompted, because it benefited from, such a mechanism, in which the assumption of a local office or role was effected in a ritual that was simple and immediate (one thinks of the similar power of the spadeful of earth cast upon the leper's feet). One readily took up an office by swearing an oath, and one as easily shed that responsibility when the court session ended or one's term was up and another person was sworn in. These transitions themselves were eased by the interchangeability of participants and on-lookers. One highly beneficial effect or cause (or both) of these practices was to facilitate the circulation of people through village offices: for the common field regime to work, all villagers had to have a stake in the village and feel a sense of responsibility toward it, and those attitudes were encouraged by the holding of office, among other activities.[45]

43 The question of greater changeability of other village offices in comparison with the jurorship is discussed fully in Olson, *A Chronicle*, especially Chapter Three.

44 See the late Ellington court of 1534–1535 (PRO SC 2 179/88), the only Ellington roll in English, where reference is made to the "payns [bylaws] made by the xii men." Interestingly, these late court rolls read very much like the Weisung texts described by Algazi, that is, they are primarily recitations of local bylaws and penalties for breaking them, and of rules governing hedge-making, fences, times when fields are open for grazing, etc. See Algazi, "Lords Ask, Peasants Answer."

45 The issue of office and identity in the Middle Ages has been discussed by Heinrich Fichtenau, *Living in the Tenth Century: Mentalities and Social Orders*, 50, who claims that "people were not accustomed to

Taken together, the court's "performance" features point to a village interest in the individual suitor's ability to identify with the people who, in any given moment, occupied "center stage" in the proceedings. It is, however, conceivable that parts of the court ritual were more compelling for some villagers than for others. Presumably, looking on while someone was sworn in as a juror, with the steward reciting "Hold up your hands. You shall loyally" etc., while the beadle holds "a book," might have been most meaningful (in the sense of being able to imagine oneself in that other person's place) for men who had done so as well. Men might also have more readily identified with the ceremony of being sworn into a tithing group and being evaluated corporately at the view of frankpledge, since these were experiences, even rites of passage, for all boys upon reaching the age of twelve. Yet it is critical to note that women also regularly participated directly in court ritual, most commonly as brewers. Ale-wives were cited in a block and (as discussed earlier) were required to step forward to have their brewing vessels measured for correct capacity.[46] They would also have had to find, announce, or accept a pledge for their payment of fines if their ale or their brewing vessels were deficient or for their future brewing activity. The treatise *De Placitis et Curiis Tenendis* gives the specific forms for the oaths to be performed when one is received into frankpledge, takes the office of bailiff, swears homage,[47] acts as champion in a suit of land (all male prerogatives), or comes before the court as a witness, an activity which certainly included women.

Moreover, individual women, like men, came before the court in many roles, as did the widow Agnes del Reues, who, ably assisted by

separating essence from appearance, nor did they perceive the latter as 'mere appearance' ... [t]he representation of the office coincided with the office itself."

46 This is evident from notations of "gpq" (*galonem, potellum, quartum*) at the end of brewing entries. As in other cases, we find a medieval procedure more clearly enunciated in much later rolls. For example, see the reference to brewers in Ellington's 1534–1535 (English) court roll: *Also al the ale wyves to breng in ther merssers in to the corwt the payn xxd.*

47 The act of swearing homage given in *De Placitis* is a variation on the more familiar hand clasp mentioned above: "With joined hands he shall offer himself and with his hands under his lord's mantle he shall say this," etc. *De Placitis* in Maitland and Baildon, *Court Baron*, 78.

her sons, had a notable career of trespass in Upwood over the period 1318–1342.[48] In several early fourteenth-century Ellington courts (1306, twice in 1308) young Alice, daughter of Bartholomew in Lynlond and beneficiary of her father's aggressive land acquisitions (cited as holding ten acres one rod *et amplius* of free land in 1311), was repeatedly brought forth in the court and pledged by several prominent villagers that she would not marry without the lord's consent. In 1311, after her father's death, the abbot allowed her to marry a freeman at the instance of the parson Robert de Bereford.[49] Other activities for which women were cited and usually pledged in the rolls of Ellington and Upwood over our period include trespass by flooding, failure to show up for labor on the lord's demesne or failure to send the proper number of men to work, default of court attendance, being fined for a servant's behavior, raising the hue and cry (justly and unjustly), pledging her husband (one occurrence), trespass in the commons, receiving land, being excused from work due to illness, demolishing trees, cutting down oaks, trespassing with animals, receiving wages, mutual pledging, trespass on the commons by enlarging a brewing shed, quarreling, and missing court *quia prengnans* (*sic*).[50] (It will be noted that only the last of these activities is truly sex-specific).

Women who took up land in the village in their own right were required, like men, to promise to fulfill the conditions of tenure by taking an oath, and when a married couple held a tenement they were considered to be co-tenants.[51] As we saw earlier, in Upwood in 1333

48 Her career is discussed in Olson, *A Chronicle*, 62–64 with n28. Note that wherever a person is given dates as here (1318–1342), these refer to the first and last years in which that person appears in the records, not the years of birth and death nor to his or her entire span of greatest activity.

49 The full text is as follows: *Postea dominus Abbas in septimam Pascham ad instanciam domini Roberti de Bereford concessit eidem Alicie ut possit maritari cuidam Galfrido Vnterhyl libero pro quadraginta solidis sicut patet per rotulum gersumarum de anno eiusdem Abbatis xxvi. Et quod habeat predictam terram in pace sine calumpnia aliquali etc.*

50 These citations and others are found in Olson, *A Chronicle*, 220–221. The question of women's integration into the court and the cultural mainstream of the village are discussed more fully below in Chapter Two.

51 See the discussion in J.A. Raftis, *Tenure and Mobility* (Toronto, 1964), 36–42, where he notes that a widowed woman did not pay an entry fine to continue on the tenement after her husband's death because she held

Agnes the widow of Stephen le Write took up her husband's tenement in her own name: *et super hoc venit Agnes et clamat et facit fidelitatem*. In a land transfer case that contains many aspects of public performance and answering to public authority, entered in the 30 July 1324 court of the Bishop of Ely at Littleport, Alice Brokenhorn "of her own free will in court before the steward after examination and without the coercion but with the assent of her husband and by the licence of the lord" quitclaimed all right she had in a certain messuage from her dowry, and gave the lord 6d for having this covenant enrolled (*pro convencione irrotulanda*). She was then pledged by two men.[52] Though not every role was open to women, they would certainly have been able to identify with most of the people on "center stage."

In the present analysis, then, village court rituals are distinguished by their emphasis on inclusion and engagement of "the many" in the routine operations of the court, especially if we think of all those present as participants in the ritual, as Kapferer has argued. Further, the model suggested earlier of an individual "weaving" into and out of the business of the court helps us understand the effects of the commonplace occurrence when a suitor changed his or her role several times in a single session, in effect taking up a number of different stances vis-à-vis the "enactment of the central ritual episodes"[53] (a phenomenon that mirrored variation in the quality of integration of individuals into the public life of the village at large). Alongside inclusion, therefore, the heterogeneity and even the intermittency of participation in the court's rituals enhanced the quality of individual involvement in the court, because they complicated it; indeed we may add a historical dimension to this picture, since a villager undoubtedly thought about the activity of the court over months and years and not simply in terms of a single session.[54] References to

---

it as co-tenant. The wife "is not said to enter the land but to hold the land after the death of her husband" (quotation at 36).

52 Maitland and Baildon, *Court Baron*, 137–138. The subject of women and landholding is explored further in Chapter Two below.

53 Kapferer, "The Ritual Process," 187.

54 An individual would not only weave in and out of the record for a single court session but also play many parts over his or her lifetime. A fifty-year-old juror, for example, would have thought and acted differently from the way he did when he was a thirty-year-old juror. This must surely have been the case for John Hicson, called at age eighty-four to be

the "last court" and the "next court," *in ultimo visu, ad proximam Curiam,* discussed earlier as reflecting a kind of "village time," occur in the court rolls in connection with matters such as an inquest which, as we have seen, required a delay before being properly heard or settled. Indeed, the treatise *De Placitis et Curiis Tenendis* of c. 1307 recommends that he who holds the court should have the rolls of earlier courts and pleas with him "so that if any plea or plaint hath not been determined he may proceed to determine it according to right and justice."[55] In villages where the court met every three weeks, as in Wakefield or Brigstock,[56] or where the court met frequently and irregularly,[57] it is hard to imagine how villagers would not have had a diachronic sense of the court. Even if a suitor did not step forward at the current court, he or she may have been active at the previous one, and might well be called upon in any number of ways when the court met again. The remembrance of past roles and anticipation of future

---

a special inquest juror in Upwood in 1428, whose previous record of regular juror service spanned his lifetime, from the age of twenty-five to the age of seventy-six. See Olson, *A Chronicle*, 151–153, for an earlier, fuller discussion of Hicson.

55 *De Placitis* in Maitland and Baildon, *Court Baron*, 68. This carryover is explicit in connection with love days (*dies amoris* or *licencia concordie*, that is, days appointed for litigants to resolve their differences), respites (that is, delays, extensions), and being at one's law (*facem legere*, compurgation), all of which are amply illustrated in the manuals for holding manorial courts. In the Ellington and Upwood rolls, the love day is usually indicated by the phrase *datus est* [*datur*] *ei dies usque ad proximam Curiam*, "he is given a day until [at] the next Court." Elaine Clark's study of debt litigation shows that villagers used the court for settling debts over time; see "Debt Litigation in a Late Medieval English Vill," in *Pathways to Medieval Peasants*, ed. J.A. Raftis (Toronto, 1981), 247–279. See Chapter Three below for a detailed discussion of document use.

56 Brigstock's court met once every three weeks: there are records surviving from 549 courts between 1287 and 1348. See Judith Bennett, *Women in the Medieval English Countryside: Gender and Household in Brigstock Before the Plague* (New York, 1987), 21; for Wakefield see *Court Rolls of the Manor of Wakefield*, published by the Yorkshire Archeological Society (Leeds, 1977–).

57 Maitland noted, for the court of the village of Littleport, that the "usage seems to have been to hold six courts in the year at somewhat irregular intervals." See Maitland and Baildon, *Court Baron*, 110.

ones, both one's own and those of others, would have helped foster a sense of identification and inclusion at each court "performance".

At a deep structural level, the court's inclusive and integrative powers rested upon the airing of a variety of matters that were more or less replicated in every home, every family, and every variety of social group found in the village. In a largely homogeneous and stable community, especially one founded upon some form of collective agriculture, one person might readily stand for other people,[58] one

58 This observation should not be confused with the older convention that peasants were such a homogeneous group, living and working in the same way, that individuals were virtually interchangeable, with "low levels of individuation" (see Olson, *A Chronicle*, 167–168, for discussion of this question and some representative citations). On the contrary, it may be that living in close quarters and engaging in the same pursuits encouraged personal differentiation. (Perhaps the "monumental stability" of village life, as it seems to modern eyes, far from lending itself to static perceptions of people, time, and place, had quite an opposite effect: the mind, not preoccupied with noting and reflecting upon surface change, as for example in technology or landscape, was freer to note and reflect upon other types of change.) While we lack immediate testimony from medieval villagers that they habitually recognized and placed meaning upon the wide personal differences between the people they knew, that, in short, they distinguished personal difference as readily as modern people might do, there is suggestive testimony in some early modern first-person narratives and autobiography. In Richard Gough's local history of the parish of Myddle, written around the year 1700, this tendency to see and categorize people by their inborn nature is extremely pronounced; indeed, it forms the basis for Gough's entire commentary. His statement that "families are made of particulars" also implicitly acknowledges the fact of individual differences. See his *History of Myddle*, ed. David Hey (Harmondsworth, 1981), 214; and see Olson, " 'Families Have Their Fate and Periods:' Varieties of Family Experience in the Pre-Industrial Village," in *The Salt of Common Life: Individuality and Choice in the Medieval Town, Countryside, and Church*, ed. Edwin B. DeWindt (Kalamazoo, 1995), 409–448. Also see the autobiography of Miquel Parets, *A Journal of the Plague Year: The Diary of the Barcelona Tanner Miquel Parets, 1651*, ed. and trans. James S. Amelang (New York, 1991). Parets, a seventeenth-century Catalan artisan who lost most of his family in a plague epidemic, grieved over the loss of his favorite son, while the one with the "worst nature" survived; and see further discussion of this text in James S. Amelang, *The Flight of Icarus: Artisan Autobiography*

person might assume a role familiar to others and become part of the ritual performance that, according to Kapferer, "objectifies the everyday life" of everyone in that court, and that calls this life forth as material for reflection. Once everyday matters are presented in court according to the prescribed rituals, they are objectified. By taking on another role, or by identifying with another who is doing so, participants gain a measure of distance from their actions and from those of others, and are able to consider the issues presented from varying perspectives. This fosters an atmosphere of reflection and deliberation that allows the important work of the court to be done.

That all suitors to the court did not play the same role or have the same powers did not detract from the efficiency of the court because the "reflexive" power of a ritual does not depend on all participants maintaining the same distance from the "enactment of the central ritual episodes." Indeed, Kapferer argues that the progression of the ritual through its various stages is in large part effected through the "changing integration of those individuals assembled in these episodes."[59] In its incarnation as a "performance arena" where the central performers "assumed responsibility" to "an audience and to tradition" as they understood it,[60] and where the audience could identify to some degree with the performers, the court could foster a powerful feeling of inclusion for all members of the village community because that feeling did not depend on the identicalness of people's experience in the court.

In its response to the demands of self-government, especially the need to diffuse power in order to achieve consensus, the court became a site for purposeful ritual where the actors could continually assume different roles. Such a court, whose business was forwarded by its suit-

---

in Early Modern Europe (Stanford, 1998). For further testimony on this point by a modern peasant, see the autobiography of Pedro Martínez, a twentieth-century Mexican peasant who generally seems to see people very much in terms of their nature, which he readily describes as "good" or "bad." *Pedro Martínez: A Mexican Peasant and His Family*, ed. Oscar Lewis (New York, 1964).

59 Kapferer, "The Ritual Process," 180.

60 This statement paraphrases John MacAloon's definition of "performance," in which he emphasizes people "assum[ing] responsibility to an audience and to tradition as they understand it." Introduction to *Rite, Drama, Festival, Spectacle*, 8.

ors' differing integration, was able to create and deploy considerable power, in the sense suggested earlier, that of rendering authoritative decisions. The interdependency and collectivism that characterized the total organization of the village created a tension, a "controlled dynamic quality,"[61] which was channeled and diffused in the court, as much in its performance aspects as in its specific mechanisms.

If this analysis has validity, then villagers' notions about authority, decision-making, and the possession of executive power, which were based on their own life experiences, must have admitted of greater variety and complexity than has been appreciated by historians.[62] Hitherto, historical analysis has often emphasized that all individuals were not "equal" in village political and social life, that lord and villager were essentially antagonistic, that "elite" villagers controlled local office, and that women were barred from full participation in the village assembly. In these analyses, exclusionary measures based on landholding, wealth, or gender are seen as a primary rule of operation in the court. How the historian chooses to interpret such matters will affect his or her reading of every detail of the court rolls.

61 *Webster's Third New International Dictionary of the English Language, Unabridged* (1976), s.v. "tension."

62 The implications of this discussion of power in the village will be more apparent if we bear in mind that an emphasis on legal status and the liabilities of serfdom dominated scholarship throughout the late nineteenth and most of the twentieth centuries, as discussed above in the Introduction. Cultural history approaches offer the opportunity to problematize this older view, as well as models that have emphasized division and conflict, indeed, posited a village oligarchy of officials and a full-fledged class system that divided villagers among themselves. See for example Rodney Hilton, *Class Conflict and the Crisis of Feudalism: Essays in Medieval Social History* (London, 1985). For a different and non-scholarly view of the medieval peasant in comparison with the nineteenth-century factory-worker, based upon close observation, see the commentary of William Cobbett, *Rural Rides*, first published in 1830 (new ed. 1853; repr., London, 1985), 125, 127: "Talk of *vassals*! Talk of *villains*! Talk of *serfs*! Are there any of these, or did feudal times ever see any of them, so debased, so absolutely slaves, as the poor creatures who, in the 'enlightened' North are *compelled* to work fourteen hours in a day, in a heat of eighty-four degrees; and who are liable to punishment *for looking out at a window of the factory*!"

In the present study, it is argued that what mattered most in the "ways of thinking" of medieval villagers was not that some were completely included and others were completely excluded, according to various criteria, but rather that the individual was held in a web of connections that organized and explained his or her life and relations with others, and that no two people had precisely the same web of connections. The analysis offered here suggests a system where the court marshaled and then circulated power through a labyrinth of individuals in a continuous but varying flow. Resourceful villagers used the performance and ritual potential of their annual local courts to govern themselves, in a way that creates a medieval parallel to the function which the drama played in classical Athenian society. Both communities would have put a premium on devising mechanisms to strengthen self-regulation, and in so doing fostered rituals in their public assemblies.

Other Village Dramas

To further substantiate this point, we may note the abundant evidence, both within and outside of the court rolls, that village society generated the raw material of performance and ritual, indeed, that village existence was profoundly informed by ritual. Indeed, the performance-related qualities of dialogue and debate have been claimed even for manorial accounts, administrative records which, as we have seen, were more narrowly concerned than court rolls with the interests of lordship.[63]

63 According to P.D.A. Harvey, these accounts were "written for the local officials before the audit by clerks of their own choosing [that is, a reeve's clerk]. The account would be presented at the audit as the basis of the official's [for example, the reeve's] claim; often his clerk would be there to help him make his case ... we see what the local official claimed, what was queried or disallowed by the auditors and very often why, for revealing notes and comments may be added to explain the alterations made on the account – 'In future so much will not be allowed,' 'In future the number of acres of each sort of corn [reaped] should be entered.'" In other words, we can distinguish between the original document and what was added on at the audit: we see "what happened at the audit" itself. "The result is that [such an] account is virtually a dialogue, a debate between local official and auditors, not a statement from a single viewpoint" which, Harvey notes, "adds greatly to its interest and historical value." *Manorial Records* (London, 1984), 32–33.

George Homans provides a clear example of village drama in the well-known practice of "beating the bounds" on Rogation Days, the Gangdays:

> Led by the priest and carrying the Cross, banners, bells, and lights the men of a village went in perambulation about the boundaries of the village. The small boys who went with the procession were thrown into the brooks and ponds or had their buttocks bumped against the trees and rocks which marked the bounds, so that they should remember them the better.[64]

Another example is found in the Plow Plays, mostly from northern England. Plow Monday, the first Monday after Epiphany, marked the resumption of labor after the winter holiday, and it entailed Plow Monday observances. E.K. Chambers describes it thus:

> Plowboys, often in white shirts, harness themselves to a plow and drag it in procession round the village. There is a Quête (or "gathering"). The churl who does not contribute runs the risk of having the ground before his house plowed up ... and many churchwardens' accounts show that the proceedings of the "gathering", or part of them, went to the maintenance of a plow light [that is, a candle placed before certain images] in the village church.[65]

Just such an observance seems to be captured in the Upwood court of 3 December 1299, which records the following youthful prank: "It is found by the jurors that John Crane of Wystow, John son of Margery, Roger Hewe, John son of Walter, William son of Hugh, Thomas le Pykeler, John son of Thomas atte Snape, and Thomas son of John Hylheyl maliciously plowed up the park of William of Raveley at Kyngwell (*maliciose arrauerunt parcum Willelmi de Rauele*), 4d damages to William, and for their trespass 12d, pledge the reeve."

The court sessions that met in Ellington and Upwood occasionally provided a stage for drama of great immediate public interest and must often have included storytelling sessions that would readily

64 Homans, *English Villagers*, 368. David Nirenberg cites a ritual employed in the fifteenth century to beat the bounds between the towns of Andújar and Jaén in Spain; this involved staging an event at each of the landmarks. One of the events involved killing a ram, cutting off its head, and burying the head in the middle of the landmark. See *Communities of Violence: Persecution of Minorities in the Middle Ages* (Princeton, 1996), 226.

65 E.K. Chambers, *The English Folk-Play* (Oxford, 1933), 90–91.

draw everyone into the central ritual that day. Indeed, the treatises of village court procedure refer to much of the substance of court discussion as *narrationes transgressionis*,[66] and contain numerous stories in the precedents they provide, as in a story contained in *La Court de Baron* (c. 1265): Walter of the Moor, called on to answer in the court for stealing fish from the lord's preserve, told the tale of

> how I went the other evening along the bank of this pond and looked at the fish which were playing in the water, so beautiful and so bright, and for the great desire that I had for a tench I laid me down on the bank and just with my hands quite simply, and without any other device, I caught that tench and carried it off; and now I will tell thee the cause of my covetousness and my desire; my dear wife had lain abed a right full month, as my neighbours who are here know, and she could never eat or drink anything to her liking, and for the great desire that she had to eat a tench I went to the bank of the pond to take just one tench.[67]

The Upwood and Ellington court rolls contain similar tales. The 1280 Ellington roll records the breach of a retirement arrangement (discussed earlier) between a father and his adult son, and the enactment of a very public reconciliation scene: William Buk acknowledges an arrears in grain deliveries owed his father, Walter, for the current and previous year. "And the said William comes and agreement is reached with Walter his father, and the said Walter graciously and at the instance of friends" (*ad instanciam amicorum*) forgives the previous year's debt, and rearranges the current deliveries due.[68] As Paul Hyams has argued, the "stage management of public reconciliations was not ...

66 Maitland and Baildon, *Court Baron*, 86. In Upwood's 1339/40 court, William Wadeloue, the bailiff, was fined because he "falsely narrated" the trespasses in the lord's wood (*false narrauit* [illegible] *Bosci*).

67 Maitland and Baildon, *Court Baron*, 54–55. Other narratives are found on pp. 65–66, where a villager tells the story of how his house was burglarized. The story of the tench is also cited in Michael T. Clanchy, *From Memory to Written Record: England, 1066–1307* (2nd ed., Oxford, 1993), 277–278, where he emphasizes the same elements of a play, spoken dialogue, and the creation of a "courtroom scene" where "[s]ome protagonists are even given star roles."

68 The reconciliation must have been complete, since Walter then turned over the tenement to William and paid the lord a fee to reside permanently outside the village with his chattel, *cum suis catallis*.

confined to the most dramatic and violent of feud situations but rather was a common need frequently felt after more mundane disputes over property and the like."[69]

In the Upwood court of 7 December 1295, the last eight lines of the roll are devoted to the jurors' presentment (*Prejurati dicunt quod*) of the activities of John Cholle, hayward, over the previous summer, in which they aver that he beat and wounded Margery Belaunce, and stole a small sum of money and some clothing from her (a hood, a hairnet, and three pairs of gloves) before she was able to escape from him (*emanibus eius euasit*). Afterwards he "made peace" with Margery, paying her 12d through his pledge, Simon de Sudbyr' (*et postea dictus Iohannes per quendam Simonem de Sudbyr' pro xii denariis pacem dicte Margarie fecit*). However, within the same month, in the fields next to the house of Hugh Lauerok (*in campis de Magna Rauele iuxta domum Hugonis Lauerok*), Cholle robbed another woman of a tunic, a hood of brown cloth, and some linen, and secretly carried them off (*depradauit quamdam mulierem de Bekeswell de quadam tunica et uno capucino de burnetto et de Linis que habuit et furtive secum asportauit*). The *narratio transgressionis* of John Cholle might have become as famous locally as the unravelling of Lynlond family history in Ellington around 1310, when Alice Lynlond, wife of a prosperous local tenant, was cited for adultery with John le Warde "and various others" (*et aliis diuersis*). Within a year or two, her husband Bartholomew died, and Alice, after an apparently brief widowhood, married a John Brymbel, whom the villagers allowed to enter the Lynlond tenement without the lord's permission, by payment of an entry fine agreed upon among themselves. Another tale embedded in the court roll narrative, one that is reminiscent of the youthful exuberance of Plow Monday observances, is found in Upwood's 1301 court. There the jurors presented ten men from the neighboring village of Wistow who had come to Upwood one evening for a vigil by the body of Simon de Sutbyr' (Cholle's pledge, mentioned earlier) and, in returning home, threw rocks at their neighbors' cattle and behaved so badly that the hue and cry was raised (*redenndo iacuerunt lapides ad bestia vicinorum et male se habuerunt*).

69 See Hyams, *Rancor and Reconciliation*, 122, where he notes the ubiquity of the feud in medieval society. Also see pp. 199–202 for a discussion of what he calls "reconciliation rituals."

That this was another crowd of mostly young men is evident in their names: two are cited as "son of" someone, two were the abbot's shepherds, and one was a servant (*seruiens*).

The connection with storytelling, telling tales, in court is also clear in connection with rumor and defamation: in Ellington's 1294 court William Aldyth charged William Buk with having defamed him and his son John by "uttering lies" (*quod idem Willelmus defamauit ... iaculsse* [*iaculo*, to utter] *in fab*[*ula*]). The public drama of defamation would have required restitution in the public forum of the village court. Indeed, as is well known, these local courts were the first to deal with charges of defamation, which later passed to ecclesiastical courts and, in the early modern period, to the royal courts.[70]

Two disputes involving land, which together take up one-third of the text of Ellington's c. 1310 court roll, clearly illustrate purposeful storytelling and evocation of memory in a collective setting. Let us take the first dispute, between a tenant named Nicholas Burgeys and a man named Richard whose father had previously held the land in question, as an example. We learn from the account given in court that Hugh in Estrate, a virgater, had three sons, Thomas, Adam, and Richard. Adam married a certain Juliana who had a virgate of land, Thomas married Juliana's daughter Agnes, and by an agreement reached among themselves Thomas and Agnes were to receive the paternal virgate when Hugh died. "And in this way the said Hugh and Thomas and Agnes lived together in the same tenement for a long time" (*simul in eadem terra per tempora longa vixerunt*). This arrangement was disturbed, however, because Thomas predeceased his father, Hugh, who survived him for a long time (*diu postea remansit et vixit*). When Hugh died, his widowed daughter-in-law Agnes continued living in the tenement for eight years and more (*per octo annos et amplius*), probably to the end

70 John S. Beckerman, "Adding Insult to *Iniuria*: Affronts to Honor and the Origins of Trespass," in *On the Laws and Customs of England*, ed. M.S. Arnold et al. (Chapel Hill, 1981), 159–181; and M. Patricia Hogan, "The Slight to Honor: Slander and Wrongful Prosecution in Five Medieval Villages," *Studies in Medieval and Renaissance History*, n.s. 12 (1991): 3–42. As pointed out many years ago, "until further researches have been made among the records of our manorial courts, we shall know little of the medieval law of defamation." See F. Pollock and F.W. Maitland, *The History of English Law before the Time of Edward I* (2nd ed., 1898; repr., Cambridge, 1968) 2: 536–538.

of her life, since the tenement in question was held at the time of the dispute by Nicholas Burgeys, against whom Richard brought the action. Since the jurors found that Thomas was never properly seised of (had never properly possessed) that land, Agnes's tenure was found (after the fact) to be "against established custom," *contra consuetudinem prehabitam*; and since Richard at some earlier time had expressly (*expresse*) used his father's goods and chattels to pay the land entry fine on three quarters of land elsewhere within the vill, the tenement was given (*comitatur*) to Nicholas Burgeys, who promptly paid a *gersuma* (land entry fine) of 40s.

The flow and rhythm of this story, the sequence of events, the reaching into individual and collective memory to retell the tale, and the adduction of *consuetudo prehabita*, are all elements of the sort of tales that villagers would have been required to recall and relate in connection with coroners' inquests, depositions, canonization proceedings, and in various inquisitional settings.[71] Villagers would also have recalled and related their store of local knowledge in the form of proverbs.[72] The same court that could create a favorable setting for

71 See A.B. White's *Self-Government at the King's Command: A Study in the Beginnings of English Democracy* (Minneapolis, 1933) for a discussion of the numerous types of inquests with which the English secular government could charge its subjects. Ecclesiastical tribunals of many sorts also clearly required information gathering and reporting by bodies of lay people. Recourse to the people as a source of knowledge was one of the principal mechanisms of medieval government throughout Europe. A well-known, early example is the polyptychs (surveys) carried out on the lands of the monastery of St Germain des Prés outside of Paris, which were drawn up sometime between 809 and 839. See David Herlihy, *Medieval Households* (Cambridge, MA, 1985), Chapter Three, especially pp. 62–78.

72 Natalie Zemon Davis, "Proverbial Wisdom and Popular Errors," in *Society and Culture in Early Modern France* (Stanford, 1975), 227–267. Common proverbs were used by suitors in "vassalic and manorial courts," indeed, mnemonic proverbs were "necessary to so much of the business of society ... we have evidence that villagers both expected an exchange of proverbs to have some role in legal argumentation and probably used them themselves before manorial courts and in village disputes." She cites a late medieval manuscript where a lawyer is advised to use proverbs in court, "for the peasants like to judge according to pro-

this recitation and exchange of proverbs also prompted the telling of stories, because stories were the prime instrument for the basic work of the court, which was fostering consensus. Just as people could variously interpret proverbs, so too there was ample room for them to relate to any given story in a variety of ways. People listened to a narration alongside their neighbors ("as my neighbors who are here know," said Walter of the Moor in the story of the tench), in a collective reception of the story, and in the knowledge that some roughly agreed-upon version had finally to be arrived at. The individual's ability to relate generally to others and to integrate his or her experience with that of others was a linchpin of the functioning of that tribunal.

Bruno Bettelheim's work, discussed above in the Introduction, suggests several parallels between fairy tales and the village court version of storytelling: the stories are set in the recent past, and the problems they refer to are ordinary ones, of the sort anyone might encounter.[73] In this respect, the court resembles the institution of the *veillée* mentioned earlier, as it is a setting where work and storytelling come together, and not simply in the sense of occurring simultaneously, but something more: each helps the other along, work moves the story forward, the story moves work forward.[74] In reading court rolls, one has the sense of many ears listening to a story that is being worked out as it goes along, of a story that is searching for assent as it unfolds, thus involving all auditors as active participants implicated in the work of achieving consensus and bound therefore to observe its terms. We might say that everyone was drawn into the charmed circle of performers, in a court where the boundary between audi-

---

verbs" (p. 244). This practice would have added to the traditional repertoire of dialogue that one would hear in court.

73 Indeed, perhaps the stories told in local courts may be thought of as belonging to the same tradition that created folk tales, myths, and proverbial wisdom, thus forming part of the "literature of preliterate societies" discussed by Bettelheim. See *The Uses of Enchantment: The Meaning and Importance of Fairy Tales* (New York, 1977), 25.

74 Indeed, the connection between storytelling and getting practical work done may lie at the very origins of myth and folk tale: Bettelheim points out that some scholars believe such stories were initially derived from initiation rites or other *rites de passage*. Bettelheim, *Uses of Enchantment*, 35. Bettelheim also emphasizes that these stories are shaped by the "consensus of many" and not by particular individuals (p. 36).

ence and actors in the central ritual was highly permeable, so that a version of recent local history acceptable to everyone could be constructed and affirmed.

The Uses of Ritual in Self-Government

What was the incentive to fashion, collectively and over time, a local court with such cultural powers? Village society and its court had numerous mechanisms to handle most of the conflicts and disorder that occurred in the community, some of which have been discussed in these pages. As we have seen, the court could enforce compliance through fining, through pledging (by another person, by one's body, or by an article of value, such as an implement), by distraint and impounding of chattels, or by confinement to the stocks, a measure rarely noted in the court rolls for Upwood and Ellington, as mentioned earlier. There was a ducking-stool in the village of Ellington, but its sole appearance in the court rolls occurred because the vill was fined 2s in 1322 for neither raising nor repairing it (*non leuauerunt nec reparauerunt Tumberellum suum*). As a more extreme measure, offenders could be expelled from the vill, as was Henry Cook from Upwood in 1294 for being outside tithing; or Hugh son of Robert Lauerok in 1318 for theft of geese, chickens, and *alia minuta* on several occasions; or as were Agnes and Alice Foot from Ellington in 1316 for theft of their neighbors' chickens (all thefts occurring in the famine era of the late 'teens). Such coercive measures have, understandably perhaps, tended to weigh more heavily in mainstream scholarship than have the village's cooperative or non-coercive structures.

But coercion was at once too much and not enough to govern the village. In a society dependent on collective agriculture and thus conditioned by collective behavior, it was not usually necessary: quite simply, "[m]utual dependence for the food supply of the village wrought mutual forbearance."[75] Most of the time, such extreme measures as expulsion from the vill or confinement to the stocks would have been more than was required to promote social order. In fact, village society was highly tolerant of the non-conformists in its midst because they were the rule and not the exception: according to J.A. Raftis,

75 Nellie Neilson, *Medieval Agrarian Economy* (New York, 1936), 19.

> non-conformity was of a wide incidence rather than the repeated performance of the few. The failure to increase small regular fines must have been an important condition for this attitude towards the law. Aberrations from the law appear as strongly with respect to obligations for work on the lord's demesne, or against the assize of ale, as in the easy encroachment on lands of a neighbour or of the common, or in civil and criminal violence in personal lives. The very fact that non-conformity should move against the family, neighbourhood, customaries, as well as against the lord, defies rationalization.[76]

The long-term stability of village society despite this widespread non-conformity suggests the individual's internalization of a body of ideas, many of them articulated and enforced in the court, where performance, ritual, and storytelling helped to integrate the life experiences of all members of the community. Frequent sessions of the court, whether it met once, twice, several times a year, or once every three weeks, provided a predictable, recurrent, open forum that focused and concentrated people's response to change in the village. The demotic art of storytelling would also aid the work of memory, upon which so much of day-to-day village life, as well as seigneurial management, depended.

Alongside its many overt legal functions, then, the court was also a performance arena for the enactment of local drama, of the sort medieval country audiences liked to see and hear. The "parish drama" of the village court becomes analogous to the pageants and plays put on in rural settings; and villagers likewise had access to such spectacles in the towns, which put on plays because they "were good business. ... Then, as now, there was money to be made from a crowd."[77]

76 Raftis, *Tenure and Mobility*, 210–211.

77 John Coldewey has discussed the staging of popular plays in town and country including, among many other things, the making and use of props, how these were rented out, and the wages paid to actors (for example, 2s to the man who played God, less to the one who played Judas). See "Some Economic Aspects of the Late Medieval Drama," in *Contexts for Early English Drama*, ed. Marianne G. Briscoe and John Coldewey (Bloomington, 1989), 77–101, especially 90–93 (quotations at 87). According to Coldewey, "the lion's share of drama performed in England for the first three quarters of the sixteenth century was not that supported by craft guilds as part of large civic enterprises; rather it was

The telling of tales in court paralleled the telling of tales elsewhere; thus, the demands of self-government participated in the traditions that created European fables and folktales, perhaps contributing to what Robert Darnton calls the "historical dimension of folktales."[78] As discussed above, the suitors to the court might also find in this ritual dimension of their court a mechanism for self-government. In the "mutual awareness," that particular kind of reflexive consciousness created by the rituals of the court, villagers moved the business that lay within their purview onto a different plane of collective reception where, in a single and continuous performance, it was objectified by all, for all. In this way, ritual supported the growth of power in the village, as it did in church, city, and royal court. We might even say that wherever we see performance and ritual we see power, or claims to power that are as good as power itself.

Thus, the performance, rituals, and storytelling of the village court were part of a local repertoire of mechanisms to govern the community: they emphasize the instrumentality of the court and the agency of the suitors to the court. In this reading, the court becomes a place where villagers do the work of government, and where ritual and performance help them do it. But village ritual and performance were more than the instruments whereby all the apparent and latent powers of collective life could be marshalled: they are also a key to structures of thought within the villager, even to villager identity. Anne DeWindt has noted that the historian's approach to the peasant over the past century of scholarship has moved gradually from an external to an internal perspective, that we began by viewing the villager from afar, from the vantage point of royal law and legal treatise to the economic demands and political power of lordship over the "manor"; then, in the village study, into the village itself; thence into villagers' homes, where we see individuals as husbands, wives, children, and widows, and can observe aspects of their family

---

the smaller local productions put on by a truly astonishing number of parishes and towns around the countryside" (p. 93).

78 See Darnton, "Peasants Tell Tales: The Meaning of Mother Goose," in *The Great Cat Massacre and Other Episodes in French Cultural History* (New York, 1985), 11.

life.[79] In this chapter we have extended this itinerary by studying the values and assumptions, the "unconscious grammatical principles," of the individual villager through the collective rituals of his and her community, and the fecund activity of swearing an oath. By doing so we have shed light on their understanding of power and the instruments they employed to forge a *pax iurata*, a peace "based on a consensus, association, or oath" in the village,[80] that also implicated the inner person.

79 From a paper given by Anne DeWindt at a Court Rolls seminar (University of Copenhagen, March 1997). My thanks to Professor DeWindt for allowing me to cite her paper.

80 Otto Gerhard Oexle, "Peace Through Conspiracy," in *Ordering Medieval Society: Perspectives on Intellectual and Practical Modes of Shaping Social Relations*, ed. Bernhard Jussen, trans. Pamela Selwyn (Philadelphia, 2001), 285–322, at 285. Oexle calls for a greater focus on study of the sworn peace as opposed to the *pax ordinata*, or "commanded peace," that is, a peace "ordered from above."

CHAPTER TWO

Peasant Names and Peasant Women

English court rolls can be seen as a medieval precursor to – and within the "universe" of writing in the village, perhaps preparation for – the parish registers of the early modern era, in the sense that they provide the full names of tens of thousands of men, women, and even children, an approximate sense of their life span, and some knowledge of their activities in a specific village. Yet the villager of the court roll is embedded in a fuller social context than the parishioner named in a parish register.[1] Indeed, as suggested earlier, the court roll shares qualities with medieval inquisition records and early modern parish registers: like the former, it has narrative qualities based on a transcript of verbal proceedings, yet like the latter it is grounded upon a body of fully-named individuals in a specific time and place.

The question "what's in a name?" in an English court roll will elicit a lengthy reply from the historian of village life: the rolls are rich in the names of persons, places, offices and actions, offences and institutions; as an on-the-spot transcript of the day's business, they also preserve the vocabulary and names that villagers used, and they preserve a community discussion anchored in time and place that progressed by continual reference to the court's suitors, who were routinely designated by their full names. Further, the late thirteenth

1 Judith Bennett, "Medieval Peasant Marriage," in *Pathways to Medieval Peasants*, ed. J.A. Raftis (Toronto, 1981), 231, has also compared court rolls and parish registers, along somewhat different lines. It is, of course, in the early modern period when the state was making novel inroads into local power that court rolls become less informative, and parish registers first appear. In other words, the state's traditional interest in recording individuals by name increases in the sixteenth century. For a study of names based on parish registers see Scott Smith-Bannister, *Names and Naming Patterns in England, 1538–1700* (Oxford; New York, 1997), which employs a data base of more than 100,000 names.

century (when the earliest surviving court roll series begin) is the same period when the surnames of individuals and families were beginning a process of stabilization and thus becoming more fixed. As we will see in some detail in the present chapter, surnames continued to exhibit significant fluctuation, influenced by place of origin, occupation, residence, parents' names, and individual personality (nicknames) and the like, up to the arrival of the plague in the mid-fourteenth century. Thus, the court rolls for Upwood and Ellington, and for hundreds of other English villages, provide materials for studying the foundations of what Cecily Clark has called the "name-creating permutations" and even the "chronology of fashions" in patterns of naming.[2] The final chapter of this book will examine the history of naming the land in the post-plague village; in the present chapter, our focus is on the names given to people, especially to women, their variations over time, and how this evidence may provide another approach to the villager's "invisible world."

From a discussion of the extent of women's participation in village life, we will proceed to explore their impact on the village as a source of names. An analysis of the metronymic surnames found in court rolls will shed light on women's instrumentality within marriage, and perhaps on the associations brought to marriage by women who held land. The court's focus on tenure and land management, which included women holding and controlling, inheriting and leasing land, just as men did, may also give us a closer look at the village tradition of "thinking with women" – in particular, how the sex of the landholder affected village ideas about tenure, the control of land, the partitioning of village space, and even the formation of personal identity, insofar as that was influenced by landholding. Finally, it will be suggested that the scholarly emphasis on the inferior status of peasant women must give way to a more complicated view incorporating the fact of ambiguity, which to some extent affected everyone.

2 Cecily Clark, "English Personal Names ca. 650–1300: Some Prosopographical Bearings," *Medieval Prosopography* 8 (1987): 31–60, at 34, 37. See P.H. Reaney, *The Origin of English Surnames* (New York, 1967), for a lucid introduction to this type of study. See J.A. Raftis, *Warboys: Two Hundred Years in the Life of an English Mediaeval Village* (Toronto, 1974), for a discussion of the pool of personal names observable in the records of that village.

As we saw in Chapter One, court rolls are most informative when studied alongside other estate administrative records: account rolls, cartularies, and extents also focused on the named tenants within a lordship, and formulary books for holding a manor court, which were composed mainly of precedents from court rolls, emerged to standardize those ubiquitous assemblies. Further, because most estate records derived from peasant informants and thus have a roughly common source, they might be said to refer readily, even organically, to each other. Taken together, this body of local materials demonstrates above all that peasants were neither nameless nor generic to the record-making institutions of the English Middle Ages, particularly those that had frequent and sustained contact with them, and that they need not be nameless to us.[3]

Women in the Court and in the Village

The all-purpose forum of the court drew the vast majority of adult villagers, men and women, into the court in connection with a great variety of business, albeit far fewer women than men. Judith Bennett, who has argued that the court disadvantaged women, estimates that only about 25 percent of the women in a village appear in the rolls; Helen Jewell, working with the court rolls for the manor of Wakefield, notes that the range of activity recorded for women was broad but their appearances were infrequent; where individual women did appear they were often *sole*, either widows or unmarried.[4] In Upwood and

3 As early as the ninth century, polyptychs (mentioned above, note 71 in Chapter One) named the members of the peasant farms that were surveyed, for example, "Teutbertus a *colonus* [farmer] and his wife a *colona* by name of Ratgundis ... have with them three children, with these names: Rantgarius, Rantgis, Teutberta." See David Herlihy, *Medieval Households* (Cambridge, MA, 1985), 66.

4 Helen M. Jewell, "Women at the Courts of the Manor of Wakefield, 1348–50," *Northern History* 26 (1990): 59–81, at 78–79. Judith Bennett's *Women in the Medieval English Countryside* (New York, 1987) is still the most comprehensive study of medieval countrywomen using court roll data. For a biography of a medieval countrywoman, pre-eminently using court roll evidence, see Bennett's *A Medieval Life: Cecilia Penifader of Brigstock, c. 1295–1344* (Boston, 1999). Also useful is P.J.P. Goldberg,

Ellington women accounted for about 30 percent of the total number of individuals named in the court rolls for each village over our period, and between 13 and 14 percent of the total number of entries. Women are conspicuous in these records, as we have seen, especially for the early rolls of the end of the thirteenth and early fourteenth centuries, and their appearances in court derived mostly from landholding and economic activity, as was also the case for men. Men appeared more frequently than women, but villagers would have been accustomed to seeing both acting in a variety of roles. Further, women were prominent in some categories of activity, notably brewing, money-lending, and the raising of the hue and cry.[5]

This picture is highly compatible with P.J.P. Goldberg's findings for women in town and country in northern England in the later Middle Ages: the prevalence of a "late companionate marriage regime," and of service (that is, working as a servant) as a "normal feature" of the life-cycle, were coupled with "significant work opportunities for

---

Women, Work and Life Cycle in a Medieval Economy: Women in York and Yorkshire, c. 1300–1520 (Oxford, 1992). For a more general discussion, one that touches upon many of the issues raised in the present chapter, see Rodney Hilton, "Women in the Village," in *The English Peasantry in the Later Middle Ages* (Oxford, 1975), 95–110.

5 See Sherri Olson, *A Chronicle of All That Happens: Voices from the Village Court in Medieval England* (Toronto, 1996), for a full discussion of women's participation in this local policing effort in Upwood and Ellington; note especially that women in Ellington had a better record for raising the hue and cry "justly" than did men in that village, and that this activity brought women into court in other ways: in Ellington's 1311 court roll there is an entry noting that Walter Faber broke into Emma Faber's house because she had justly raised the hue and cry on him (*Walter Faber fecit hamsoken super Emmam Faber' in domo sua per quod dicta Emma iuste leuauit uthesium super eundem Walterum*). In that same court William le Foulere was cited for beating the wife of Laurence de Bedford because the latter had justly raised a hue and cry on William. Yet another variant is found in a 1307 Upwood entry noting that Sarra Waryn beat Alice Bygge because Alice justly raised the hue and cry upon her; Sarra's pledge, Thomas Godes, was fined because he didn't have her in court that day, and it is ordered that Sarra be distrained to answer the charge. For a recent discussion of women and the village hue and cry, see Sandy Bardsley, *Venomous Tongues: Speech and Gender in Late Medieval England* (Philadelphia, 2006), especially pp. 70–77.

women to support themselves independently prior to marriage, or even independently of marriage."[6] Indeed, Goldberg argues that "women's work identity tended to be rather fluid" because "[u]nlike the male apprentice, most female servants would have experience of several different types of household." A wife might also learn her husband's trade, thus "would build up through life a range of experiences and skills." In short, women were "seldom wholly engaged in a single employment."[7] Indeed, court roll entries regularly show women appearing alongside men, or being involved in the same or similar activities, women like Elena Wright, referred to in a 1361 York cause paper as a woman who "served her husband by winnowing and selling grain and ... 'in other tasks which pertain to a *materfamilias*'."[8] In Upwood, Matilda Neuman provides a good example of the integration of women in village society by virtue of landholding: in 1339 she appropriated land, dug turves, reaped badly, and plowed badly; in 1344 she trespassed with geese, and was fined for not coming when called (*non venit quando vocata*); and in 1347 she cut into the royal way, made hedges badly, and trespassed with horses. In 1311 Alice Haukyn sent *insufficientes homines* to an autumn work, was fined 3d, and was pledged by the beadle. The 1297 court roll lists nine people fined and pledged for various infractions involving the taking or cutting of wood, trees, and rushes, and includes Beatrix le Horseman who sold rushes from the common and Julyana wife of John Toleboy who reaped and carried the lord's wheat. In 1295 Matilda daughter of

6 Chapter Five, "Marriage in Town and Country," in Goldberg, *Women, Work and Life Cycle*; quotations at 204, 272–273.

7 Goldberg, *Women, Work and Life Cycle*, 335–336. Goldberg assigns a different meaning to such fluidity from the one suggested in the present book (where we have argued for a fluidity of personality as existentially necessary or desirable): he describes women as lacking a "well-developed work identity" (p. 336). This characterization could apply equally well to a typical merchant of Prato who tended to ply more than one trade, if not several, at one time. See Richard K. Marshall, *The Local Merchants of Prato: Small Entrepreneurs in the Late Medieval Economy* (Baltimore, 1999).

8 Cited in Goldberg, *Women, Work and Life Cycle*, 137. The cause papers used in Goldberg's study are another type of evidence that relied upon the depositions of witnesses, here, in ecclesiastical court and concerning testamentary, defamation, and matrimonial matters. See his discussion, ibid., 217–218.

Serlo Faber, Ida sister of William Faber, Lucia Wauke, Philippa de Monte, Agnes le Turnur, and Agnes le Vtler, as well as "Little William" (*Parvus Willelmus*), are cited as bakers who were fined for breaking regulations governing bread production (*assisam panis*). In 1307 Robert Ayse is cited, though not fined, for allowing his daughter Margery to marry without licence; in the next entry it is noted that she (not her father) is to be distrained to settle this matter by paying the customary fee to the lord, and that afterwards she had done so, "as appears in the Roll of Land Entry Fines" (*Et preceptum est quod dicta Margeria distringatur ad factam finem cum domino. Et postea fecit finem sicut patet in Rotulo Gersumarum*).

Other cases exemplify the multiple strands of women's participation in the public legal life of the village. In Ellington's 1299 record, Emma daughter of Henry le Bok is pledged that before the next court she will build a house on a piece of land formerly her father's, and for the construction of that house she took one-half mark from William son of Bate (*plantabit vnam domum super placeam*).[9] In 1306 Iulyana le Neweman, *nativa domini*, sublet one-half acre of "servile land" to one Matilda Kount, an outsider (*dimisit Matilde Kount dimidiam acram terre servilis ad firmam extra feodum domini*); the land was taken into the lord's hand and Neweman was to answer for the issue. In c. 1310 the jurors found that Elena Aldyth defaulted on a debt to Simon son of John: she was fined for unjust detention, pledged by William Aldyth and Galfridus Buk, and was to pay before the feast of St Michael (29 September). In the same court Beatrix le Brewster purchased an acre of land from Simon de Elyngton, and she made fealty to the lord for that land (*fecit domino fidelitatem*) with William de Spaldwyck as her pledge. In 1311 Margaria wife of William Leonard had not yet emended a charter for one-half acre of land which she had bought from Thomas Pylcok and Joan his wife. She was fined 6d and was to be distrained to emend her charter (*ad emendam cartam suam*).

Women's participation in the regional labor market is illustrated in a 1280 Upwood entry where Milo de Leyhtone was fined 6d for "housing" women from outside the village (*quia hospit' extraneas contra assisam*). With respect to labor within the village, Matilda

9 J.A. Raftis explains this entry as a sale of land from Emma to William son of Bate, where the "capital investment on the tenement may have provided the main terms of the sale." See *Tenure and Mobility* (Toronto, 1964), 71, 74.

daughter of Serlo and Alice daughter of Robert le Plouwrytte were fined in the 1294 court because they didn't come to the lord's work at harvest (*precarium domini*); in addition, William Tyler was fined because Alice le Plouwrytte took her neighbors' turves from the marsh and did damage in the lord's wood against custom (*ex consuetudine*). Tyler had been her pledge that she not do damage again (*ne de cetero dampnum facit*). Also in Upwood in 1295 Agnes widow of John le Vacher in cleaning her ditch cut into the king's road at le Heyerode Weye to the nuisance of passers-by, and cut into a marker between her land and that of Simon le Vacher while plowing. She was fined, pledged, and ordered to fix what she had damaged.

Women's activities in local industry is indicated, as we have seen, by the routine jurors' presentment of the brewers, which sometimes included interesting details on this facet of women's "agency." In 1301 Alice Brun, brewer, was fined because she didn't "send for the tasters" (*quia non misit pro tastatoribus*) when she brewed (a routine public responsibility, associated primarily with women, that took place outside the court's jurisdiction). A variation on this kind of agency was exercised by Agnes Bygge (1307) who watered down her ale after the tasters left (*Et post tastacionem deteriorauit*), as did Matilda le Reue (1308) who, in addition, "falsely kept back" and didn't bring her quart measure to court because it was "broken and useless" (*fraudulenter detinuit quartam suam et secum non tulit eo quod fracta fuit et inutilis*).[10] Women were also active as debtors and creditors in local money-lending: Muriella le Newman (Ellington 1321) defaulted on a debt of 16d which she owed to Emma le Neuman. Her fine was excused because she was poor and she was pledged by her body (*plegius corpus*). Isabella le Wodeward (Ellington 1322) acknowledged two separate debts of 10s and 3s 4d owed to Petronilla le Bere, herself a money-lender who was cited that same day by the jurors for a false charge against Isabella (a finding with which she evidently disagreed because she quarreled with the jurors) as well as for a false charge of debt against Walter Beumeis. This small sample of entries provides a picture of the scope and variety of women's daily activity in the public village arena and offers further evidence for the argument made in Chapter One that the court relied

10 As discussed earlier, the public association of these implements with the brewer in court reinforced women's participation in the culturally-charged arena of work, implements, agency, and identity formation.

upon its powers of inclusion to get its work done. Women were included in court as they were included in most aspects of village life.

While few historians working on medieval women today would agree with Eileen Power's observation (made in 1926) that married people of the medieval countryside existed within a relationship of "rough and ready equality,"[11] many of those scholars still frame analysis around the issue of equality. Scholars speak of the "basic legal and political rights" of women, of their "legal disabilities" in the village, and of women's "power and status" within marriage.[12] In this view countrywomen's "inequality" inside and outside the home, particularly married women's inequality, had a fairly monolithic character: their activities, and the public appraisal of those activities, were preeminently driven by notions of gender. At the core of the idea of "legal disability" there lies an assumption that man is indeed the "measure of significance." Whether women in the medieval village shared the view of modern scholars that this is so is a point that cannot simply be assumed. As we shall see in the present close reading of court roll data, interpersonal evaluation on the basis of gender, while significant, cannot be described as the most important dynamic in the public response to women and their activity; rather, the meaning assigned to gender is best interpreted within a context of "local knowledge" that contained numerous constituent parts.

As records of practice focused on a community of farmers, where farming was a family, not an individual, enterprise, and thus included

11 Eileen Power, "The Position of Women," in *The Legacy of the Middle Ages*, ed. C.G. Crump and E.F. Jacob (Oxford, 1926), 401–433.

12 Judith Bennett, "The Tie That Binds: Peasant Marriages and Families in Late Medieval England," *Journal of Interdisciplinary History* 15 (1984): 111–129, at 123. For the related view that village men defined and controlled women's "space" see Barbara A. Hanawalt, "Medieval English Women in Rural and Urban Domestic Space," *Dumbarton Oaks Papers* 52 (1998): 19–26. In an essay on village women, Rodney Hilton frames the question along similar lines: "Was their status at this time, when general personal unfreedom was still widespread, such that subsequent history has seen a progressive improvement in their condition? Was their situation within their own class comparable with that of women in other classes, such as the bourgeoisie and the aristocracy, or better, or worse?" See Hilton, "Women in the Village," in *The English Peasantry in the Later Middle Ages* (Oxford, 1975), 95.

men and women,[13] court rolls provide a unique vantage point from which to address these issues. We will begin by focusing on metronymic surnames, which are formed from women's names, and thus are subject to village ideas about women.

Studying Village Surnames

According to P.H. Reaney, all surnames "were given spontaneously and not according to any fixed rule," thus "all surnames are really nicknames" (from *ekenames*, meaning "additional names").[14] As mentioned at the beginning of this chapter, English surnames tend to fall into one of several sometimes overlapping categories which Reaney identifies as local surnames (for example, place names or toponymics), surnames of relationship (for example, patronymics and metronymics), surnames of occupation or office, and nicknames (from physical, mental, or moral characteristics). Among these, local surnames are most numerous in town and country alike, followed (in the country) by surnames of relationship, occupation, and finally nicknames.[15]

According to Charles Bardsley in his *English Surnames,* first published in 1873, metronymic surnames were a "considerable class" of surnames that derived from a variety of sources. His close study of thousands of surnames enabled him to reject the prevailing late nineteenth-century notion that metronymic names derived primarily from illegitimate descent (indeed he counters this idea in the preface to the second edition "on account of the mischief it may do"),[16] and to look for other explanations. He writes:

13 See George Homans's discussion of the etymology of "husband," "anilepimen," and "anilepiwymen," which makes this point quite clear. The denotation of "anilepiman" is "single man, unmarried man," but its connotation is "a landless man." *English Villagers of the Thirteenth Century* (1941; repr., New York, 1975), 136–137.

14 Reaney, *Origin of English Surnames*, 19–20.

15 See the table "Distribution of the Classes of Surnames in Middle English" on p. 22 in Reaney, *Origin of English Surnames*. This table is based on over one hundred thousand surnames drawn from various royal, regional, and local documents over the period 1066–1459, although most (about 90%) are from the period 1290–1340.

16 Charles Bardsley, *English Surnames: Their Sources and Significations* (4th ed., 1889; repr., Rutland, VT, 1968), xvii.

adoption of children by women, posthumous birth, and other peculiar circumstances would often cause a boy or girl to be known in the community by a metronymic. Especially, too, would a child be thus styled in a family where the mother was notoriously, and in an emphatic sense, the better half, in a family where the husband was content to sit in the chimney nook, and let the bustling Margery, or Siss, or Emmot take, whether in or out of doors, the lead in all that concerned the domestic relationship. Thus, I doubt not, a large mass of them have arisen.[17]

P.H Reaney, commenting on this passage, cites such names as Geoffrey Liggebyethefyre (Yorkshire 1301) and Henry Lenealday (Yorkshire 1336) as examples of "men of this type." Indeed, Upwood had its own Robert Dryngallday (Old English *dringle*, "to waste time in a lazy, lingering manner").[18] Court roll evidence enables us to reframe and continue this inquiry, and to consider whether the prominence achieved by women and suggested by some village surnames proceeded from other causes, in addition to Margery's bustling about the chimney nook.[19]

We begin by recalling Helen Jewell's observation that women's range of activities was great, but their court appearances were infrequent, that women were somehow both ubiquitous and unusual, a

17 Bardsley, *English Surnames*, 80. Reaney, *Origin of English Surnames*, 78, cites other possible sources of metronymic surnames: "the children of a widow; in the case of second marriages, the distinguishing of the two families by their mother's names; the adoption of orphans by females relatives; and [citing E. Weekly] … 'in a village which counted two Johns or Williams, and few villages did not, the children of one might assume, or rather would be given by the public voice, the mother's name.'" Note the functional orientation of that "public voice."

18 Reaney, *Origin of English Surnames*, 78; *Oxford English Dictionary*, s.v. "dringle".

19 Indeed it may be said that court rolls provide a context for names that is not present in other types of sources such as assize rolls or charters, a point of some importance since, as Reaney points out, "[l]ack of context may prevent us from discovering the real meaning" of a name. See *Origin of English Surnames*, 224. For another example of names whose fuller context is retrievable from the documents, see R.K. Marshall's discussion of nicknames in an Italian urban setting, *The Local Merchants of Prato*, 66–67, 154 n16.

fact that accords well with a commonplace of current scholarship (as it was not in Bardsley's day) that the domestic arts were not "privatized" in medieval Europe.[20] While women occupied the central role in the household economy, they were also integrated into the web of village life outside their door: women were conspicuous in the major concerns of village life, that is, family and landholding; as argued earlier, the court included all its suitors in its work and required their participation to some degree – a principle of operation strengthened, perhaps, by the presence of the very people who could not hold local office, that is, women. By this reading (and because people "thought with women"), the latter needed to be present for the court to function properly.[21] In addition, as we have seen, women answered for themselves in court, brought complaints, swore oaths, and paid fines. Extremely rare but not unknown are instances where women were elected to local office or acted as pledge in court (the sole occurrence of this in our evidence is found in Upwood's 1350 court roll where Adelina Wauke, who had justly raised the hue and cry on her husband, Osloc, then had to pledge for him, probably because no one else was willing to).[22] In the village, in short, the realities of women's and

20 That all villagers spent most of their time out of doors is evident in general surveys and specialized studies alike. For example, see Barbara A. Hanawalt, *The Ties that Bound: Peasant Families in Medieval England* (New York, 1986); Frances and Joseph Gies, *Life in a Medieval Village* (New York, 1990); Bennett, *A Medieval Life*; and Bennett, *Women in the Medieval English Countryside*. Rodney Hilton has drawn attention to the phenomenon of women everywhere present in the world of village work in *The Economic Development of Some Leicestershire Estates in the 14th & 15th Centuries* (London, 1947), and again in "Women in the Village," in *The English Peasantry*, 95–110. Also see M. Patricia Hogan, "The Labor of Their Days: Work in the Medieval Village," *Studies in Medieval and Renaissance History*, n.s. 8 (1986): 75–186.

21 If we can show that villagers (men and women) "thought with women," it follows that they also "thought with men." The present author is planning a study of the links between monastic lords and peasants and the phenomena of "monks thinking with peasants" and "peasants thinking with monks." For a recent exploration of some aspects of the interface between lord and peasant, see David Stone, *Decision-Making in Medieval Agriculture* (Oxford, 2005).

22 For an earlier discussion of Adelina Wauke in the context of plague in the village, see Olson, *A Chronicle*, 87. There are many examples of

men's lives helped to shape the local community, the historical setting in which most hereditary surnames were formed.[23] Our evidence will help us explore the role of women's names in surname formation and disappearance, and the factors influencing these processes.

Women's Names in Surname Formation and Disappearance

As mentioned at the beginning of this chapter, the years around 1300 provide an interesting juncture for the study of surnames: although a substantial proportion of village surnames were fairly stable, with one surname being used most of the time for a given person, there were still fluctuations in certain village names, fluctuations that are all the more interesting to the historian given that they were exceptions to the growing tendency towards stabilization of names in the village. Court roll evidence is particularly well-placed to reveal the variety and innovation "within traditional patterns" which Cecily Clark has noted for English naming practices in this period.[24]

---

women being elected or allowed to fill some office or perform some function one time only, or very rarely. For instance, Judith Bennett, *Women in the Medieval English Countryside*, notes that women did pledge in Brigstock but that it was extremely rare (p. 25 with n9). Warren Ault, in his discussion of what types of men were elected warden, notes that a woman, Johanna Barber, was elected warden in the village of Great Horwood in 1436. See *Open-Field Husbandry and the Village Community: A Study of Agrarian By-laws in Medieval England* (Philadelphia, 1965): 44 n71. Eileen Power gives other examples for women of the upper classes in her seminal essay, "The Position of Women."

23 According to Bardsley, *English Surnames*, 107, and in agreement with P.H. Reaney, in most countries where hereditary surnames have developed, the majority were of local origin and, further, the surnames of local origin were the first to become hereditary. This point counters somewhat the usual claim that the growth of the state and its increasing record-keeping practices promoted surname stability. Perhaps it would be more accurate to emphasize a mutual influence between state and locality in surname formation.

24 Cecily Clark, "English Personal Names," 34. One can get a sense of this debate in Zvi Razi's village study of Halesowen: see *Life, Marriage and Death in a Medieval Parish* (Cambridge, 1980), and especially his discussion on the difficulties in identifying individuals who were known by

The serial nature and time-sensitivity of court rolls make them a valuable witness to the multiplicity of surnames and their "changing fashions," which have their own story to tell. For example, the fleeting appearance of some occupational surnames in court roll data clearly has something to do with the mobility of laborers, artisans, and skilled laborers in the late thirteenth- and early fourteenth-century countryside. This mobility can be amply illustrated from our evidence, as in a 1308 case where William le Combere, an outsider, was to come to Upwood's court that day either to put himself in tithing or "to show his Warrant that he is in tithing somewhere else" (*ad ostendum Warrantum suum quod alibi est in decenna*). Mobility is also indicated in the many citations in the early court rolls that refer to men working as butchers "outside the fee," that is, beyond the manor. For example, John Shoemaker is cited in Ellington's 1292 court roll as a tanner outside the town giving one capon per annum for permission to be absent (*Iohannes Sutor utitur officio tannatoris extra Burgum sed dat domino per annum i capo*), and William Twyt and John Suyft are cited as butchers *extra Burgum* in the same year. At the end of the heavily damaged 1308 Ellington roll, it is noted that *Walterus Carpentarius* makes a payment for so long as he remains outside the village (*dum manet extra feodum domini*), and *Thomas Pelliparius* (Skinner) is cited for payment made for exercising his craft (*pro officio suo excercendo*). Thomas N[e]lly, cited in 1332, will pay a capon per year and come to court for so long as he works as a skinner (*dum utitur officio pellipar'*).

---

more than one name. For more recent scholarship, see the introduction to *The Court Rolls of Walsham le Willows, 1303–1350*, ed. Ray Lock (Woodbridge, 1998), 23, where the variability of surnames is presented as a problem. The editor states that occupational surnames can be "misleading," and that use of the article "le" is often "superfluous" and can result in "absurdities" such as "Agnes the Man, John the King and William the Typtot." Larry R. Poos, "Peasant 'Biographies' from Medieval England," in *Medieval Lives and the Historian: Studies in Medieval Prosopography*, ed. Neithard Bulst and Jean-Philippe Genet (Kalamazoo, 1986), 201–214, refers to the "difficulties arising from surname variability" (p. 208). P.D.A. Harvey, "English Estate Records, 1250–1330," in *Pragmatic Literacy, East and West, 1200–1330*, ed. Richard Britnell (Woodbridge, 1997), 117–118, also alludes to surname instability as a "particular problem at this period, for which there is no simple solution."

What other factors play a part in the history of surnames before 1350 in Upwood and Ellington, and what role does gender play? Since men were dominant in the village court, was there a "survival of the fittest" mechanism that favored men's names over women's in surname formation and survival in our two villages?

Surnames based on a parent's first name tended to disappear as a person moved through his or her life cycle. Thus, in the Coten family in Ellington, Richard son of *Alicia de Coten* is also cited as *Ricardus filius Alicie* in the earlier part of his career in the village, which spanned the period 1290–1316, but he is usually called Richard *de Coten* towards the end. A surname derived from a woman named Dulcia le Hunte nearly established itself as a surname in Ellington. Although her name survives only in a single citation as a brewer in 1310, thirteen people in the village between 1278 and 1332, nearly half of whom were women, have been identified as members of the le Hunte family. The earliest known representatives of this family are a *Ricardus le Hunt'* and *Mabilla le Hunte*, listed in the *Hundred Rolls*[25] under *Coterelli* (cottage-holders), each holding one messuage. A Richard *le Hunte*, possibly also styled *Doucesson* (the text is damaged), is cited as giving one capon to be outside the fee in 1332. Dulcia's son Robert (*Robertus filius Dulcie*), appeared between 1311 and 1340; he is cited as *filius Dulcie* or *filius Douce* up to 1322, appearing thereafter as Robert *Doucesson*, *Ducessone*, and again as *filius Dulcie* in the lay subsidy roll for 1327.[26] In the court of 1340 *Robertus Ducessone* is cited twice for receiving women who gleaned badly, but when his own son is cited in the same court for having had a hue and cry justly raised against him, and again for finding a swarm of bees in the lord's wood which he then concealed, he is called *Iohannes filius Roberti Hunte*. The surname that the father had acquired as a younger man did not in this case pass to his own son. Moreover, while *Hunte* survives as a surname in Ellington after 1340,

25 The *Hundred Rolls* are the records generated by a royal survey taken (based on information given by local juries) in the 1270s of the privileges held by lords throughout the country. For Ellington see *Rotuli Hundredorum tempore Henrici III et Edwardi I*, ed. W. Illingworth and J. Caley (London, 1812, 1818), 2: 630–631, at 631.

26 *Early Huntingdonshire Lay Subsidy Rolls*, ed. J.A. Raftis and M. Patricia Hogan (Toronto, 1976), 165.

the surname *Doucesson* does not seem to have attached to anyone other than Robert and, after a thirty-year run, it disappeared with him.

The fleeting character of women's names as formative elements in surnames is apparent in other cases: Helewys, Mabbison (from Mabel, short for Amable), and Muriel are examples of surnames that surfaced briefly but did not survive in our two villages. The given name *Mariota* came close to establishing itself as a surname in Upwood, clearly drawing from the life career of *Cristina filia Mariote* (1279–1308), whose surname was so given in 1279, but which had become Maryoth (also spelled Marioth, Maryot, Maryoch, and Mariot) by 1290. Her daughter, whose arrears of 3d in fines were noted in the account roll of 1290, was known as Cecilia Marioth. This surname attached only to women: Emma Mariot was cited for gleaning badly in 1299; Juliana Maryot (1294–1329), a prominent brewer, engaged in trespass, credit dealings, and assault. She was also a married woman, but her husband's name is unknown, since he is cited by the conventional tag *vir eius* ("her husband") every time that he pledged for her in 1308, 1320, 1322, and 1329. The 1308 entry recording that *Mariota* wife of Alexander de Camera was fined as a brewer and pledged by her husband contains the additional – and unusual – information that she didn't come "because she is pregnant" (*Non venit quia prengnans* [*sic*]). In various forms, then, Mariot circulated as a surname in Upwood for at least forty years but ultimately disappeared. In Ellington, disappearing metronymic surnames include Deneys (from a woman named Dionysia, cited three times between 1321? and 1332/3), and Edesson (from Edith), where the notoriety of the eponymous individual extended only to his or her immediate offspring. That these and other surnames disappear in one village but survive in another reminds us of the importance of local and adventitious factors in the history of names and naming systems, factors that are most often impossible to recover.

While the preceding examples have focused on metronymic surnames, in the early fourteenth century disappearance was undoubtedly the fate of most patronymic surnames as well. Analysis of the surnames that disappear from the court rolls of Ellington and Upwood between c. 1280 and 1350 does not suggest that surnames formed with women's given names were more likely to disappear than others: names formed with elements either of local topography or geographic place names, occupations, nicknames, and women's and men's given names are all represented in the combined total of 150 surnames that disappeared from these villages before 1350. These surnames include those based on topographic elements such as Abovestrate, Atehyl, Attechirche, Atte Peretree, and Mersch; place names such as Cumberton, Essex, and St Ive; occupational names such as Fleichhewer, Horseman, Heryngmonger, Carpenter, Bocher, Shepherd, Sawyer, and le Wright; surnames derived from women's given names, such as Mariota, Maysent, Sarra, Helewys, and Catelyn (from Katherine); and men's names such as Patryck, Martin, Herbert, Olyuer, and Adam.

In short, during the period when changes in surnames are quite pronounced, men's given names have no apparent advantage over women's when it comes to surname formation or survival. The formation, evolution, and disappearance of patronymic and metronymic surnames can be understood in part as proof that people's names, whether women's or men's, were another local resource that circulated in the village labyrinth, and were used to do the work of structuring social relations by emphasizing one parental connection over another.

Thus far, the evidence suggests that surnames based on women's and men's given names operated in roughly the same manner, although we know that the naming systems for men and women, and the use made of men's and women's names in those systems, could differ in other ways. For example, it has been shown that while women's given names were restricted to a smaller pool of very popular names, their names showed more variation outside that pool, both between regions and within villages, than was the case for men's names. Also, as Peter Franklin has shown for fourteenth-century peasant names in Gloucestershire, women's given names exhibited more regional variation than did men's.[27]

The court rolls preserve two other naming conventions which apply to both men and women, but more frequently to men. The junior/senior designation is used almost exclusively for men, but there are instances where it is also used for women. In our data this occurs only twice, in Ellington's 1340 court roll, where Alice Milnere

27 Peter Franklin, "Normans, Saints, and Politics: Forename-choice among Fourteenth-Century Gloucestershire Peasants," *Local Population Studies* 36 (1986): 25.

junior and Millicent Godman *junior* are cited for gleaning badly. Men's given names were also used somewhat more frequently than women's in the *filius/filia* construction: that is, *Iohannes filius Ricardi* (John son of Richard) is more common than *Iohannes filius Margerie* (John son of Margery). Interestingly, however, in Upwood's record for the plague year 1349, we find the names *Iohanna Collisdoutere* (Collis, diminutive of Nicholas), and *Agnes Richardisdouter*, the exact reverse of the name *Robertus Doucesson*, and even more fleeting.[28]

The *filius/filia* construction flourishes in the period before the Black Death but declines somewhat thereafter, with the result that most surnames in the later fourteenth-century village are not based on men's or women's given names. The post-famine years (after c. 1325) and, a generation later, the Black Death framed the period in which the main design for surnames began to solidify. In that era, the dominant local naming practices, which created England's bedrock of hereditary surnames, shifted away from the use of given names as elements for surname formation. All mechanisms that relied on the names of individuals were de-emphasized, a development intensified by the plague. Names continue to come and go but do not demonstrate the same quality of active development within the village as had been seen in the period before about 1340. After 1350, real vitality in the village culture of naming passes, significantly, from surnames to place names, as we shall explore in detail in Chapter Five below.[29]

Agnes del Reues and Alice Lynlond

Case studies of women whose actions affected the evolution of surnames within their families in the pre-plague era provide a glimpse of the public recognition of women's instrumentality. A surname like Hosebond (Husband, "house-dweller") and the designation *filius* or *filia* clearly suggest the marital status of the individual, and a surname such as Newhosebond even conveys a sense of a person's chang-

28 The names, which occur in a list of women fined for committing *leyrwite* (sexual misconduct), are the only examples of the suffix *-daughter* being used in name formation in the court rolls for these villages.

29 Reaney's emphasis on parish registers as the earliest surviving documentation that records English surname formation might be revised if court roll evidence were more widely consulted.

ing marital status (or perhaps their recent arrival in the village, that is, to distinguish a new Hosebond family from another one already resident). Changes in widows' names may be equally suggestive, as in the case of Agnes del Reues, widow of William Reeve, who outlived her husband (dead by 1318) by at least twenty-five years in early fourteenth-century Upwood. Over that quarter of a century she continued working the traditional reeve's tenement, probably with the help of her sons John and William, and engaged in all the usual forms of trespass characteristic of major landholders, such as appropriating commons and demesne land by plowing, tearing up grain, digging pits, trespassing with sheep and pigs, sending insufficient labor for the lord's work, and insulting the bailiff. Her most spectacular occasion of trespass occurred in 1329 when she and her son John (*Agnes le Reue et Iohannes filius eius*) cut down an oak tree, a feat equaled for its egregiousness in our records only by William, the priest's brother, who cut down an oak tree in 1320. That this act was viewed as an exceptionally bad form of trespass is evident in the fact that on these occasions del Reues and William were each pledged by two officials, the reeve and beadle, a form of pledging used rarely and selectively before the 1330s, and reserved for serious offenders.

Agnes clearly controlled the tenement, described as a virgate (twenty-four acres) in the account roll of 1342, where it was also noted that she was forgiven, that is, excused from, works for two deaths "in her house" (*in domo sua*) and for illness. An entry in the roll for 1320, within the first few years of her widowhood, also specifically names the tenement as hers: Nicholas Curteys was fined 3d and pledged because "he stopped up a Rivulet [water-course] of Agnes Widow of William reeve which runs through the middle [of the] courtyard of the said Agnes" (*estupauit Riuulum Agnetis Relicte Willelmi prepositi qui ducit per mediam curiam dicte Agnetis*). As an independent head of a substantial tenement, she not only achieved a high profile in trespass (ably assisted by her sons), but was also the catalyst for meaningful changes in her surname, which was given variously as Reues, le Reue, le Reues, atte Reues, and del Reues over her twenty-five-year widowhood. Le Reues, atte Reues, and del Reues obviously function as both a locative and personal identifier in her surname, a name given her by the "public voice" which emphasized the effect of her long-term occupation and working of a tenement traditionally attached to a village office. Her neighbors had come to identify her with that tenement, not as an interim placeholder between male tenants, but as an independent head of household.

Alice Lynlond was the last holder of that name in Ellington, although her descendants continued in the village for one-hundred and thirty years after the original surname disappeared. Her father, Bartholomew Lynlond, a prominent customary tenant in the late thirteenth and early fourteenth centuries, acquired land in piecemeal fashion to provide for his daughter.[30] After her father's death Alice paid 40s for licence to marry Galfrid Underhill, a freeman. This 1311 entry states that she will hold her tenement in peace without contest (*in pace sine calumpnia aliquali*). The 1310 roll that records her father's death also cites his wife, Alice, for "losing the lord's chattels" before the bishop on a charge of adultery with John Warde *et aliis diversis*. The surname Lynlond disappeared: Alice senior continued in the village as Alice Brymbel,[31] Alice junior married Galfrid, and the Underhills continued in Ellington to c. 1450.

Thus, the surnames by which people were known could change over time, and these changes were linked to their constantly changing social relations, among other things. Further, names were linked to the land and to divisions in space that were also constantly changing, perceptible in our evidence in the connections between women's names and the formation of neighborhoods in the village.

Women and Neighborhoods: The Division of Space

Application of the strategy of "disaggregation" to names of all kinds in Ellington's court rolls provides suggestive evidence about the history of neighborhood formation there. The appearance of named clusters of habitation in Ellington over the first six decades of the earliest court rolls (that is, c. 1280–1340) suggests that residential nuclei in that village were undergoing a change significant enough

30 It might be noted in passing that the entries in the 1306 court roll that record land acquisitions being made on Alice's behalf also state that the swearing of fealty is postponed because she is not of age: *Et feoditas illius ponatur in respectu quia est infra etatem*, a confirmation of the legal validity of a woman swearing an oath.

31 It is in connection with Brymbel taking over Bartholomew's tenement that we find the conventional (though still highly suggestive) legal language of entering into the land by the widow (*intrare in predictam terram ad Relictam dicti Bartholomei*). See discussion below and note 48.

to enter into village discourse, and thus into the minutes of the court. Local neighborhoods were being reconfigured possibly in response to relative overcrowding in a time of high population levels in the late thirteenth and early fourteenth centuries. If so, that reconfiguration would have changed again as a result of the famines of the late 1310s and early 1320s, and the readjustments that followed. Interestingly, and in spite of their under-representation in the village court, women are sometimes conspicuous as residents in these rather fluid local subdivisions.

That medieval villagers readily thought in terms of neighborhoods is suggested, in court roll evidence, by the existence of tithing groups (local policing groups of great antiquity that were drawn up on the basis of proximity of residence) and by the formation of bodies of *vicini iurati*, "sworn neighbors," in connection with specific cases.[32] Family groupings that jointly owned plow, harness, and draft animals, or that engaged in various land-sharing arrangements could also follow neighborhood lines.[33] We might also suspect that in a society where both seigneurial and peasant interests were served by "keeping the family's name upon the land"[34] the naming of regions within the village could, literally, be connected with specific individuals and their names. Coten and Sybethorpe are examples of local place name elements that found their way into villagers' surnames in Ellington in the years around 1300.

There are sixteen people associated with the name Coten in Ellington between 1280 and 1332. Coten (Old English *cot*, "cell," "chamber," as in "cottage")[35] clearly refers to a cluster of houses, undoubtedly occupied by smallholders (cottagers), which for a brief period in the 1290s was cited as a distinct entity along with the submanor Sybethorpe in Ellington: indeed, the heading of the court rolls for the years 1292, 1294, and 1299 is given as *Elyngton cum Sybe-*

32 There are three such cases of panels of *vicini iurati* in Ellington's 1280 and 1290 rolls, over issues of debt, threats, defamation, and physical assault. See Olson, *A Chronicle*, 133.

33 An urban parallel is seen in late medieval Godmanchester, where the rotation of certain town offices followed lines of residence based on streets. See J.A. Raftis, *Early Tudor Godmanchester: Survivals and New Arrivals* (Toronto, 1990), 29–31.

34 For a discussion of the "blood right" to land, see Raftis, *Tenure and Mobility*, Chapter Two.

35 *Oxford English Dictionary*, s.v. "cot."

thorp et Cotene ("Elyngton with Sybethorp and Cotene"). Coten also, briefly, had its own ale-taster: in the early court rolls, those for 1280, 1290, 1292, 1294, 1299, and 1306,[36] two men (referred to as *Tastatores de Elyngton*, "Tasters of Elyngton") "present" all the brewers who brewed against the assize in Ellington and its subdivisions, but in the courts of c. 1310 and 1311 two men are named as ale-tasters for Ellington, while Coten has its own ale-taster, *Ricardus filius Alicie Tastator de Coten'*. In 1316 Richard de Coten' is listed with the Ellington tasters William Wyne and Galfrid Buk, and the brewers of both places are presented together, a pattern repeated in 1321 where *Walterus Faber de Coten'* is cited with *Walterus in le Mersh* and *Willelmus le Hunte* as tasters.[37] In 1322 the same three men are given, but the presentments for Coten are listed separately under *Walterus Faber de Coten*. In 1325 the same men are again listed as tasters for Ellington, and *Walterus de Coten' tastator ibidem* ("taster in the same place") is fined and evicted from office for not coming to the presentment of the brewers (*quia non venit ad presentacionem braciatricium*). *Galfridus filius Ede* [Edyth], another Coten name, is elected in his place. In the next surviving roll, for the court of 17 January 1329, and thereafter, two men are named as ale-tasters, with no separate listing for Coten.[38] Indeed, we might surmise that thereafter the court-based monitoring of local brewing becomes subject to new pressures and disturbances that no longer emphasize a careful distinction between Coten and "greater Ellington."

Thus, from about 1310 to at least 1325, the court acknowledged the brewers of Coten as a separate group of women whose brewing

36 The November 1308 court roll has large sections that are illegible, including the list of brewers.

37 In the *Hundred Rolls* there are four tenants listed under the heading *Coterelli*: William Leonard, Richard le Hunt', Agnes de Beaumeys, and Mabilla le Hunte. Note the small size of their tenements: one messuage and two acres of land, one messuage containing one rod of land, one messuage, and one messuage, respectively. Also note the surname Hunt, which shows up as a Coten name in the court rolls. *Rotuli Hundredorum*, ed. Illingworth and Caley, 631.

38 There may be a third man listed as a taster for the court of 1332/3, but the text is not clear. These separate listings for Ellington and Coten allow us to isolate without a doubt names of the families living in Coten, from both the tasters and brewers: *filius Alicie, filius Edyth/Ede, in le Hirne (in Angulo), le Hayward, de Coten, in Estrate,* and *Peuerel*.

activities were presented in court by ale-tasters from their own neighborhood. Those dates could be considered as marking the articulation of an emerging public awareness of changes in the division of space in the village, in this case, the emergence of Coten as a recognizable neighborhood. There are signs of such a consciousness before 1310, but it was not explicitly articulated. For example, in the court of 1306, although all brewers are presented together, the first three women presented are all from Coten: *Alicia Peuerel, Clemencia de Cotene,* and *Beatrix vxor Galfridi* [*de Coten*]. This grouping together of Coten names continues with some slight interruptions down to the 1332 court roll, in which the first election notice for tasters includes a well-known Coten name, *Adam filius Dionisie*. Clearly Coten was a neighborhood, possibly gathering numbers in this period and thus assuming a more distinct identity, however temporary or slight this identity may have been. However, even the transient history of that place name may have left some clues that shed light on the village "history of ideas" relating to women, family, and marriage.

One of the discernible features that gave a shape to the neighborhood of Coten was precisely the high profile of women associated with it. In the group of sixteen people cited with this name between 1280 and 1332, six were women (*Alicia, Edith, Roysia, Agnes, Beatrix,* and *Clemencia*), and of the ten men, six were cited as "son of" a woman: Richard and William were sons of Alice; William, Galfrid, and Kynnemann (*Kynnemannus*) were sons of Edyth; and Walter was son of *Roysia*. One of these men, Galfrid, a very high profile villager over the period 1294–1332, was cited variously as *Galfridus filius Edythe, filius Ede, de Coten,* and by the 1320s and 30s, as *Galfridus Edesson* and *Edithsone* (that is, "Edison," which did not survive as a surname in Ellington).[39] The preponderance of women, and of men

39 As a surname, Coten does not survive past the court roll of 1332, but the place name Coten continues to appear in the records as a residential area in the village. In 1373 John Gymbel is cited for having "an opening at Cotene next to the field" (*vnam aperturam apud Cotene contra campum*), and he is cited again in 1391 (as John Gymbel de Cotene) for not putting a barrier at the front of his garden (surely at the same place). The court rolls of 1443 and 1446 report villagers being fined for cutting the lord's timber *apud Coton'* in the lord's underbrush; in 1446 Henry Stale "took and carried off" one half acre of barley from the demesne at Coten (*cepit et abduxit extra dominium apud Coten vestituram dimidie acre orde* [*sic*]).

cited as "son of" a woman (there is only one person cited as the offspring of a man, *Agnes filia Roberti de Coten* in 1294), points to some village equation at work linking women, names, and neighborhood.

If the earliest references (those found in personal names) are to a residential area in the village proper, the name Coten may refer to a collection of cottages, perhaps a hamlet, housing families of modest means, probably smallholders. In these families the profile of the *materfamilias* might well be fairly high in comparison with her men folk, because cottagers owed fewer labor services (which were performed mostly by men) than tenants with larger holdings, thus rendering men's and women's contributions to the domestic economy more nearly equivalent in village estimation.[40] This high female presence may have played some part in shaping this area into a recognizable community, one that, as we have seen, had its own tasters from c. 1310 up to 1325 and possibly beyond. Furthermore, court roll citations clustered in the 1320s and 1330s point to numerous links between the people bearing Coten names, both those based on women's first names such as Dionysia, Edith, Dulcia, Alice, Matilda, and Muriel, and surnames such as *in Angulo*, *Faber*, Buk, and de Coten). Such a web of interpersonal connections among bearers of the same small pool of surnames suggests an association based on proximity.[41]

Thus, in the court of c. 1280 Richard son of Alicia de Coten' was cited, fined, and pledged for having failed (*nichil inde fecit*) to make

---

Thus Coten also appears as a separate portion of the arable as well as the residential space of the village, as seen clearly in citations in the account rolls of the 1440s (1443, 1444, and 1449) regarding the decline or default of rent from the five virgates and one quarter of land *in Coton*.

40 That the different types of work were subject to evaluation is clear not only from wage rates, but also from the high esteem attached to the central figure in agricultural labor, the plowman.

41 It must be remembered that the reconstruction given here does not show all the links that could be recovered between the people of Coten, using the existing sources, and that the court roll series for Ellington has numerous gaps (as a glance at the bibliography of primary sources at the end of this book will show). A complete reconstruction of all such connections for a village with an intact sequence of rolls, especially one whose court met every few weeks (as is the case for Brigstock, Northamptonshire), would be a sizable book in itself.

satisfaction to Edith de Coten' for a sow which he [injured? stole? the text is illegible here] (*ad satisfaciendum Editham de Coten' de una sua que* [—]). In the next entry William son of Alice de Coten' was similarly cited, fined, and pledged for having failed to make satisfaction to Edith de Coten' for having beaten her son (*super eo quod uerberauit filium dicte Edithe*), whether William, Galfrid, or Kynemann is not specified. In 1321 William son of Dyonisia is fined 6d for false claim against Richard *in Angulo*, and is pledged by Walter Faber. In 1322 the reeve (probably *Galfridus filius Ede*) and Richard *in Angulo* were pledges for Walter *Faber de Coten*' because Walter had not repaid a debt of 8s 6d to Alan le Buk, a judgment which the latter had won against Walter "in the last court" (*in ultimo visu*). In a very dense entry in the same court it is recorded that the same Walter "comes and gives" one-half mark by pledge of Galfrid le Buk for having the Court's inquiry and verdict upon "whether he may have a greater right to three acres of land and a part of one messuage in Coten." In this case, Walter asked that William son of Faber (*Willelmum filium Fabris*, Walter's own son) be allowed to hold this tenement, saying that Richard son of A[lice] de Coten held the said three acres of land (illegally).[42] Robert *filius Dulcie* and Galfrid le Buk were pledges together. In 1332 brewers *Margaria de Cotene* and *Beatrix de Coten* were pledged, respectively, by William *filius Dionisie* and *Galfridus Edithsone*. Walter *le Shepherde de Cotene* gleaned badly, Stephen *de Cotene* received him, and he was pledged by Adam *de Coten*. Richard *Doucesson* and Richard *filius Matill'* were both out-

42 The meaning is clear, although the last two lines of the entry are illegible. The surviving portion reads as follows: *Walterus Faber de Coten' venit et dat domino dimidiam marcam per plegium Galfridi le Buk pro consideratione Curie habenda ad inquirendum utrum maius ius habeat in tribus acris terre et quadam parte unius mesuagii in Coten', sicut petit quam Willelmum filium Fabris sicut tenet, dicens idem Walterus quod Ricardus filius A*[*licie*] *de Coten predictas tres acras terre* [remainder illegible]. It is worth noting that this entry exemplifies one variant of the divisibility discussed earlier in the introduction: here a single messuage (a house-and-yard unit) and its attendant acres in the open fields are divided into more than one tenement, each tenement having a part of the messuage as well as three acres in the fields. Note the language in the entry: *sicut petit quam Willelmum ... sicut tenet*, he seeks or requests that his son be allowed to hold the tenement *sicut*, "in this way."

side the fee and were pledged by Adam *Muriel*[43] that they will pay one capon a year to be absent, and will periodically return to the court (*Et veniet*). This type of association, where pledging plays such a conspicuous role, resembles the action of the tithing group, whose membership was usually based on the residential proximity of families in the village. The data for Coten, in short, suggest some of the local factors, such as working arrangements and family ties, that influenced the formation of this neighborhood.

Sybethorpe, another hamlet or collection of houses in Ellington, contained lands attached to the priest's house (rectory), with which it preserved a number of associations.[44] As in the case of Coten, the profile for women is quite high. Six of the nine tenants of the rector, who are listed in the *Hundred Rolls* of 1278–1279, were women, including two who held a messuage together: *Mabilla Gerold, Cassandra, Helewys, Mabilla Cus* (short for Custancia) and *Matilda filia Matilda* (*tenent i messuagium*), *Willelmus Capellanus* (Chaplain), *Johannes Foulere, Willelmus Bate*, and *Edytha Gerard*.[45] Galfrid

43 The metronymic surname Muriel survived in the village for a century, appearing first in the court roll of 1290 when William Miryel served as juror, and ending with Robert Muriell who was a juror in 1373, 1375, and 1391.

44 Sybethorpe included a smaller manor situated on lands that had been given to Ramsey Abbey in the early thirteenth century. This manor was held of the lord abbot by members of the Grim family throughout the period covered in the present study. For a fuller history of the manors of Ellington, see *The Victoria History of the County of Huntingdon*, ed. W.W. Page et al. (London, 1926–1936), 2: 44–48, especially pp. 45–46. As we have seen, the people of Coten and Sybethorpe attended the abbot's court in Ellington.

45 *Rotuli Hundredorum*, ed. Illingworth and Caley, 2: 631. Mabilla Gerold held the most sizable tenement, nine and a half acres and a messuage, for which she rendered to the rector a rent of 30d per annum, four chickens, and four days of work with one man, on which days they are fed by the rector (*ad cibum Rectoris*). Cassandra held one-and-a-half acres of land and the remaining tenants held one messuage apiece, except Mabilla and Matilda who held one messuage jointly. Since the evidence for Ellington does not permit a full reconstruction of the landed holdings of individuals, these people may have held more land elsewhere in the village; however, the overall impression is that these were smallholders, given their low profile, the preponderance of women, and the frequency with

Gerold (Geraud, Geroud) appears as the capital pledge of the homage of the parson (*de homagio persone*) in 1290, and was cited for men being outside tithing, including Walter son of Amycia, Adam son of Amicia, Robert Helewys, William Helewys, and Richard son of Amicia, among others, in 1290, 1292, 1299, 1306, and 1325.[46]

Unlike *Coten*, *Sybethorpe* rarely attached to people's names, possibly crowded out by associations with women and with the rectory lands. Where it did figure in a name it did so only briefly: for example, Theobald Gerard, an ale-taster in c. 1280, 1290, 1292, and 1294, is called Theobald de Sybethorpe in the c. 1280 court roll, and a Walter de Sybethorp served once as juror in 1308 (and must have had other surnames which cannot be linked with this individual). An *Edytha de Sibthorpe* is known from only one citation, and that was outside the village court rolls in the records of royal justice, the Huntingdonshire Eyre court of 1286.[47] Sarra de Sybethorpe is known only from two indirect citations, first for her son John (*Iohannes filius Sarre*), who was a special inquisition juror twice in 1310, and second for her grandson, Nicholas son of John son of Sarra de Sybethorp, who was allowed to leave the village in 1306 to study and take holy orders (*concessum est Nicholo filio Iohannis filii Sarre de Sybbethorp litteras ad discendum et primam Tonsuram suscipiendam*), with the support (*ad instanciam*) of the rector of the parish church of Ellington, who probably also had taught him some Latin. This citation brings together a number of culturally "deep" elements, the "unconscious 'grammatical' principles ... which underlie and shape behavioral response," as discussed earlier: the public notice of a three-generation relationship which began with a woman (who is not known by any other citations), holding land of the rector in a well

---

which young men from these families were outside tithing, which usually meant they were outside the vill, and thus probably seeking their fortunes elsewhere.

46 That is, Gerold was cited as capital pledge of the parson's "homage" in most of the courts that included a "view of frankpledge" (a verification that all men over the age of twelve were in their tithing groups) and for which records survive and are fully legible for the years 1290–1325. Note also the existence of a "homage" or tithing for the lands of the parson; these groups operated on the basis of the neighborhood.

47 See *Royal Justice and the Medieval English Countryside*, ed. and trans. Anne R. DeWindt and Edwin B. DeWindt (Toronto, 1981), part 1.

defined area in the village where the high profile of women has been noted. Her tenancy on the rector's lands may have formed the basis for a further connection with him since he, in his turn, acted in Sarra's lifetime as a sponsor for her grandson, Nicholas, whose public name, like his father's, derived from her own.

Teasing out patterns in the practices that informed naming people and things in the village is a delicate task, as we have seen. The picture pieced together here suggests that women and their names played a role in the division of "space" in early fourteenth-century Ellington: just like the presence of a sub-manor, rectory lands, and tithing divisions, the presence of a group of female tenants holding modest-sized tenements in close proximity, and the interpersonal connections they formed, may have contributed to the emergence of Coten and Sybethorpe as reasonably distinct, even named, neighborhoods. Among the villager's unconscious principles there may have been a particular kind of idea or response triggered when women and land were associated with each other.

That association may have informed the language used, in the court rolls and other estate management records, when a man received a customary tenement by marrying a woman who held land: that is, he was said to "enter to" her, or to "enter into" the land "through her." For example, in 1311 when the customary tenants of Ellington allowed John Brymbel to marry Bartholomew in Inlond's widow and take up her lands, they were said to have "permitted [him] to enter into the said land to the Widow of the said Bartholomew" (*permiserunt ... intrare in predictam terram ad Relictam dicti Bartholomei*). Similar entries are readily found in other court roll series: in the court rolls of Hemmingford Abbots (another Ramsey Abbey village, located some five miles to the east of Ellington) it is noted that "William Warde entered to Christina Carter, virgater," and that "Alan Syer entered to Matilda White, virgater."[48] The strength of the principle of female inheritance,

48 For the Latin original see Appendix 4 in Raftis, *Tenure and Mobility*, 220, where other examples are given; and for a discussion of this formula see ibid., 40–42. Also see *A Slice of Life: Select Documents of Medieval English Peasant Experience*, ed. and trans. Edwin B. DeWindt (Kalamazoo, 1996), 87, for an example from a 1309–1310 list of land entry fines from the abbot's manor at Warboys: *De Henrico Brun pro ingressu habendo ad Johannam Gosse in dimidia virgata terre xlj s.* DeWindt notes that a literal translation of this citation would be: "41 s. from Henry

in the peasant and seigneurial world, is well known.[49] Even though male inheritance was preferred, female succession to land was fully sanctioned by customary rules of inheritance, rules that sought first and foremost to safeguard the family claim to land. However, male and female succession were not treated identically: when a male tenant married, his wife was not said to "enter into" him or his land. This difference in terminology is another piece of evidence that the association between women and land was not the same as the association between men and land in the minds of villagers.

Taken together, the importance of descent of land within the family, the proximity of resources – including social resources – in circulation in the village labyrinth, and the necessity of assigning meaning in order to promote consensus and action all point to the existence of an association of people and land as a mechanism for ordering local society. Such a generalized linking of people (especially women) and land should not be thought of as a cultural straightjacket, however. As with the use of proverbs, interpretation varied over time, from person to person and from case to case. The longevity of such principles indicates their usefulness in the village stock of ideas.

The Uses of Ambiguity

The somewhat ambiguous position of women as a ubiquitous minority (in legal, if not demographic, terms) provided abundant material always on hand and ready for use in enforcing a rule, securing a right, defining an office, or, as discussed in the present chapter, putting a name to a person, a family, or a place. Such a use reveals the interplay of idea and agency in naming practices, and is a particularly vivid example of "culture as process."[50] The traditional pattern within

---

Brun for having entry into Joan Gosse in a half-virgate of land" which, he observes, "for all its titillating indelicacy, is actually a quite accurate statement of the facts." See ibid., 87 n268. This language, which frames the transfer of customary land and may well reflect the peasant view of these matters, has no equivalent in cases involving a male tenant.

49 See Eleanor Searle, "Seigneurial Control of Women's Marriage: The Antecedents and Function of Merchet in England," *Past and Present* 82 (1979): 3–43, at 7.

50 Again, Ellen Meiksins Wood's study of Athenian democracy provides an example of another historical process of exclusion along gender lines:

which innovation occurred in connection with naming practices is the family claim to land, a claim so powerful that "female property rights and lineal inheritance were strong enough to prevail against males of collateral lines," as Eleanor Searle observes. But the force of such a mechanism might still differ if the receiver of that land were a man or woman – a woman inheriting and controlling land was just unusual enough to activate a response that differed from the response to male tenure of land.[51] Women's ability to influence their social setting differed from that of men, in a manner that is perhaps best understood as different, rather than as lesser. One hint of this is seen in the evidence that women in early fourteenth-century Ellington had a better record of raising the hue and cry "justly" than men, as has indeed been found for other villages.[52]

As we have seen, one reason for the court's success lay in its performance and ritual aspects that expanded its powers of inclusion – not equality, but inclusion – so that all those present played some role in the work of self-government. These "roles" were not static, however: because each individual was apprehended as a person of many parts, he or she might play many parts in local society. The heterogeneity of individual responsibility and public action mirrors the divisibility of land and rights in land and movable property (leasing, subleasing, joint ownership of plows, etc.), even different names

perhaps "pressures for the cultural devaluation of women were reinforced as the extension of citizenship [early sixth century B.C.] carried with it a concomitant ideological impulse to *harden the remaining principles of exclusion*" [emphasis mine]. See *Peasant-Citizen and Slave: The Foundations of Athenian Democracy* (London, 1988), 118.

51 An entry from the Bishop of Ely's court of Littleport (*The Court Baron, Being Precedent For Use in Seignorial and Other Local Courts ...* , ed. F.W. Maitland and W.P. Baildon [London, 1891], 137–138) preserves a sense of the ambivalence surrounding this customary procedure: *Alicia Brokenhorn spontanea sua voluntate in curia coram senescallo examinata absque cohercione ex assensu mariti sui et per licenciam domini remitt' et quietumclam' dicto Radulfo totum jus quod habet in dicto mesuagio ut in dotem ad totam vitam suam, et dat domino pro convencione irrotulanda vid. pl*[*eg*] *Robertus Cartere, Iohannes Typeto*. See above, p. 76, for a translation of this text.

52 Sandy Bardsley makes this point in her discussion of the hue and cry in *Venomous Tongues: Speech and Gender in Late Medieval England* (Philadelphia, 2006), 70–77.

for the same person, as described above in the Introduction. Ready transition between roles, a requisite in village life, led to the formation of a heterogeneous peasant "self" that eased all such transitions by, paradoxically, emphasizing commonalities (interchangeability) between people. The "manner of man" and "manner of woman" that this produced forms quite a contrast with the modern integrated, discrete "self" described by Geertz and others.[53]

By this reading, gender was another component in a multi-faceted village "logic," in its repertoire of instruments that enabled it to distinguish, to decide, and to act.[54] Women's position in the village, less tied to tenure and public power (though not divorced from them), was more flexible, at times ambivalent, and thus attracted meaning because it required assessment. The work by historians of medieval countrywomen supports this interpretation of women as members of a ubiquitous minority that at times must act in roles more readily associated with men. Thus, Judith Bennett's study of the 426 merchet (marriage licence) payments recorded in the *Liber Gersumarum* of Ramsey Abbey shows that the bride paid for the licence in fully one-third of those cases (probably with money she had earned independently) and, further, that when she made this payment she had a personal pledge, which did not occur when the groom or the bride's

53 This "heterogeneous self" looks like the one targeted by the early modern state in David Sabean's study of the village of Neckarhausen (see the Introduction above).

54 Wood also suggests that the principle that women could not inherit in their own name in Athens may have been pre-eminently an expression of the "logic of the smallholders' regime," that is, not driven by the logic of gender. If (quoting G.E.M. Ste Croix) "property is fairly widely distributed in the first place, and if ... marriage is patrilocal ... then to keep women propertyless may well help to prevent property from accumulating rapidly in the hands of the richer families." This would "help to preserve family property and would work against automatic accumulation by the already rich through the processes of marriage and inheritance." See Wood, *Peasant-Citizen and Slave*, 119. In the medieval village, in a situation where a family had no sons, the principle of keeping the name upon the land would direct the family toward naming the daughter as heir. According to Wood, the Athenian woman's "condition" was shaped particularly by her role as "conserver of family property, in a society where peasant strategies of self-preservation were unusually prominent in custom, politics, and law." See ibid., 120.

father purchased the merchet. According to Bennett, then, a merchet payment by a woman was a "real and significant occurrence."[55] By analogy, a woman inheriting and controlling land was a phenomenon that inhabited a kind of frontier of significance in village culture. While it was perfectly legal for a woman to hold land in her own right, it was unusual, and perhaps even slightly undesirable, according to mainstream village opinion. This kind of activity, by its slightly atypical nature, necessarily activated the sources from which villagers drew their symbols and ideas – ideas about gender, but also about land, family, and the organization of local society.

We have noted, in another context, the case in Ellington's c. 1310 court roll where a woman (probably deceased by this date), Agnes wife of Thomas in Estrate, who had held a tenement for eight years, was now found to have had a weaker claim to it than a male villager who had been present in the village all along and who now laid claim to it. Her long tenure, known to all, was suddenly (and safely) rendered unacceptable when the right to that tenement fell into dispute in the era of land scarcity in the early fourteenth century. In this c. 1310 case, the chronology of demographic crowding was the reality, and the meaning attached to gender was used to address it. Here may be a case where an existing norm was allowed to lie dormant, and was activated only when needed.

Thus, even though a woman's landholding, a "real and significant occurrence," was invested with a meaning that differed from that assigned to a man inheriting land, this meaning was subject to gradations in both cases, depending on age, personality, and other factors less easy for us to isolate than gender. That difference provided material for villagers' enduring needs to name, define, limit, and assign power, property, importance, and place in local society: here was a lively sphere of activity that allowed great flexibility. Perhaps women's names were used more heavily in naming local space. Perhaps a woman upon the land, whether married, widowed, or as a single head of household, was seen by her neighbors as having a stronger link with that land than even a man with a competing claim, as the stories

55 Judith Bennett, "Medieval Peasant Marriage", 197. Eleanor Searle has described merchet as a control over inheritance, not marriage, thus as an "entry fine in the case of peasant heiresses," replicated for males in the "merchet-like" payment a father made when his son went away to school. See "Seigneurial Control of Women's Marriage," 20–21, 24, 30.

of Agnes del Reues and Agnes wife of Thomas in Estrate suggest. The demands of self-government and the fact of village autonomy favored creation of a varied stock of ideas, symbols, and ways of assigning meaning. The purposes to which ambiguity could be put would favor its widest application: indeed, everyone in the village, man and woman alike, must have been an ambiguous figure at one time or another, or in some respect.

The analysis in this chapter has been driven by the evidence concerning women and names that surface in court roll data. The use of women's given names in surname formation, the evolution of women's names over time, the role of metronymics in carving out neighborhoods within the village, and the pivotal roles played by women in the longevity of names are phenomena that Bardsley's work foreshadowed nearly a century and a half ago, when he claimed that metronymic surnames did not derive principally from illegitimate births. The ways in which women's names were used as the raw material for the formation of surnames, and thus were woven into the fabric of broader village culture, suggest that women's integration as individuals into local society was similar to that of men, subject to much the same cultural processes. We saw in Chapter One that performance, ritual, and storytelling achieved an integration of audience and actor that was vital to the work of the court: women's participation in that assembly – that is, the inclusion of those whose ambiguous position induced tension – was a dynamic that focused public attention and helped all suitors to the court reflect on and assess the issues before them.

CHAPTER THREE

Latin in the Fields: Farmers and Court Rolls

In his preface to *The Renaissance in the Fields: Family Memoirs of a Fifteenth-Century Tuscan Peasant,* the study of a unique account book for a late medieval peasant, Duccio Balestracci challenges the common notion that the pre-modern countryside was a "universe without writing," while conceding how "rare it is to find firsthand testimony of any kind from someone who lived in the world of the fields."[1] As has been emphasized in the present book, in the continuing search for an authentic view of medieval rural society we must re-evaluate, even re-assess, traditional sources. Following the lead of recent scholarship that has moved away from narrow notions of literacy and literate activity,[2] the present chapter explores the countryside as a "universe with writing," where peasants' use of documents was a well-established practice. The nature of the court as a document-creator in its own right suggests the desirability of rethinking village literacy.

Historians have shown that there was a connection between self-regulation and document use in medieval society, including the vil-

1 *The Renaissance in the Fields: Family Memoirs of a Fifteenth-Century Tuscan Peasant,* ed. Duccio Balestracci, trans. Paolo Squatriti and Betsy Merideth (Chicago, 1995), xx, xviii; Edward Muir calls Benedetto's account book a "farming diary," a perfect name for this text (introduction, p. xii).

2 Michael T. Clanchy, *From Memory to Written Record: England, 1066–1307* (2nd ed., Oxford, 1993), especially the section entitled "Documents at Village Level," pp. 46–51. For further relevant discussion see Brian Stock, *The Implications of Literacy: Written Language and Models of Interpretation in the Eleventh and Twelfth Centuries* (Princeton, 1983); and *Medieval Latin: An Introduction and Bibliographical Guide,* ed. F.A.C. Mantello and A.G. Rigg (Washington, DC, 1996), especially Richard Sharpe, "Latin in Everyday Life," 315–341, and John Langdon, "Agriculture, Animal Husbandry, and Forestry," 459–464.

lage. Michael Clanchy's study of document proliferation and the growth of government in England over the period 1066–1307 reveals a conjunction of claims to power and document use that mirrors the conjunction of claims to power and ritual discussed above in Chapter One. The court rolls, and their associated records, reveal peasants' need for and use of documents, and their local participation in the "literate modes" of thinking and working that flourished in high medieval Europe.

Pragmatic Literacy

Richard Britnell defines "pragmatic literacy" as the type of literate activity that produced not a literary manuscript (such as a work of philosophy, theology, history, law, poetry, or romance) but rather "contributed to some legal or administrative operation."[3] Such a document was drawn up for the use of an administrator or property-owner, was written in cursive, often hurriedly, was only copied for administrative convenience, and was preserved in some office store rather than a library (unlike literary texts). Britnell stresses the organizational impact of pragmatic literacy, arguing that it "could not create political, economic, or religious authority, which rested upon a wider range of traditional beliefs and practices, but it was a means by which almost any type of authority could be better safeguarded or stretched to new limits." He identifies pragmatic literacy as a "cultural resource that agents in all dimensions of power, political, ideological or economic, were able to exploit and develop," and views the increase in the amount and variety of documentation in twelfth and thirteenth-century Europe as emblematic of a "general hope that record-keeping would give increased control."[4] As we will see, villagers, too, participated in the practices of pragmatic literacy,

3 *Pragmatic Literacy, East and West, 1200–1330*, ed. Richard Britnell (Woodbridge, 1997). Remarks here follow his discussion on pp. 3–6; quotation at p. 3. Note that all of the essays in this collection concern literate activity in royal, elite, or urban circles. The only one that touches upon the countryside, and thus includes some discussion of court rolls, is P.D.A. Harvey's essay "English Estate Records, 1250–1330," 107–118, where the court rolls are in no way connected to the peasants' use of the court.

4 Britnell, *Pragmatic Literacy*, 3, 6.

even Latinity, and shared that "general hope" that keeping and accessing records would improve their position.

According to Britnell, a pragmatic text expresses intentions on the part of those who issue it, and its purpose must be clear since it "exists to direct the behaviour of other people." While especially true of the "written command," it is true also of what he calls "non-mandatory documents such as deeds, accounts and court records" (the three major types of estate records) that were "drawn up to facilitate or regulate action in accordance with particular institutional practices." He writes further – and note his assumption – "[n]ot all the increases in power resulting from pragmatic literacy were to the advantage of governments and the detriment of the governed," an observation that seems to discount pragmatic literacy as a "cultural resource" being used by a variety of "agents." As proof that the "recording of obligations could have advantages for all ranks of society," he cites written agreements between lords and villagers in Italy and France, and the granting of urban liberties. "[E]ven the recording of servile customs and tenures, though it did nothing to abolish serfdom, fixed the claims that lords could make, and constituted a base from which in favourable circumstances tenants might negotiate better terms."[5] Such a top-down model of power, which makes the abolition of serfdom the *locus classicus* of peasant agency, leaves little room for peasants' participation in pragmatic literate activity, for the fact of "Latin in the fields" (to parallel Balestracci's title, *Renaissance in the Fields*).[6]

5 Britnell, *Pragmatic Literacy*, 4–5.

6 The question of peasant benefit from pragmatic literacy raises the issue of our understanding of "power" in medieval Europe, and how much the effort to uncover what has been "invisible" may benefit scholarship in this area. Along somewhat different lines, the continued effort to understand court roll evidence, as in the present study, may contribute to the study of all types of medieval English estate records. As Harvey points out, estate archives are "far from having been fully exploited. Partly because there are no continental parallels to most of these records, historians have tended to work on them purely in an English context, and with some notable exceptions have generally failed to place in its European setting the wealth of information they provide ... [t]hey have yet to contribute significantly to the medieval history of Europe as a whole." See Harvey, "English Estate Records, 1250–1330," 118.

Pragmatic literate activity was indeed widespread in medieval Europe. As we have seen here, while court rolls were among the most important and most informative witnesses to the formation of a "universe of writing" in the English countryside,[7] they were not the only documents with which peasants had contact. The records of royal government, such as the *Domesday Book*, the *Hundred Rolls*, lay subsidy lists, coroners' reports, and the records of local lordship, such as lists of tenants, custumals, terriers, and account rolls, all were based on detailed information provided by panels of local jurors, as stated earlier.[8] Individual villagers, notably officials, might be called on to play other roles in connection with record use: reference has been made to the account rolls enshrining a kind of dialogue between the auditors and the presenting official, usually the reeve. According to Clanchy, the "presumption that officials [of the central government] knew some Latin ... by 1200, extends to manorial and village stewards, bailiffs, beadles, and reeves by 1300."[9]

Most of the documents created locally by tenant informants have not come down to us. As P.D.A. Harvey has pointed out, there were many "ephemeral records" drawn up in connection with the court's activities, such as notes of cases to be heard at a forthcoming court, frankpledge lists, and the like, the survival rates for which are much lower than those of court rolls; a similar situation exists for account rolls.[10] Moreover, a body of literature developed around the manor court that included glossaries of terms used, sets of questions for the steward, and specimen texts for the clerk who drew up the court roll.[11]

7 Zvi Razi and Richard M. Smith, "The Origins of the English Manorial Court Rolls as a Written Record: A Puzzle," Chapter One in *Medieval Society and the Manor Court*, ed. Razi and Smith (Oxford, 1996), 36–68, points out that while similar courts existed on the continent, the "shift from oral to written procedures" seems to have occurred only in England's manorial courts (p. 36).

8 One of the most thorough-going treatments of this issue remains A.B. White's *Self-Government at the King's Command: A Study in the Beginnings of English Democracy* (Minneapolis, 1933).

9 Clanchy, *From Memory to Written Record*, 236.

10 P.D.A. Harvey, *Manorial Records* (London, 1984), 38–40. According to Harvey, records that were used to draw up accounts and that were discarded after use included draft accounts, views of account, particulars of account, lists of estreats (extracts), indentures, and tally sticks.

11 Harvey, *Manorial Records*, 44.

To these must be added the long-lived tradition of treatises on how to hold a manor court discussed in Chapter One. In short, the proliferation of records characteristic of high medieval Europe also occurred in the village within the "universe" of estate management records.[12] The question as to who "benefited" from this has heretofore been answered mostly in the favor of lords and state governments, especially by historians who view the village court principally as "an obvious instrument for browbeating and punishing discontented peasants."[13] What the present discussion will show is that peasants were also beneficiaries.

The court rolls reveal villagers' need for and use of a wide range of documents (including the court roll itself): deeds of land transfer, charters, tenant lists, wills, personal seals, letters granting permission for village boys to study elsewhere and take holy orders, lists of estreats (extracts), and, later, "copy of court roll," that is, an extract copied from a court roll that records a tenant's admission to a holding. The development of copy of court roll, which would later serve as proof of a tenant's possession, reflects "the increasing use of written records in manorial administration and the growing formality of procedure in the manorial courts."[14] Here is an example of a new type of document drawn from the action of the court itself, whose development resembles the history of agrarian bylaws that, once agreed upon, were "promulgated in open court, and in late medieval and early modern times, were then usually, though not always, recorded in the court books and rolls."[15]

12 A good French example of a wealth of diverse documents produced at the behest of villagers would be the letters, formal complaints, affidavits, charters, and the like drawn up for the tenants of Rosny-sous-Bois in their legal quarrels with the abbots of St Geneviève in the twelfth and thirteenth centuries. See Marc Bloch, "From the Royal Court to the Court of Rome: The Suit of the Serfs of Rosny-sous-Bois," in *Change in Medieval Society: Europe North of the Alps, 1050–1500*, ed. Sylvia L. Thrupp (New York, 1964), 3–13.

13 Peter Franklin, "Politics in Manorial Court Rolls: The Tactics, Social Composition, and Aims of a pre-1381 Peasant Movement," in Razi and Smith, *Medieval Society and the Manor Court*, 162–198, at 185.

14 See Harvey, *Manorial Records*, 43–44, for this definition and discussion of copyhold. The earliest examples he cites there of "copy of court record" or "copy of court roll" date to the early fourteenth century.

15 Eric Kerridge, *The Common Fields of England* (Manchester, 1992), 88. Kerridge goes on to say that the laws would then be "published," that is,

Wills, personal seals, charters, tally sticks, and court rolls were not the only "documents" regularly employed by peasants.[16] Objects too could be "read," such as the brewer's vessels used for measuring and selling ale that were to be brought to court to be checked and marked with a seal. In Upwood's 1443 court four women are cited for selling ale "by unsealed measures, that is, by cups" (*vendiderunt cervisiam per mensuras non sigillatas videlicet per ciphos*). We might include sheep brands as a type of document, since they left a mark to be read to determine possession: in Upwood in 1450 [Richard?] Gebard was fined 1d for putting the lord's sign on a sheep belonging to John Bracer (*posuit signum domini super Ovem Iohannis Bracer*). Participation in document creation also occurred in the court itself, as we have seen, where the testimony, findings, and inquiries generated by villagers formed the substance for the record of the proceedings that was drawn up then and there, often by a scribe of peasant social origins.

Peasant participation in court roll creation necessarily raises and complicates the question of authorship of the document. The notion of "many voices" suggests that the origins and purpose of the court roll derive from the village and lord-tenant relations, and that both lords and tenants relied on the court, its mechanisms, and its rolls to protect their interests in the village because their interests were interwoven in that forum.[17] Moreover, since a growing number of lords, including the abbot of Ramsey, engaged in widespread leasing of their demesnes by the end of the fourteenth century, and thus increased the traditional distance between themselves as lords and agricultural operations, villagers' connection with the record may have intensified over our period. Thus, not merely the fact of pragmatic literacy, but also a chronology of its development in the village, may be recovered by studying court rolls.

One manifestation of a lord-tenant relationship of mutual dependence specifically reinforced by the court roll has been described by

---

posted in the church porch and announced by the town crier. Announcements were, of course, also made in the court itself, just as strays, vacant tenements, and calls to men to serve as juror were announced in court and recorded in its rolls.

16 See Clanchy, *From Memory to Written Record*, 46–51.

17 For an opposing view see Razi and Smith, "The Origins of the English Manorial Court Rolls," 36–68.

Warren Ault, who was intrigued by the evidence he found of a new fining practice attached to the breaking of agrarian by-laws, whereby half the fine was given to the lord and half to the parish church fabric.[18] This practice, which flourished over the first half of the fifteenth century, was widely represented in the forty-eight manors in thirteen English counties that Ault studied and is found in Upwood and Ellington as well.[19] In the 1450 Ellington court roll it is recorded that tenants are to clean their ditches, under penalty of 20d to the lord and 20d to the church; in 1459, no one is to carry off greenwood or demolish hedges except on his own holding, under penalty of 40d to the lord and 40d to the church. Ault interpreted this mechanism in the light of a mutually beneficial arrangement between lord and tenant: "in return for the use of his court to enforce their harvest rules the villagers agree to give the lord half of the fine, reserving the other half to the use of their church."[20] This fining practice enhanced the village's powers of control, and also allowed it to maintain and even modernize the local church.[21] The lord's willing participation was secured, and the measure was reinforced with court sanctions noted in the minutes. Using the court to publicize the bylaw and the court record to enroll the fine exemplifies the village community's reliance on pragmatic literacy to "carry on its life."[22]

18 The issue cannot be fully explored here, but there may be some question as to the absolute novelty of this fining practice, since a 1325 court roll for the village of Littleport, belonging to the Bishop of Ely, makes reference to such a mechanism: any man, "free or bond", who mows beyond the amount of six thousand sedge must give "for each thousand 32d to the lord and to the men of the vill for the repair of the church, so they say, in equal portions." (Maitland notes, "i.e., one such portion to the lord, one to the men.") See *The Court Baron, Being Precedents For Use in Seignorial and Other Local Courts* ... , ed. F.W. Maitland and W.P. Baildon (London, 1891), 145.

19 Ault, "Manor Court and Parish Church in Fifteenth-Century England: A Study of Village By-laws," *Speculum* 42 (1967): 53–67.

20 Ault, "Manor Court and Parish Church," 56.

21 See Colin Platt, *The Parish Churches of Medieval England* (London, 1981), for a discussion of the proprietary instincts of medieval villagers; and, more recently, Eamon Duffy, *The Stripping of the Altars: Traditional Religion in England, c.1400–c.1580* (New Haven, 1992).

22 As we saw in Chapter One above, the formularies for holding a manor court suggest a meeting that bears a strong resemblance to the actual

Farmers and Latin

Exploring the realities of pragmatic literacy in the village, and in particular the fact that suitors to the village court were actors in an arena where Latin literacy was present and powerful, has much to contribute to the present debate. Although some historians continue to view Latin as a "foreign language" to the great mass of medieval people, recent scholarship has challenged the once accepted wisdom that insuperable barriers existed between peasants and Latin written culture.[23] Few historians would posit a simple divide between understanding and not understanding Latin as did H.S. Bennett, who, in 1937, voiced a then current view that church services themselves were

> mysterious to [peasants] for the most part, since the vast majority of medieval congregations were unable to follow one word of the Latin in which they were said. The priest rehearsed the words and performed various actions, while they repeated such prayers and devotions as they knew. Not that these were many.[24]

Since the laity's inability to understand the Latin they heard in church is often presented as going hand-in-hand with the poor training of the parish priesthood, the improbable image is conjured up of peasant parishioners attending services whose rites were performed in a language they did not understand, by a priest who may not have understood the language much better.[25] Such a view contrasts with

---

courts that were held, and the lord's steward and scribe fostered order in a meeting which served both villagers and their lords. It is difficult to say where lord and peasant interests divide, since both were engaged in the making of the rolls.

23 In an essay on the manor courts of the sixteenth century, Christopher Harrison describes the courts as regulating activities that were "minor perhaps but nevertheless crucial to everyday life," and asks how "illiterate and uneducated peasants and townsmen" used these courts, which had "complex procedures" (that "aped those of the royal courts") and whose records were "in a foreign language: Latin." See "Manor Courts and the Governance of Tudor England," in *Communities and Courts in Britain, 1150–1900*, ed. Christopher W. Brooks and Michael Lobban (London, 1997), 43–59, at 45.

24 H.S. Bennett, *Life on the English Manor* (Cambridge, 1937), 323.

25 A recent survey of the English village reiterates this traditional point. Referring to the impoverishment of parishes in the post-plague country-

most current scholarship, which emphasizes the links between priest and parishioner, indeed argues that the outlook of the local priest was essentially that of a farmer in the village, and makes no "necessary" deduction about the "negative impact" this would have had on the "quality" of religious service or belief.[26] Indeed, according to Michael Clanchy "most scholars agree that by the thirteenth century, when information becomes sufficiently abundant to make generalizations, parish priests were often of peasant, even servile, origins and also that the standard of learning of the priesthood was on the whole quite high."[27]

---

side, Phillipp Schofield, *Peasant and Community in Medieval England, 1200–1500* (New York, 2003), avers that "generally speaking, religious expression in the countryside lacked the sophistication of that in towns" (p. 186). Where a rector was "actually present" instead of a "lesser cleric," parishioners "benefited from the spiritual leadership of a man who may, perhaps, have had a university education" (p. 194). For a similar viewpoint see Robert C. Palmer, *Selling the Church: The English Parish in Law, Commerce, and Religion, 1350–1550* (Chapel Hill, 2002), 1, where he argues that once "a more educated, substantial clergyman was present in the parish" due to Henrician clerical reform, the parish became "an organization more oriented to spiritual needs." Survey literature repeats these views: Joseph H. Lynch, *The Medieval Church: A Brief History* (London, 1992), 128, in discussing rural churches around A.D. 1000, observes: "We do know some of the basic conditions in which ministry took place. The congregation was utterly illiterate and the priest was probably of peasant origin and poorly educated." A current Western Civilization textbook states that altar screens had "special peepholes so that many people could gawk at the elevation" of the host. See Brian Levack et al., *The West: Encounters & Transformations* (New York, 2004) 1: 301.

26 Warren Ault, "The Village Church and the Village Community in Medieval England," *Speculum* 45 (1970): 197–215.

27 H.S. Bennett also observed that the parish priest was "frequently of peasant stock" which made him "more capable of understanding his parishioner's point of view." See *Life on the English Manor*, 325–336. For Clanchy's discussion, see *From Memory to Written Record*, 241–243, at 241. John Boswell's discussion of monastic oblation suggests that parents from every walk of life gave children to monastic communities to be trained as clergy. See Chapter Eight in Boswell, *The Kindness of Strangers: The Abandonment of Children in Western Europe from Late Antiquity to the Renaissance* (1988; repr., Chicago, 1998), especially pp. 302–304. According to Boswell, by the fourteenth century the "influx [into monas-

The scribes of the village court, the intermediaries between record and villager, were probably also mostly of peasant origin. According to Zvi Razi, who has worked with the court rolls of Halesowen and Redgrave, the late thirteenth-century decentralization of estate administration involved an "increased use of literate lower-order bureaucrats who operated from bases that were firmly planted upon the manors." This created a "small army of jobbing clerks" large enough to "have created a notable occupational category in rural communities."[28] These men would also have engaged in farming and officeholding, often bearing the surname *Clericus*, le Clerk, and were frequently of villein status.[29] They also provided clerical services to their neighbors as well as to the manorial administration, and were cited as keepers (that is, holders) of records, thus indicating another possible repository for documents within the village itself. Alongside such local clerks, the lords and tenants of the manors of Halesowen and Redgrave may also have used the services of itinerant, possibly poor clerks (thus mirroring the migration of seasonal agricultural laborers who also surface in the court rolls). An "army" of clerks of peasant origin, farming background, and frequently local affiliation constitutes just the sort of personnel required to produce and sometimes house the vast amount of English estate administrative records under discussion here.

---

teries] of illegitimates, primarily the children of priests, was staggering." See p. 302 with n22 where he cites figures for dispensations from illegitimacy for men wishing to enter religious orders.

28 Razi and Smith, "The Origins of the English Manorial Court Rolls," 58–59, 60.

29 Razi and Smith, "The Origins of the English Manorial Court Rolls," 60, also provides some details regarding the fourteen people who acted as clerks and were described as clerks in the Halesowen court rolls between 1270 and 1349, and the thirteen clerks identified in the Redgrave manorial courts between 1260 and 1300: a total of eight men from that group of twenty-seven can be positively identified, and of those eight, three were of villein status. The authors also rightly point out that these people have been "undervalued and under-researched" by students of the village. That clerks came from various backgrounds helps to explain the differences in scribal practice in drawing up the court rolls, even within the same lordship. As J.A. Raftis has pointed out, "local clerks differed in style from manor to manor in the amount of detail recorded." See *Peasant Economic Development within the English Manorial System* (Montreal, 1996), 205 n18.

We find confirmation of the peasant origins of clerics in the records for our two villages. Clericus, le Clerk, occurs as a surname in both Ellington and Upwood, and there are also references to the brother and niece of the priest, *frater, nepota presbyteri,* which indicate his family connection to the village. In Ellington's 1306 court it is recorded that Abbot John grants licence to Robert son of Geoffrey Buk and John son of William Buk to be promoted to holy orders, at least to first tonsure (*saltem ad primam tonsuram*), and they are each to say twenty-four psalters. As mentioned in Chapter Two, at the instance of the rector of the parish, the abbot also granted to Nicholas son of John son of Sarra de Sybethorp letters to study and to take up first tonsure (*litteras ad discendum et primam Tonsuram suscipiendam*); and in 1329 Simon [surname illegible] and William Walter were permitted to proceed to first tonsure, "as is clear by a licence of the lord" which is in Simon's possession, "in his hand" (*ut patet per licenciam domini que est in manu dicti Simonis*). In what may be another case of a local boy heading off to school to study "and take up first tonsure," in 1438 Nicholas Albyn of Upwood was fined 2d for placing his son William at school without licence (*posuit Willelmum filium suum ad scolas sine licencia*). All of these men were of villein status. Such a practice was common enough to warrant regular inquiry: in the court of Middleton, Essex, one of the questions to be put in court was "whether any bondman has been ordained clerk without licence."[30] The social links between peasant, scribe, and parish priest were greater than anything that might have divided them.

The image we must dispel, one that would necessarily follow from a view of the court and its record as punitive instruments of the lord, is that of the scribe present in the court as a remote figure, sitting apart, embodying the power of the lord, and busily drawing up a kind of village Domesday Book which would bind tenants in mysterious and undesirable ways.[31] On the contrary, the scribe's taking of the

30 Maitland and Baildon, *Court Baron*, 102.

31 If conceived of in this manner, village court rolls do bear a resemblance to inquisition records, except that the latter were special tribunals convened under very different circumstances and under the aegis of an external power. Moreover, the documents generated by the inquisitions were not as accessible to the peasants who provided the testimony as court rolls were. Indeed, inquisition records have powerfully reinforced the prevailing view that written records were not only "weapons" in elite

minutes in the court during its proceedings, in view of all, indeed, frequently making entries into the record at the behest of individual villagers, must have played a role in promoting among the English peasantry what Clanchy has called "literate modes," particularly in the matter of "trusting writing."[32]

Alongside the use of Latin, our investigation into peasants' pragmatic literacy should also consider, first, the court roll evidence for villagers' use of other types of documents, to situate court roll use within a larger framework of document use; second, villagers' use of the court rolls in particular; and third, the appearance of English vocabulary in the court rolls, read as a measure of increasing peasant control in the village in the late fourteenth and first half of the fifteenth centuries.

Villagers' Use of Other Documents

Court roll data further reveal modes of pragmatic literacy in the village that have also been glimpsed by historians in peasants' routine use of seals, charters, and wills. We have seen here numerous entries revealing villagers' use of these other documents: as discussed earlier, villagers were sometimes required "to come and show" charters prov-

---

offensives against peasants, but that their coercive capabilities were heightened by being cast in an arcane and mysterious language. For another view that emphasizes villagers' fear of written records see William Langland, *Piers Plowman*, ed. J.A.W. Bennett (1972; repr., Oxford, 1979), 90, note on 'ragman' and the etymology of 'rigmarole': "In Langland's time [late fourteenth century], then, a long parchment tagged with episcopal seals would be likely to evoke the same awe in a simple-minded villager as that produced by the inquisitional visits of the royal justices." As Clanchy points out, the villagers "who had thought Domesday Book to be the Last Judgement ... had charters of their own (the *Cartae Nativorum*) by the 1300s" (p. 329).

32 Nevertheless, Clanchy himself referred to court rolls as "laconic" and often "little more" than lists. For his discussion of "trusting writing" see *From Memory to Written Record*, Chapter Nine, 294–327; for his comment on court rolls, see p. 98. Given the stability of the record over many generations, the scribe who sat in the court and took the minutes in the thirteenth century must have operated under a mandate similar to the one held by his fourteenth- and fifteenth-century counterparts – this might have enhanced villagers' "general hope," their ability to "trust" his writing. Thus, the conservatism displayed by court rolls could have been due to the requirements of villagers as much as those of the lord.

ing land acquisitions. In Ellington in 1299 Robert Miller brought his charter showing his purchase of land from another villager two years earlier, and the scribe notes that the charter is correctly drawn up (*que quidem carta recta forma est confecta*). Even the presentation of a properly drawn up charter did not resolve all issues, for the entry continues: "the said Jurors are uncertain whether that land ought to be held in chief of the lord Abbot or of Ranulph Grym" (*Et Iurati predicti sunt incerti vtrum dictam* [terram] *debeat teneri in capite de domino vel de Ranulpho Grym*). The parish priest in a 1310 court is required (and has a pledge) to show his charter for the purchase of one-half acre at the next Court: *ad ostendam cartam suam ad proximam Curiam*. In Upwood in 1311 Alexander son of Alexander le Chamberleyn has a pledge to show his charter (*ad ostendam Cartam suam*) for a messuage and two acres he holds from the gift of his father. Villagers are also required to have warrants for various claims, most frequently if they are outsiders: in Upwood in 1299 John Trasscus, *cissor* ("scissor," hence "tailor"), is noted as having been received without being in a tithing and must have a local man stand as his pledge that he have his warrant before the next court, proving that he is in a tithing in his village of origin (*ad habendum Warentum suum citra proximam Curiam quod est in decenna apud Somersham*). In Upwood in 1307 William le Comber is outside tithing and John Bygge is his pledge for having his Warrant that he is in tithing at "Huntyngdon."

Cross-references to other documents, like the abbot's letters granting permission to study, suggest that villagers' reliance on the court roll was situated in a web of inter-related Latin documents. In Upwood's account roll for c. 1299 it is noted that Sarra daughter of Serlo Faber is "released" (that is, forgiven) a payment of 18d *per breuem Abbatis*, "by a letter of the Abbot." In 1301 Geoffrey le Pykeler was fined 6d for refusing to provide carrying services, and for failure to consult the Register at Ramsey on this point as he had been "charged to do at the last Court" (*Et quia non quesiuit Registrum apud Rammesia sicut ei iniunctum fuit ad ultimam Curiam*). Presumably this meant that he was to bring back a document, an extract (or estreat) from a custumal, enumerating the services attached to villein tenements of the sort that he held (a good example of an "ephemeral record" that would have been discarded or recycled after use). Villagers not only understood how and why these records were kept but even where they were kept; and they could be charged to consult them, procure an extract, and report back at the next court, indeed, they could be fined if they failed to do so. References are also made to records related to officeholding: in 1299 Upwood's reeve was ordered to answer in his next account (*in proximo compoto suo*) for chattels distrained from a villager who hadn't yet paid his entry fine for land recently acquired.[33] Notices could also be entered in the court rolls in response to traditional fines or renderings recorded elsewhere: in Upwood in 1307 it is ordered that Margery daughter of Robert Ayse be distrained to make fine with the lord for marrying, which she later did "as appears in the Roll of land entry fines" (*Et postea fecit finem sicut patet in Rotulo gersumarum*), the same roll used to record the payment of 40s when Alice, daughter of Bartholomew in Inlond, married a freeman. In the court for Upwood of 1325(1), three tenants pay 12d for licence to exchange land, as contained in the Roll of the manor (*pro licencia escambiandi terram pro* [*sic*] *ut continetur in Rotulo manerii*).[34]

Such references to records to be consulted outside the court are commonplace in the court rolls of other villages, and reveal the integration of different types of texts into daily life.[35] In short, we can

33 A 1313 Upwood entry provides another example of a tenant who is to go to the central offices: Alexander Galion is "given a day" to "come before the lord at Ramsey" to answer the charge that he is a naïf (that is, serf) of the lord and not of John Clerevaus (*ut veniat coram domino apud Rames'*).

34 Peasant testimony based on document use occurred in other venues as well. Joel T. Rosenthal, *Telling Tales: Sources and Narration in Late Medieval England* (University Park, PA, 2003), in his discussion of Proofs of Age (late fourteenth, early fifteenth centuries) mentions numerous examples of villagers' retrieving information about the age of an heir or heiress by reference to some kind of text, usually one where a date of birth or death had been recorded: a book of martyrs in the church, a missal, a chapter book of the abbey, a "great missal," written charters, court rolls, even writing on the wall of a hall. See Chapter One in *Telling Tales*, especially pp. 13–14, nn29–32.

35 In the Bishop of Ely's village of Littleport, whose rolls (1285–1327) were selectively edited by Maitland, several such instances occur: the jurors assert that their subtenants ("undersettles") have right of common for mowing and reaping a half acre of corn for the lord, and that "this is so in the terrier" (*et hoc per terrarium*); a group of tenants give the lord 40d for an inquest regarding widows' claim to lands alienated by their hus-

explore the contours of a "universe of writing" whose texts have mostly not survived, in the same way that we "catch glimpses of some thirty other account books and diaries kept by Sienese people" revealed in the pages of Benedetto del Massarizia's farming diary.[36] Indeed, the routine nature of such charges, and the dependence placed on being able to consult the rolls and other records, raise the question whether the village itself may be described as having a clerk in the same way that the reeve had a clerk (*clericus prepositi*) "to help him make his case" when he presented his account to the auditors.[37] That is, the court roll may be viewed as a kind of *clericus*

---

bands without the wife's consent, an inquest is taken of twenty-four villeins, and it is noted that "judgment [as to this custom] is suspended [while search is made in the court rolls]"; the bishop orders his steward, in connection with a complaint of dower wrongfully withheld, to "have your rolls and memoranda diligently searched that the truth may be known, and if perchance you can find nothing, then do you have this inquired by good and lawful folk of Littleport ... so that right may be done"; a tenant claims he holds a fishery "in several" (that is, as an individual), "and thereof he vouches the record of the terrier [*inde vocat recordum terrar'*]. And the terrier being inspected it is witnessed that the said fishery is several." In one very complicated and instructive case, a tenant whose claim to one-half acre is contested "vouches to warrant the rolls of the said [bishop]; which duly testify this" (*inde vocat ad warantum rotulos ejusdem, qui hoc bene testantur*). Her opponent "says that no matter what the rolls may say against him [*qualitercumque rotuli testantur contra ipsum*], he none the less says that this half-acre was never surrendered in court, but that the clerk, who then was, falsely made mention of this half-acre instead of another ... and he craves that this be inquired of the neighbours," who find against him. Here, multiple witnesses and authorities are searched: demandant, defendant, record, clerk, and neighbors. Such examples suggest that searching people's memory and searching manorial documents complement each other almost seamlessly. See Maitland and Baildon, *Court Baron*, 146–147, 121–122, 132–133, and 133–134, respectively. Phillipp Schofield cites a 1338 case at Birdbrook (Essex) where the question arose whether widows holding their land as dower were liable to heriot (that is, were required to pay a death duty), and an inquest jury inspected the court rolls for earlier examples. See *Peasant and Community in Medieval England*, 42. For the role of memory see Chapter Five below.

36 Balestracci, *Renaissance in the Fields*, xix.

37 See Harvey, *Manorial Records*, 26, 33.

totius communitatis, a "clerk of the whole community," a point to be developed further below.

The network of links between records included the lord's use of the court roll to post notices just as villagers did, as in the case involving bylaws described above. In Upwood's 1297 court roll the full text of a *scriptum* is found containing the terms of an agreement worked out between the abbot of Ramsey and another local landholder, both of whom had tenants in the village, regarding the holding of the court and the paying of fines. A nearly exact version of this document appears in the Ramsey Cartulary. Thus, the issue at hand, which involved two lords and their bodies of tenants, generated a document that was copied into the central records of the monastic landholder and into the minutes of the villagers' court.[38] Finally, some of the early fourteenth-century rolls include various memoranda at the end, as in the 1311 Ellington record where the last item (placed alongside the notation *memorandum* in the margin) contains a prohibition against *nativi* leaving without permission to reside on another fee, or receiving strangers without the lord's permission (*sine licencia domini speciali*). Any Customary tenants found to be acting against this *forma* (order, notation) are to be heavily fined (*si predicti Custumarii contra predictam formam ... fuerint conuicti facientes*). The word *forma* seems to mean both the notation on the parchment roll and the prohibition itself.

It can be seen from these examples that villagers and lords alike made use of a variety of documents, but that court rolls occupied a central place in village record-keeping.

Villagers' Use of the Court Rolls

Peasants used the court rolls regularly, both as individuals and collectively, as historians have long known. Thus, villagers came into court and used a variety of familiar rituals to enforce their rights and to protect themselves against future disputes by registering the terms of loans of money and leasing of animals and tools, as well as the conditions of retirement arrangements for the elderly, defaults on debts, land exchanges, accusations and redress for personal assault

38 This agreement is explained fully in Raftis, *Peasant Economic Development*, 36–38.

and slander, and the commissioning of panels of local men to inquire into some point of dispute, usually tenure of land. In 1311 two elderly Upwood tenants turned their tenements over to their heirs, "as is clear by the Roll of land entry fines in the previous year" (*sicut patet per Rotulum gersumarum in anno preterito*), and the conditions of their retirement arrangements were noted in the roll, specifically, what space they were to have in the house (*hospitium rationabilem*) and what grain deliveries they were to receive annually (both arrangements were violated, hence their citation in the rolls). In 1295 Juliana the widow of Adam son of John gave the lord 6d for the Court's judgment (*pro consideratione Curie habenda*) regarding her rights to land formerly belonging to her husband. The jurors said that according to the custom of the vill (*dicunt quod secundum consuetudinem ville*), she was to have a house with a small curtilage (yard) and annual deliveries of grain, wheat, and beans. The reason for her commissioning the inquest is evident in the next entry, where it is noted that her son Nicholas is in arrears for her grain deliveries.

Villagers also paid to have the results of dispute resolution and local inquiries entered into the court record, thus using the court as people would use the service of a notary. In Ellington in 1310, William of Coten gave the lord three shillings to have the court investigate his claim to two messuages and two virgates of land against his half-brother, Walter of Coten, who then held them. The dispute centered on whether the children of a first wife had a better right to their father's land than the children of a second wife, and in this case Walter, the child of a second marriage, prevailed. The court roll spells out quite clearly that, in order to protect this favorable decision, Walter paid two shillings to have the judgment "properly enrolled" in the court roll: *Et dat idem Walterus domino ut bene irrotuletur ii s.*

Over the course of nearly two centuries, villagers in Upwood and Ellington used the court and its record-making capacity to register and thus stabilize all sorts of agreements among themselves: villagers pay for licences of concord (*licencia concordie*), acknowledge debts to each other for the public record (*recognouit se teneri, fatetur se teneri*), record instances of defamation, and place themselves upon inquests (that is, request an investigation by jurors, and agree to accept their findings). In Ellington in 1290 a special panel of jurors found that Walter son of Stephen had slandered Richard Beaumeys by calling him a thief. Walter had to pay Richard damages of 6d and pay a court fine of 6d (*Conuictum est per vicinos Iuratos quod Walterus filius Stephani dixit oprobria Ricardo Beumys vocando ipsum latronem ad dampnum suum*). In 1294 the jurors found that William Aldyth did not defame the wife of William Bok as he had been accused of doing, and William Bok was charged with false claim and fined (*Conuictum est per Iuratos quod Willelmus Aldyth nunquam defamauit vxorem Willelmi Bok sicut inposuit eidem. Ideo dictus Willelmus Bok pro falso clamore in misericordia*). The same court of 1294 contains a series of entries concerning a dispute over a service contract (*convencio*) to salve sheep between Richard le Beaumeys and Richard *Messor*.

A mix of collective and seigneurial use also appears in the court records, as in the 1322 Ellington entry where it is ordered by the steward and with the assent of all free and customary tenants (*et per assensum omnium liberorum et Custumariorum)* that no one is to go to a local "penny tavern" which is over-charging *(ad tabernam de denariis)*. A 1307 Upwood entry records that a wood called Roundewode belonging to another manor (John de Deen) has grown onto the lord's land to his damage and his disinheritance if it is allowed to grow further (*ad exheredacionem domini si ulterius permittatur*). In that same court the roll seems to share some of the properties of an account roll, when Robert Tolleboy gives the lord 12d in advance as earnest money (*premanibus ingersuma xiid*) and undertakes to give each year at Christmas one chicken (*unam gallinam*) that he might lawfully remain outside the fee. (Such renderings in kind may be read as symbolic of a tenant's continuing tie with that manor). A 1427 Upwood memorandum fixes the amount of turves tenants can dig according to allotments established under Abbot John, some 130 years earlier, that were found in "an old book of the steward" (*in antiquo libro senescalli*).

In the later courts new entry types appear to address the new realities of the fourteenth- and fifteenth-century village. Thus, along with publication and enrollment of the bylaws referred to earlier, the rolls also record cases where villagers placed matters in arbitration (*ponitur in arbitracione*), including the selection of arbiters, to resolve disputes among themselves.[39] Another new type of entry appearing in

39 For licences of concord, see examples in the Upwood court rolls of 1299, 1301, 1307, 1322, 1325, 1344, 1365, 1372, 1378, 1382, 1386, 1391; for debt

the later rolls is the specification of the procedures for election to village office: for example, in the Upwood court of 1418 it is recorded that Robert Myles, Richard Payn, Thomas Peny, and John Gouler were elected to the office of beadle by the homage (here, the jurors), and of that group, Robert Myles was chosen to fill the office by the Steward (*electi sunt ad officium bedelli per homagium de quibus predictum Robertum electus est per Senescallum*). Indeed, in looking at the late fourteenth- and early fifteenth-century rolls one has the sense that a variety of matters were still being handled in traditional ways, but were being enrolled in the court's minutes for the first time in the form of election procedures, arbitration arrangements, and bylaws.[40] As well as reflecting continued growth in "trusting writing," the explicit recording of traditional practices would have been useful in a period when increased tenant turnover was challenging collective practice and memory in new ways.

In short, it may be said that villagers' use of the court roll parallels for an entire community the use that Benedetto del Massarizia made of his private account and diary papers in the fifteenth century: to record agreements and the findings of local inquests regarding debt, land acquisition, and various personal arrangements. There seems to be an emerging viewpoint among the villagers that these traditional practices should be confirmed and protected by being "properly enrolled" in the community's most important record.

---

and other "recognitions," see examples in 1322, 1325, 1326, 1339, 1344; for cases of defamation, see examples in 1326; and for various examples of people placing themselves upon the findings of an inquest, including *pro consideratione Curie habenda*, see examples in 1294, 1295, 1375, 1390, 1391, 1402, 1438.

40 The appearance of bylaws, methods of electing local officials, and arbitration arrangements, and the meaning that might be attached to this change in recording procedure, are discussed more fully in Sherri Olson, *A Chronicle of All That Happens: Voices from the Village Court in Medieval England* (Toronto, 1996), Chapters Three and Four. Ault noted that offences against the bylaws were recorded in the court rolls before the bylaws themselves were set down; see *Open-Field Husbandry and the Village Community: A Study of Agrarian By-laws in Medieval England* (Philadelphia, 1965), 17. At the same time that these new entries were appearing, older types were disappearing, notably retirement arrangements for the elderly.

The Appearance of English Vocabulary

Close analysis of the evidence reveals a relative increase in the amount of colloquial speech in the minutes of the court over the late fourteenth and fifteenth centuries. This change must be read as significant given the interpretive framework employed here, which emphasizes the density of court roll evidence and its time-sensitivity.

What, then, are some of the areas in which English terminology is preferred to Latin? When the types of trees and vegetation that have been illegally cut are specified, this information is sometimes given in English: *pro quadam arbore que vocatur mapele* ("for a certain tree that is called a maple"), *fodit hassokes infra mariscum* ("he dug hassocks [sedge grass] in the marsh"), *parum Crabbetres in bosco domini* ("a pair of crab trees in the lord's wood"), *tres Crabbetres, pro i arbore ull'* ("for one elm tree"), *i asshe* ("one ash tree"). Stray animals may be named in English (*i sherehog*[41]), and the color may be noted, especially of horses, in order to identify them (*unus equs coloris bay, coloris gray, coloris greselyd*). Local artisans may be identified in English, such as *pewterer, cissor, carpentyr*, and *gannokers* (ale-wives). In Upwood in 1411 it is ordered that no one dig in the marsh without permission of the *Fenreffs* (fen reeves). In Ellington 1440 Nicholas Ba[rley?] was fined 2d for trespass with animals and "because he gathered peasecods" (*quia collexit pescodd'*). The names of distrained items, usually agricultural tools used in cutting wood illegally, also appear (as discussed earlier), as in the 1294 and 1299 Ellington entries referring to bills (*byll'*), knippers (*knypulis*), and hatchets (*hathiis*). A 1446 entry lists attachment by (*per*) *i Twybill*[42] *et ii Aynvill.* In 1306 there is an entry that lists the chattels belonging to Hugh son of William in le Mersch which were found after his outlawing (*post utlagacionem*), including *unum anfeltum, unum Grynston cum vno axe ferrea, vnum slekcrow cum uno par de tonges* ("an anvil, a Grindstone with an iron axe, a slekcrow? with a pair of tongs"), all of which are to be held by the reeve.

Some fines or payments occur in the vernacular in court rolls and other local records across different lordships, such as *leyrwite* (lying

41 Shearhog: the "name given to a lamb after the first shearing and until the second." *Oxford English Dictionary*, s.v.

42 Twybill: "a kind of ax with two cutting edges; formerly used for cutting mortices." *Oxford English Dictionary*, s.v.

+ fine; the fine levied, usually against an unmarried woman, for sexual misconduct), but occasionally tags of local provenance are also preserved, such as the payment called *monkyeld*, which seems to be an Upwood term (monk + payment) for the fee to pasture one's animals, an apt name for a rendering to a monastic landlord.[43] There are references to a wide variety of workaday items: the *chopins*, or illegal measures, of the alewives (*cum chopino*), customary agricultural renderings (*cornbote* in 1295 and 1297), merestones (*mareston'*) between tenants' holdings (1450), and baskets (*lepes*) used in fishing illegally (1411). In 1452 and 1453 Richard Aleyn was fined for not throwing open a croft in front of his tenement to commoning *in le Schactyme* (*in tempore de shaktyms* in 1453) (shock + time). In 1439 Robert Preston was fined 1d for not cleaning *gutture sua* [*sic*] *vocata Cowgripe*, and Peter Bray did not clean a dungheap near his door (*unum Mukhilpit uersus hostium suum*) in c. 1430. In Upwood in 1347 it is noted that Cristina Cowherd *est squabblyre*.[44] The court roll text even preserves alternate spoken forms, as in a reference to the parcel of wood mentioned in the testimony of the elderly John Hicson in Upwood in 1428(2), which was "called le Rowesway or Rowes" (*parcella bosci in Roucegroue vocatur le Rowesway vel Rowes*). As we have seen in Chapter Two, villagers' surnames, still in flux over the late thirteenth and early fourteenth centuries, are another evolving source of English vocabulary in the court roll before 1350.

Other English usages in the later rolls speak more directly to the troubles of the post-plague village, and provide a telling contrast to the earlier period. The bills, knippers, and hatchets used in illegal woodcutting found in the court rolls around 1300 are, in the 1420s to

43 The names of certain fines and customary renderings always had their vernacular as well as Latin forms, such as fishsilver, maltsilver, woodsilver, and the like; see Nellie Neilson, *Customary Rents* (Oxford, 1910), for a full discussion.

44 There are no citations in the rolls for Upwood and Ellington that are as colorful as an entry concerning slander found in a c. 1450 court roll for the village of Broughton, in which it was ordered that "no one henceforth should call anyone else living there by the name of horribel horeson or kokold" (*nullus decetero appellat aliquam convicinorum ibidem comorancium hoc nomine horribel horeson vel kokold*) under penalty of 40d, half to the church fabric and half to the lord. See citation and discussion in Ault, "The Village Church and the Village Community," 197–215.

1450s, sometimes mirrored by citations which name the weapons that villagers are using against each other, as in the 1428 Upwood entry that John Freston "came into the lord's manor armed with a pitch-fork" (*venit in manerium domini vi et armis cum uno pykefork*) and attacked the bailiff. In 1454 the constable assaulted a tenant "with a pitchfork drawn in his hand and beat him, wounded him, and treated him badly" (*cum i pyckefork in manu sua abstract' et ipsum verberauit, vulneravit et male tractauit*). Several villagers attacked each other *cum daggar' abstracte*.[45] Yet another new source of English vocabulary in the later rolls involves villagers who are fined for lapses in upkeep, such as failure to clean a watercourse, repair a room in a house, build a hedge, or mend a gap giving onto the fields: *non mundavit guteram suam* (1430), *non reparauit le Insethous* (1418, 1420, 1430), *non fecit le grouehegge* (Ellington 1446), *tenet i gap apertum et non emendauit* (1435 in Upwood, 1429 in Ellington).[46] While colloquial speech occurs more or less throughout the rolls for arable and pastureland, in names such as *Fenfurlong, Duffhousdole* (dole meaning "field strip"), *Kylnehousdole, Foxholdes, Riecroftwelldole,* and *Heymadefeld,* by the end of the fourteenth and first half of the fifteenth centuries, new applications of English are being found in the place names for areas of human habitation. (These new composite place names, which combine family surnames and topographical features, will be discussed more fully in Chapter Five.)

The increased profile of English can be read as a measure of increasing peasant intervention and control: although lord and tenant interests continued to influence the court roll, the fifteenth century court becomes more fully a villagers' court with the lowering of seigneurial involvement due to the leasing of the demesne. Establishing tenure, and thus one's place in the web of land-use rights, was always important in a common field village, but it became

45 Other entries involving weapons cited in English occur in the Upwood courts of 1454 (four entries total) and 1456 (two entries).

46 The account rolls of this period also abound in citations of ruinous properties. Ault, in *The Self-Directing Activities of Village Communities in Medieval England* (Boston, 1952), 3, commented upon this interweaving of English and Latin, observing that "when documents relating to rural communities do appear in English the spelling is so bizarre, and the vocabulary so bucolic and difficult to understand that the student wishes the document was in clear and familiar Latin."

increasingly so when, in addition to increased tenant instability, hundreds of acres of demesne, no longer *in manu domini*, were added to the tenant lands. Once villagers began leasing the demesne it was subject to the same set of safeguards and rights as other tenant holdings. As will be seen in detail in the remaining two chapters, the gradual disappearance of a historical dynamic between lord and tenant, who each had a stake in the village but held different kinds of land, undermined a kind of tension that had supported the rights of both by permitting argument and negotiation within the limits of a long-established relationship. Such analysis is far removed from the traditional focus on the abolition of serfdom as the chief event in lord-tenant relations in the late medieval period.

Ultimately, there is a larger historical context within which we may place this peasant participation in Latin document culture. Most obviously, peasants were accustomed to hearing the Latin mass and saying Latin prayers.[47] For them, as for all medieval Christians, more or less, Latin was an enigmatic language that made mysteries familiar. Latin allowed people to confront directly what was most exalted, without the alterity of the most exalted being in any way diminished.[48] When the court was held in the parish church, peasants would have been in a setting where they were accustomed to hearing and speaking Latin, and their use of the court roll might have drawn support from these other routine contacts with that language.[49]

47 See Clanchy's discussion regarding the knowledge of Latin among the laity, *From Memory to Written Record*, 234–240, where he argues that by the eleventh century, "the people at large," which of course means mostly peasants, knew and could recite at least the Lord's Prayer and the Creed in Latin; quotation at 237.

48 For a discussion of the medieval understanding of miracle, the "drawing out of the hidden workings of God within a nature that was all potentially miraculous," see Benedicta Ward, *Miracles and the Medieval Mind: Theory, Record and Event, 1000–1215* (Philadelphia, 1987); quotation at 3.

49 Another dimension is raised here of the issue discussed earlier with respect to storytelling. Here we may see a kind of intersection of religious belief, story-telling, and the articulation of power. See Bruno Bettelheim, *The Uses of Enchantment: The Meaning and Importance of Fairy Tales* (New York, 1977), 13–14, where he points out that fairy tales "abound in religious motifs; many Biblical stories are of the same nature as fairy tales." According to Bettelheim, most fairy tales "originated in periods when religion was a most important part of life" and thus they

Thus, peasants' inability to translate the language was not a barrier to the development of a variety of "literate modes" in the village. Latin was, in their experience, a language of authority, a language that got things done – the language of charters, wills, seals, court rolls, tax lists, and the sacraments. In this light, perhaps court roll Latin was *just arcane enough* (a quality that Duffy describes as "the decent obscurity of a learned language")[50] to enhance the authority of the measures villagers employed to "carry on" daily life: the remove of Latin was of a piece with the remove of the written record. As in the case where a woman controlled land in her own right, a perfectly acceptable but not most frequent occurrence, "pragmatic Latinity" was at once familiar and unusual, hence it was also just arcane enough to attract notice, commentary, and the assignation of meaning. Latin in the village resembles what Rosamond McKitterick has called the "symbolic uses of literacy"[51] (such as the clump of earth or twig placed on a charter of land transfer), uses which stand on their own yet also "qualify the ostensibly practical [uses]" by adding new layers of meaning to them.[52] At another level, the Latin of estate

---

"deal, directly or by inference, with religious themes." The interweaving of Latin and vernacular speech occurred in other kinds of texts, for example within the tradition of macaronic sermons that have been studied by Siegfried Wenzel, *Macaronic Sermons: Bilingualism and Preaching in Late-Medieval England* (Ann Arbor, 1994).

50 Duffy, *Stripping of the Altars*, 110.

51 That symbolic literacy might also be allied with power is illustrated, in more recent American history, in the story of a fugitive slave who took a large, unwieldy Bible with her. "Though she was unable to read, she 'had got her old mistress to turn down the leaves at the verses she knew by heart, and often she would sit down in the woods and open the big Bible at these verses, and repeat them aloud, and find strength and consolation.'" See "Bible Christians" in Albert J. Raboteau, *Slave Religion: The "Invisible Institution" in the Antebellum South* (1978; updated ed., New York, 2004), 239–243; quotation at 240.

52 *The Uses of Literacy in Early Mediaeval Europe*, ed. Rosamond McKitterick (1990; repr., Cambridge, 1995), 9. Such a usage might also be seen as a factor in peasant religion; thus our study may add to the "research into the authentic history of medieval Christianity – the contribution of the affective and intellectual life of broad strata of European populations and its role as a powerful factor in social behavior" which, according to Aron Gurevich, should be "one of the tasks of future historians." See

administrative records mirrors the pervasive textual bilingualism (and, when they include French, trilingualism) which a variety of medieval people apparently found not only efficient but necessary. Peasant pragmatic literacy was fostered by Latin.

We have seen that documents were part of normal village culture. As suitors to the local court, as in all the fora where they provided information, peasants were producers of records and their engagement was facilitated by Latin; and while pragmatic literacy could not create authority, "it was a means by which almost any type of authority could be better safeguarded or stretched to new limits," as Britnell said. Lords were certainly powerful people, more powerful than their tenants, but there were popular "cultures of power" alongside elite ones.[53] The relationship of farmers and Latin can be partly seen in this light, as part of a relationship of power that derived from the life of a community whose survival depended on a common center, a "concentric" constellation of power not of the lord's making, though supported by his authority. The common center of that community, made up mostly of peasants, was reinforced in the court and in its Latin record. The confidence with which Balestracci's Tuscan peasant made and relied upon his "farming diary" may in fact be less of a "Renaissance" in the fields than a deeply embedded tradition of practical peasant reliance upon the written record, a tradition that changed again with the expansion of literacy and texts in early modern European history.

Gurevich, *Historical Anthropology of the Middle Ages*, ed. Jana Howlett (Chicago, 1992).

53 Thomas N. Bisson, introduction to *Cultures of Power: Lordship, Status and Process in Twelfth-Century Europe*, ed. Thomas N. Bisson (Philadelphia, 1995), 7.

CHAPTER FOUR

Trespass Against Whom? Transgressio *and Its Meanings*

According to Eric Kerridge, the "fundamental cause of common fields" is the "division both of the land itself and, just as importantly, of the livestock, among a mass of small occupiers."[1] In the present study it has been argued that this "smallholders' regime" of common-property rights in the arable, meadow, wood, and marsh formed the economic base and informed the cultural life of thousands of medieval villages. In a common field village, matters of right and of injury, of access and trespass, of use and misuse would require continual management and adjustment, and thus the "habits of mind" to support such decision-making, so that Alice Typeler (a regrater, or reseller, of ale), Richard Netherde (a shepherd), William Sadeler, Alice Cook, John Sondey the village priest, John Stale (a baker), Agnes del Reues, Robert Dryngallday, and Bartholomew Inlond could manage farming operations cheek-by-jowl.

For medieval common field farmers, the arenas for such constant management were the "assemblies of cultivators," the village court as well as various other types of extra-curial gatherings that did not generate records. No documents provide systematic evidence of common field arrangements or even of their presence, although court rolls abound in entries about trespass which plainly reveal common field agriculture. For example, in Ellington's 1311 court roll Roger in le Hale was fined for not having repaired a "purpresture" (enclosure, encroachment) which he had made "by appropriating to himself two balks [ridges of unplowed land] serving as boundary markers next to

1 Eric Kerridge, *The Common Fields of England* (Manchester, 1992), 4. He goes on to say, "[c]onversely, the supersession of small occupiers by a small number of large ones, sounded the death-knell of the common fields." Implicit here, of course, is the idea that the smallholders enjoying such common property rights were also fundamental to the continuing vitality of that system.

his croft" (*appropriando sibi duos sulcos de diuisa iuxta croftum suum*). In Upwood in 1318 Thomas Aspelon was fined and pledged for appropriating the lord's land by plowing and removing (*subtrahendo*) a boundary marker placed between his land and the lord's land at Duffhousdole. In the same court John de Wenyngton was fined because he placed Boundary markers (*posuit Bundas*) between the lands (*terras*) of Agnes le Reves, Robert Cook, and John Crane. In 1320 William le Frere appropriated a furrow (*unum sulcrum*) of Alice le Pikelere's land. The 1369(1) court records a bylaw that no one should allow animals into the fields until all the grain of one field is completely in the barn (*omnia blada unius campi sint plenarie in horr*[*eo*]). As a final example, in 1375 John Houghton was fined 3s because he burdened Upwood's common pasture with outsiders' animals (*superonerauit communam de Upwode cum boviculis extraneis*). These entries and others make clear that, as Joan Thirsk has observed, while "there are few hints of crop rotation or common pasture rights," the court rolls provide "much evidence of penalties imposed on those who damaged the property of others, particularly at harvest time."[2]

Still, citations concerning trespass, that is, the movement of people, animals, or both on the landed interests of others, in fields, woods, meadow, and yards, are a valuable source of information about the common field regime and its imprint on the fabric of village life. It is also an activity well represented in the records of estate management, especially court rolls.[3] Because notices of trespass routinely name the perpetrator and the place, and appear so regularly throughout the duration of the court roll series, we may take the evidence of trespass in Upwood and Ellington as being a fairly complete record of such behavior in the years for which we have records. More generally, the court rolls also attest to the setting, the mechanisms, and the local climate that villagers created for achieving the rough consensus so essential to common field agriculture. Trespass, which is probably universal in farming societies, was a highly charged activity in a common-property rights community. A focus on villagers

2 Joan Thirsk, *The Rural Economy of England* (London, 1984), 39–40; see especially Chapter Four, "The Common Fields." The phrase "assembly of cultivators" used earlier is hers, as noted above, p. 16.

3 As has been noted earlier, the kinds of cases and terminology presented here can readily be found in the court rolls for other villages.

in transgressione, however, can also provide us with a window onto their understanding of personal rights and thus onto the shaping of individual personality and group culture alike.[4]

Explaining Trespass

Not surprisingly, some scholars have favored a politicized view in their analysis of the court roll data on trespass. Peter Franklin, in an essay on peasant "movements," cites trespass as an example of an "individual action" that, like theft, may "well have included significant political content" even if it is hard to link it to an "organized movement." Ralph Evans, in a discussion of seigneurial "control" of tenants, sees the protection of the lord's interests as the "primary purpose" of the court: the presentation of trespass on the demesne is a "very common item of business" and the "frequency with which trespasses with animals came into court" is significant because it "implies an active guardianship of the lord's interests."[5] In this analysis, focus is on trespass against the lord, which is interpreted primarily as a political commentary whose origins lie in social (that is, class-based) grievances. Whether such an interpretation can account for the varied and changing picture of trespass, its range and meanings, and the numerous victims and perpetrators that emerge from court roll evidence will be one of the issues raised in the present chapter.[6]

4 Historians interested in the morality of the many have tended to rely upon ecclesiastical prescriptive literature. On this point see Paul R. Hyams, *Rancor and Reconciliation in Medieval England* (Ithaca, 2003), especially his chapter on Social Emotions. Hyams instances as sources the Decalogue, confessors' manuals, and proverbial sayings as sources for uncovering the moral codes of the laity. See especially p. 48 n66.

5 For the essays by Franklin and Evans, see *Medieval Society and the Manor Court*, ed. Zvi Razi and Richard M. Smith (Oxford, 1996); quotations at 182, 204, and 227, respectively.

6 J.A. Raftis, *Tenure and Mobility* (Toronto, 1964), 97, cites the case of a villager "treated as a veritable traitor" in the Hemmingford Abbots court roll for 1332 because he had betrayed the village to royal tax officials by revealing hidden things of his fellow villagers (*secreta vicinorum suorum*). The collective outrage at having to pay a higher tax took the form of accusing him of trespass against lord, common, and neighbors: he appropriated a furlong to himself by plowing, took land from the com-

Historians of trespass have drawn attention to the broad and flexible meaning of the term. According to John Hudson, "trespass" in the medieval period had the same meaning that it has today, of a general wrong, as in "forgive us our trespasses."[7] More specifically, Paul Hyams, working with the records of the common law courts, has argued that the usage of the term "trespass" was "flexible enough to invite the speaker to inject his own sense of the breached norm without definition." According to Hyams, "the word's initial attraction was perhaps its very imprecision, which suited the ancient undifferentiated procedure because it left the complainant's options open." He argues for a lively "lay or popular, vernacular not official, usage" of the trespass charge that may be proof of the "favored status" it had achieved by the late thirteenth century, though that status may not be "visible" in common law records.[8]

Fortunately, the serial court rolls exist at precisely the level where that "vernacular usage" is visible. The density of the evidence makes it possible to reconstruct changes in the use of the trespass charge over time (changes that make the institution visible), and in particular to show how villagers came to manipulate the power attached to the term to protect their interests in the post-plague era. As we shall see, in the early court rolls the term was used infrequently and for a variety of "wrongs"; by the middle third of the fourteenth century, usage was narrowing to target personal matters such as assault and defamation. More especially, the use of the charge of trespass became reserved for landed trespass (perhaps partly because landed trespass occurred more frequently than any other type of wrong encompassed by that term), and in particular trespass on the lord's demesne. In other words, by the middle of the fourteenth century, the charge of *transgressio* in the village shows the same tendency to adhere to the

---

mon, caused damage to the lord's meadow by digging, and mowed unceasingly (*continuatim*) with his servants on his neighbors' lands to the damage of the whole homage. This entry suggests that people certainly distinguished between the victims of trespass (lord, common, or individual tenant), but what is striking here is the sense of an offence committed against the entire community, treating its constituent parts as one.

7 John Hudson, *The Formation of the English Common Law: Law and Society in England from the Norman Conquest to Magna Carta* (London, 1996), 164.

8 Hyams, *Rancor and Reconciliation,* 236, 277.

rights of lordship that it demonstrated in the "higher courts."[9] Then, over the later fourteenth and into the fifteenth centuries, in the era when the abbot of Ramsey (like lords everywhere) leased the demesne to the villagers, the charge of trespass was still used to defend that same land, though the interests being defended were now those of tenants instead of the lord. This suggests not only that villagers traditionally saw demesne land as different from customary land but also, and more importantly for the present chapter, that this distinction generated meaning that could be used to protect personal rights as well as the common field regime itself. We will explore the implications of these developments at the end of the present chapter.

Hyams and others see trespass as arising out of a "culture of enmity and vengeance," thus emphasizing its personal application.[10] While social conflict had its part to play in everyday village life, court roll data show a variety of associations attached to the trespass charge. The "flexible usage" and "imprecision" that contributed to the popularity of trespass as a charge are apparent in the many different types of trespass and in its capacity to carry weight both as a personal charge and as a mechanism for shoring up common field arrangements in an era of great stress. That the meaning of trespass as an activity, as well as *transgressio* as a working label, would be flexible in a common field regime dovetails with our earlier characterization of village resources as fluid and circulating continually.

Who Committed Trespass?

Court roll evidence shows that reeves and other officials were among the most efficient purloiners of the lord's resources. While their "insider status" made this easy, their actions suggest a fine line

9 According to Hyams, *Rancor and Reconciliation*, 234, well into the thirteenth century "legal records use *transgressio* (and its cognates) almost exclusively for wrongs committed against the king or some other superior." While Hyams's book deals principally with common law courts, and not the courts of private jurisdictions, his analysis helps to elucidate the evidence from village court rolls.

10 See also John S. Beckerman, "Adding Insult to *Iniuria*: Affronts to Honor and the Origins of Trespass," in *On the Laws and Customs of England: Essays in Honor of Samuel E. Thorne*, ed. Morris S. Arnold et al. (Chapel Hill, 1981), 159–181.

between an illicit taking of the lord's goods and the traditional perquisites attached to office. In Upwood's 1297 court, Richard *Messor* (Hayward) was cited for a stunning series of offences under the term *ad dampnum domini* ("to the lord's damage," rather than *transgressio*), including stealing blankets made locally, removing the lord's hedges, allowing his animals to feed upon the lord's grass, badly guarding the lord's grain, and allowing outsiders to cut hedges around the lord's assarts (pieces of land cleared of trees and brush). He was also cited in connection with his wife's destruction of the lord's peas and his own servant's theft of meadow grass which was used to feed his animals *in domo sua*. Finally, he returned twelve impounded animals to their owners without the pound-keeper's permission. In fact, his offences are very similar to the kind of privileges that lords traditionally granted to officials to encourage good service.[11] That same court (1297) includes a citation of William the son of the reeve who cut down alder trees belonging to the lord (*amputauit alnet' domini*), and the entry notes precisely that he carried them off to his house with his own cart (*cum Carreca sua domui sue cariauit*).

Some thirty years later in 1329 the bailiff and reeve were cited for selling timber that been blown down by the wind to R[obert?] and William le Couper – an excellent example of official opportunism. In 1332 Thomas Bailiff gathered eight cartloads of thorns in the lord's wood, took them to his house, and paid nothing for them (*et nichil soluit*). William Edward, Jr, *prepositus marisci* (fenreeve), led the carts of outsiders into the marsh to steal turves in 1427 and 1435. William Frere, cited as "recently reeve" in the account roll of c. 1324, had an extremely active career as trespasser: his activities included scaling the lord's fence at night and breaking into his pea stack (1299) as well as trepassing against both lord and villagers in meadow, woods, and field on at least eleven occasions, including appropriating his neighbors' land by plowing and taking the lord's wagon outside the manor without licence (1331). Much later, in Ellington, William Gymber, also cited as "recently reeve" in the account rolls of 1407, 1411, 1415, and 1416, extracted boundary markers, trespassed against the commons (with animals and by plowing and appropriating land),

11 For an earlier discussion of this phenomenon, see Sherri Olson, *A Chronicle of All That Happens: Voices from the Village Court in Medieval England* (Toronto, 1996), 74–75 with n42.

"snatched land secretly" (*furtiue*) by plowing, and closed a headway that blocked pasturelands. The 1391 entry regarding his trespass by plowing shows a fully developed vocabulary of trespass: "And that the same William is a common trespasser against his neighbors by plowing and appropriating land, to their harm" (*Et quod idem Willelmus est communis transgressor vicinis suis arando et appropriando sibi de terra* [illegible] *ad nocumentum*).

Common field agriculture is the framework within which this historic encroachment was perpetrated by officials against the lord as well as others, an encroachment that bears comparison with other expressions of economic self interest: for example, Thomas Brokenhorn and Ralph Shepherd were cited in the court for the village of Littleport in 1319 for taking hay from the lord's rick and setting it "before their impounded beasts" without the lord's permission.[12] Note that in this case the men did not attempt to free their animals from the pound (which of course could also occur). Perhaps Brokenhorn and Shepherd saw the pound as part of the public arena of the village where their rights of access continued, and availed themselves of the lord's hay to care for their livestock. Whose pound was it; whose precise interests did it protect? The answers to these questions are complicated in a constructive way when this episode is considered within a continuum of resource management that includes the perquisites enjoyed by officials, the liberties that officials often took with the property committed to their care, meals provided to workers during boonworks (extra tasks that tenants performed for the lord), the gleaning rights of the village poor, perquisites granted to tenants in "sporting chance" competitions, portions of court fines being used to pay for improvements to the parish church – and of course the flow of resources that sustained common field farming.[13] These village

12 *The Court Baron, Being Precedents For Use in Seignorial and Other Local Courts, Together with Select Pleas From the Bishop of Ely's Court of Littleport*, ed. F.W. Maitland and W.P. Baildon (London, 1891), 57.

13 For the "sporting chance" competitions, see Andrew Jones, "Harvest Customs and Labourers' Perquisites in Southern England, 1150–1350: the Corn Harvest," *Agricultural History Review* 25 (1977): 14–22; "Harvest Customs and Labourers' Perquisites in Southern England, 1150–1350: the Hay Harvest," *Agricultural History Review* 25 (1977): 98–107. As an example Jones cites the custumal of the manor of Barton, a Ramsey Abbey manor, c. 1255: "On the day when the virgaters mowed

traditions (some more obscure than others, and all deserving of further study), so clearly planted in both the seigneurial and tenant spheres, were rooted in the same common resource use mentality that facilitated practices that served tenant or lord more narrowly: in the case of tenants, these practices included the sub-leasing of land parcels among themselves, and in the case of the lord, the commutation of labor services into money payments (and vice versa), and the leasing of the demesne, which is of special interest in the present chapter.

That the actions of Brokenhorn and Shepherd were quite unremarkable is suggested by the procedural treatise, *La Court de Baron* (c. 1342?), which provides model language for a similar case in which a tenant takes his animals out of the lord's pinfold (that is, pound), alleging they had gone several days without food and water.[14] Similar incidents in Upwood illustrate other variants that suggest this common use mentality: in 1297 the twelve jurors were cited for concealing the fact that William Frere had rescued animals belonging to his father Thomas Frere, which had been found in the lord's stubble, at night against the gamekeeper and other servants of the Abbot's demesne courtyard (*fecit Warennario et aliis famulis Curie domini Abbatis*). For this William was ordered to the stocks (*quod adiudicatur in compediis*), a penalty rarely imposed, which he afterwards paid a fine of 40d to avoid (*et postea fecit finem*). In 1299 the same William by night climbed over the lord's wall (*noctanter transiuit murum domini*), broke into the lord's pea stack, and carried peas to

---

the lord's meadow they received a sheep ... the sheep was placed in the meadow with the tenants looking on; if they caught it they kept it, if not, they had to wait until the next year for better luck" ("The Hay Harvest," 102). The custumals and account rolls of the great ecclesiastical estates of East Anglia, the west Midlands, the south, and the West Country that Jones relied upon for these articles provide evidence for other avenues of research that cannot be explored here: for example, medieval notions of the body could be studied by villagers' practice of measuring many of the perquisites of the harvest (size of the harvest sheaf measured by using a binding equal to the "circumference of the reeve's head" or to "stretching twice round the hayward's head," the handful as a measure, etc.) by the "size of their limbs [or] the strength in their bodies" ("The Corn Harvest," 14–15; "The Hay Harvest," 106–107).

14 Maitland and Baildon, *Court Baron*, 60.

his father's impounded horses. He was to be put in the stocks and again afterward paid a fine of 2s.

"Shareholder's Logic"

Such routine activities by people like William Frere arose in part from a kind of shareholding mentality, that is, a set of assumptions about having a common stake in village wealth. Since the orientation of the entire agricultural regime would be weighted towards what Kerridge called the "mass of small occupiers," the traditional location of demesne land as scattered strips alongside tenants' strips in the open fields would also have fostered the working notion of the lord, the abbot of Ramsey himself, as one among a body of shareholders. This "shareholder's logic" held that rough equivalencies existed – and new ones could always be readily found – between lots or shares; and by its very nature that logic extended to include parts of animals, human labor, land, grain, implements, etc., parts that could then circulate, that could be leased, sold, exchanged, loaned, or traded upon, as part of the "diversified portfolio" of village resources. As discussed above in the introduction, agrarian partibility assumed an immense range of forms, mirrored strikingly in such practices as multiple ownership of plows or, in a case cited by Kerridge, of holding half-year meadows, "where one man had the hay and another the aftermath." [15] That labor functioned readily within such a system is apparent, of course, in the account rolls in the entries concerning *opera*, especially sales of *opera* in years when the lord commuted labor services to cash payments. Indeed, the etymology of the word "job" (which the *Oxford English Dictionary*, hereafter *OED*, defines variously as "a small compact portion of some substance," "a cart-load or what a horse and cart can bring at one time," "a piece of work," "a small definite piece of work done in the way of one's special occupation or profession," etc.) points to this same mentality to divide, subdivide, and trade upon: according to J.A. Raftis, the word derives from the notation

15 Kerridge, *Common Fields*, 5. Long-term piecemeal acquisition and management of tiny parcels of land are practices profusely illustrated in Benedetto's fifteenth-century farming diary; see *The Renaissance in the Fields: Family Memoirs of a Fifteenth-Century Tuscan Peasant*, ed. Duccio Balestracci, trans. Paolo Squatriti and Betsy Merideath (Chicago, 1995).

"one work," *unum opus* = *i. op.* = *jobbe* = *job*[16] (note that the *OED* gives the origins of "job" as "unascertained," "obscure," and, notably, "prob. in colloquial use some time before it appeared in literature"). Similarly, the word "task," from Latin *taxare*, originally referred to a fixed payment and came to mean a piece of work, a specified quantity of work or labor imposed or exacted (see *OED*, s.v. "task"). These etymologies are particularly interesting because they point to a conscious measuring of the work that one person does, thus investing that work with additional meaning, and perhaps contributing to the development of a "sense of selfhood" discussed earlier.

Under the common field regime, a large number of "small occupiers" governed their own access to portions of land, whether they held lots in the meadow, worked their one-acre parcels sometimes *separaliter*, sometimes *communiter*, pastured livestock together on the stubble, or exchanged these lots and working arrangements among themselves. These conditions required that the partibility and fungibility of local resources be active, both in terms of the real use of those resources and the understanding that lay behind that use.[17] The parcelling up of land, labor, dues, crops, and implements by sale, lease, or trade may be seen as a mechanism to gain the greatest possible use from resources by promoting their divisibility, interchangeability, and recombination; such an approach to wealth management would have emphasized the brisk circulation of resources throughout the "market" of the village (fluidity was also encouraged by the rural monetary system, with its coins in small denominations being everywhere present, in high velocity and wide circulation – a fact certainly attested to by the ubiquity of money in court and account rolls for the English village)[18] and would have offset hardship by increasing the

16 See Raftis, *Tenure and Mobility*, 15 n9.

17 See Michael M. Postan, *Essays on Medieval Agriculture and General Problems of the Medieval Economy* (Cambridge, 1973), for an older but still evocative discussion of the divisibility of fields and the almost infinite variety of field management arrangements, a phenomenon he describes as a kind of field "metabolism"; and for an exhaustive work on field systems, see *Studies of Field Systems in the British Isles*, ed. Alan R.H. Baker and Robin A. Butlin (Cambridge, 1973).

18 These features point to a type of "economy of expedients," of the kind discussed by Olwen Hufton, *The Prospect Before Her: A History of Women in Western Europe*, vol. 1: *1500–1800* (New York, 1996), especially 156–164.

economic leverage of the villagers.[19] This practical mentality may be interpreted as the rural equivalent of the "economy of expedients" that economic historians have long understood for urban settings.[20]

This fundamental circulation of resources was a central principle of village life, affecting not only traditions of trespass, but also personal interactions and even individual identity, thus providing the historian with materials to study village morality. The existence of a "culture of enmity and vengeance" in which a dynamic "vernacular" use of trespass developed, as described above by Hyams, suggests that village ideas of morality incorporated the notion of vengeance. Straightforward evidence of vengeance is certainly present though not voluminous in the court roll narrations: clear instances would include those cases where a villager attacks the spouse of someone who had raised the hue and cry on him or her. But alongside ideas that some villagers had about vengeance was an idea that almost everyone had about the desirability of having a good reputation. If having "face to lose" is a sign of the personality makeup of the nobility, it seems to be replicated among the peasantry.[21] John S. Beckerman, working with the records of village and hundred courts, formulary books, and fair court records from St Ives (materials at approximately the same judicial level as the court rolls studied in the present book), has shown that claims for shame or dishonor suffered were frequently heard in local courts (indeed that claims for dishonor may lie behind the ubiquitous entry *ad dampnum suum* when it appeared with a sum of money). He emphasizes the "variety of wrongs" for which the allegation of dishonor could appear: "from defamation to forcible injuries to breaking obligations to defaulting on transactions. Any of these offences could be counted a contumely, insult, affront to personal honor."[22] Thus, the protection of personal rights and personal

19 Along these same lines, see Donald N. McCloskey, "English Open Fields as Behavior Towards Risk," *Research in Economic History* 1 (1976): 124–170.

20 See Richard K. Marshall, *The Local Merchants of Prato: Small Entrepreneurs in the Late Medieval Economy* (Baltimore, 1999), 43–44, for an urban example of the economy of expedients, seen in the multiple sources of income for the druggist Benedetto di Tacco in a single year (1370).

21 The more usual perspective is found in Hyams, *Rancor and Reconciliation*, 251: "The nobility was *certainly not exempt* from these *mundane* human emotions [anger, resentment, fear of losing face]; *great men*, after all, possessed the *most face to lose*." (Emphases mine).

22 Beckerman, "Adding Insult to *Iniuria*," 174.

honor fell within the purview of the village court. Indeed, a concern for personal honor seems to underlie many of the early citations for trespass, as we shall see.

The Chronology of Trespass

Trespass was enacted within the labyrinth of village wealth, a continuum embracing land, goods, people, labor, and rights, "parts or specimens" of village wealth that circulated easily because, in part, of the readiness with which equivalency was determined between them. The history of landed trespass (from the fuller records of Upwood) shows that it was a traditional village activity that took many forms both over the years and at any given time: trespass was committed by individuals and groups, natives and outsiders, with and without animals, by unclean ditches, by unclosed gates, in the arable, woods, and marsh, by day and night, by stealth and openly, by a wide variety of acts of both commission and omission, by officials, villagers, the lord himself, on demesne, customary, free land, and common. Such diversity requires a detailed reconstruction.

In the earliest surviving Upwood rolls actions which are clearly cases of landed trespass are described and fines are attached, but there is no standard vocabulary, no one word for landed trespass. For example, in 1294 Alice the daughter of Umfrey the Sawyer was cited for damage in the woods and was fined 6d (*De Alicia filia Umfr' le Sawyer quia fecit dampnum in Rokesgroue*). In 1295 Alexander Godes and his brother Thomas were fined for pasturing six animals in the lord's grain (*pro bestis suis blado domini pascentibus videlicet cum vi bestis*). As noted earlier, the court scribes of the late thirteenth and early fourteenth centuries did use the term *transgressio*, but they used it sparingly, and when they did they applied it to a variety of cases, including physical assault, slander, and defaulting on debt. A 1307 court roll entry records that John Crane unjustly defamed (*defamauit*) another villager by accusing him of stealing woolen cloth, with damages set at 12d and a fine of 12d (*pro transgressione*), a case of "trespass" that links the offences of defamation and theft. In 1308 the jurors found that John de Burgg had badly treated Agnes Horseman by pulling her nose (*male tractauit Agnetem Horseman capiendo ipsam per nasum suum*) and was fined 3d *pro transgressione*. In 1311 Nicholas son of Adam acknowledged that he had broken an agreement (*fregit conuentionem*) with John son of Robert Attewodestrate regarding the crop of a half-acre of wheat, and *pro transgressione* he was fined. Thus, in the first decade of the fourteenth century, defamation, personal assault, and a broken agreement are all cited under the heading of trespass. The three cases cited all concern a sense of the individual, of his or her "personal honor" as discussed by Beckerman, or of rights that might be said to operate on an intimate level.

In the pre-plague era, as we shall see in some detail, the term *transgressio* for landed trespass showed a strong, though not exclusive, tendency to refer to trespass against the lord's landed interests. Thus, in one of the early rolls (1279) the jurors present that the tenants from the manor of William le Moyne in Upwood had cut and carried off sixteen oak trees, a "trespass" against the lord Abbot that had not yet been corrected (*non dum est transgressio domino Abbati correcta*). However, an unusually informative entry (1297) regarding trespass against the interests of two lords does not employ that term: Simon Cowherd was fined 4d and pledged because he mowed and carried off the lord's grass at Aunham from the strip of land marking the boundary between the lord Abbot's land and that of William le Moyne, although Simon claimed that he had bought a portion of that "boundary marker" from the reeve of William le Moyne.[23] The 1301 Upwood court roll contains a total of sixty entries, half of which concern trespass, yet the term *transgressio* is used only once, where Geoffrey le Pykeler is cited for unjustly cutting in what were obviously the meadow lots of seven other people, *ad dampnum*. When referring to cases of landed trespass against others, these early records use varied language, for example, "to [someone's] nuisance" (*ad nocumentum*), "for damage done" (*pro dampno facto*), and "it is ordered that it be repaired" (*preceptum est quod emendetur*), and the main focus is usually on the fine. In the record of 31 January 1307, there are sixty-nine entries, nineteen of which deal with trespass, but only one use of *transgressio*, this time in connection with defamation.

23 The entry reads as follows: *De Simone Vaccario quia falcauit et asportauit herbam domini apud Aunham de diuisa* [boundary marker] *domini Abbatis inter ipsum Abbatem et Willelmum le Moyne ratione quod emit portionem illius diuise de Messore dicti Willelmi iiiid.*

The 4 December 1307 court roll is overwhelmingly concerned with turf-digging and general trespassing (86 of its 121 entries deal with trespass), and thus invites a special consideration of the terminology used. Specifically, more than sixty people are cited for digging turves, including numerous outsiders.[24] These cases also include thirteen citations of trespass with animals, a form of trespass that occurred regularly but less frequently than trespass by individuals, at least in the pre-plague years. Yet, in this court roll with such a sharp spike in the incidence of trespass, the term *transgressio* is used only three times. It is used once for William Aubyn, who cut wood and an oak sapling worth 2s to be paid to the lord, for which he is in mercy 6d *pro transgressione*. This is followed by citations of others cutting wood in le Holt, breaking and taking off the lord's hedge, carrying off acorns, doing damage with cattle in Rokesgroue, and carrying wood off the same, none of which is referred to as a *transgressio*. The other two uses of the term concern a single case, cited in two different places in the court roll (yet appearing with the phrase *pro transgressione* each time), in which Richard son of Philipp and Thomas son of Geoffrey each tore the other's hood (*dilaterauit capuc'*). Perhaps the element of contempt for the person, discussed earlier, triggered the trespass terminology. Similarly, in the 1308 court, twenty-eight of seventy-four entries deal with trespass and *transgressio* is used only twice, once for nose-pulling and once for reversal of a water course. The general pattern here again is one where high levels of landed trespass are cited using a varied vocabulary, but where the term *transgressio* is rarely used, being reserved for unusual cases (defamation, cases where amount of damage done is very high, and trespass against the "king's peace"), or for trespass on the lord's land.

In the 1320s and 1330s *transgressio* continues to be used rarely, although landed trespass is frequent. The term's tendency to attach to cases between individuals continues, at somewhat elevated levels, in the 1326 roll, where *transgressio* is used in connection with eight separate instances. John son of Sarra is fined for false claim against Galfridus Swon in a plea of trespass; the jurors find that William

24 Outsider status is known either because it is stated specifically or, in cases where the person's name is not readily apparent as a local surname, is suggested by artisanal surnames (often a sign of itinerants), or the use of distraint (a method usually employed when the perpetrator cannot be fined because he or she comes from another lordship).

Pikeler and his wife committed trespass (*fecerunt transgressionem*) against Matilda Baroun, to her damages, and are fined *pro transgressione*, and Matilda Baroun in her turn defamed (*diffamauit*) the wife of William Pikeler to her damages, for which she is fined *pro transgressione*, as is William Pikeler for defaming Matilda. The interpersonal quality in trespass citations (indeed their adherence to the ongoing actions of just a few people) is also seen in Alice Dikoun's citations for beating both John, son of Stephen Collessone, and Agnes the wife of Stephen Collessone, damages and pledges being assigned in both cases. In the remaining two entries in this series of eight, the charge of trespass occurs in conjunction with distinctive arrangements for settling the case. Thomas Aspelon, who had defamed (*diffamauit*) two other villagers to their damage (*ad dampnum ipsorum*) of 6s 8d, was to pay 3s 4d to the scribes (*clericis*), and the remaining amount was to be placed in respect (that is, set aside) under the charge of Thomas (*ponatur in respectu sub latura eiusdem Thome*), with the provision that if he behave well to those two villagers, he would pay them nothing (*nichil eis soluat*). Thomas was also fined 40d *pro transgressione*. Finally, in a rather detailed arrangement between two villagers that uses *transgressio* twice, Stephen Crane acknowledged a debt of a measure of drage (a mix of oats and barley) to Elena Atte Hul for a trespass committed against her (*pro transgressione facta eidem Elene*), which he was to pay in two installments, one half this year and one half in the following year, in return for which Elena "released him from all actions that she could have against him by reason of trespass for the said grain" (*dicta Elena relaxat eidem Stephano* [*omnes*?] *actiones quas erga eum habere potuit ratione de transgressione pro blado supradicto*).

In 1329 the use of the term continues to increase to eighteen cases, here with an emphasis on protecting the lord's interests: an initial citation of *transgressio* in Rokesgrove, the lord's wood, followed by nine *pro eodem* ("for the same thing") notices (for example, *De Willelmo le Couper pro eodem vi d*), and three for trespass in the lord's grain with pigs (one entry followed by two *pro eodem* citations). The remaining trespass notices concern default on a debt payment and two cases of false plea, the first of which concerns the servant (*manupastus*) of Alice Wenington who committed trespass against Geoffrey Heringmongere. The next entry deals with the second case: the jurors state that Geoffrey was fined for a false plea against Alice in a plea of trespass (*in placito transgressionis*). The tendency found in the 1320s rolls, that is, reserving use of the trespass charge for acts of personal violation and for protection of the lord's interests, still seems fairly clear.

The fifteen trespass citations found in the brief 1331 roll all target trespass in the lord's wood, grain, and meadow. These notices are interspersed with entries about failing to come to the lord's work and about working badly in the lord's fields, thus emphasizing the connection between the protection of seigneurial interests and the use of the trespass citation. The 1332 roll is particularly full, and full especially of a wide variety of delicts: we read about tenants gathering acorns, cutting greenwood, cutting birches, appropriating the lord's land by digging, stopping up ditches, enlarging ditches, destroying a quickset hedge (*quamdam vivam hayam ad capud crofti sui*), cutting and carrying turves, gleaning badly, and committing hamsoken (assaulting someone in his or her own home); for example, Stephen son of Nicholas cut an oak and William Newman *Nativus domini* carried it off in his own cart outside the lord's wood (*in carecta sua propria extra boscum domini duxit*). There are also notices of default of suit to the lord's mill (using hand-mills and not the lord's mill) and receiving strangers. William Twyne made waste in his garden with trees (*fecit vastum in gardino suo de arboribus*, that is, wasted land for gardening by letting trees grow there), as did Geoffrey Siwelle, and Sarra wife of Henry encroached on the commons by enlarging her cowshed (*elargando vatatorium suum*).[25] Robert de Wenyngton didn't keep vigil the previous summer, that is, he didn't take his turn acting as night watchman (*non servauit vigiliam in estate*). Amid these numerous and varying entries, there are only seven *transgressio* citations: these concern villagers being fined for not prosecuting in a plea of trespass, for false claim in a plea of trespass, or for trespass in the lord's grain and wood. One of the more detailed cases using the trespass citation concerns the jurors' finding that Stephen Hurre "lost the lord's chattels" (that is, settled this case in another lord's court)[26]

25 Note the frequent use of the possessive pronoun in these entries: his croft, his own wagon, his house, his garden, her cowshed.

26 The Upwood court of 1339 contains an interesting entry along these same lines: that William de Wenington "by praising drew his neighbors to a court Christian" (*adulando traxit vicinos suos in curia Christianitatis*), that is, an ecclesiastical court, whereby they lost the lord's chattels.

by making an agreement (*pactum*) for trespass committed against lord William Moygne. In short, while it would not be correct to speak of a narrowly focused use of the trespass citation, it would be defensible to say that by the end of the first third of the fourteenth century certain selective applications or tendencies can be seen.

At this point perceptible changes appear in the history of the trespass charge. In 1333, there are twenty-three cases that feature the *transgressio* label, eighteen of which are trespass with animals in the field or trespass in the lord's wood. In this court roll and that of 1334, again, all sorts of trespass are recorded, by natives, by foreigners, against the lord, against other villagers, and against the common, and the charge takes many forms: misplacing dungheaps, reversing water courses, not cleaning ditches, illicit plowing, making purprestures, building an oven on the common (*Iohannes Bonde fundauit unum furnum in communa*, Upwood 1334), enlarging ditches by digging, encroaching on the king's way, and leading the carts of outsiders into the marsh at night to steal turves (*noctanter duxit extraneas carectas in marisco*). However, the term *transgressio* is only used in certain cases. Thus, in 1333, two men (the names are mostly illegible but one of them is referred to as *Dominus*) are fined for not having John the parson of Wistowe to answer to the lord for trespass with his (John's) cart in the lord's wood, an entry that perhaps attracted the trespass label because another lord (*Dominus*) was involved, and because the trespasser was a cleric. In 1334, an entry citing William le Coupere for trespass with his horse at le Frith (*pro transgressione cum equis suis apud le Frith*) is followed by ten names *pro eodem* sometimes specifying with animals, sometimes not, some specifying *in blado domini* ("in the lord's grain") with animals. Then a listing (that begins with the rector of the church of Wistow, that is, another reference to John) "for trespass made in the lord's wood" (*pro transgressione facta in bosco domini*) is followed by nineteen *pro eodem* citations. The next two citations name John Kyng for disturbing the lord's workers and for withdrawing early (*ante tempus*) from the lord's work; neither contains the *transgressio* charge. Then follow five more citations of *transgressio in blado domini*, mixed in with citations that Richard Baroun broke the lord's park, that John Kyng plowed badly and that Robert Flemyng disturbed the lord's workers. Thus, clearer groupings are emerging in the text of the court roll around *transgressio* in the lord's grain, in the meadow, and in the wood; in addition, the placing of other entries concerning the lord's business (for example, work defaults) among these *transgressio* citations suggests a closer pairing of *transgressio* with his landed interests. No such citation occurs in connection with encroachments on the king's way, the oven on the common, or trespass in the marsh, all of which are dealt with in the first part of the court roll, along with defaults and assize of ale, and monitoring of the hue and cry: the "tenant" section of the court roll does not employ the term *transgressio*, which begins to be used quite suddenly in this roll for landed trespass on the lord's interests.

The 1339 court roll repeats this structure and elaborates upon it: indeed a new (although short-lived) organizational mood pervades the minutes of this session, and the deliberate assignation of *transgressio* to the lord's business is clear. The entry section of the court roll begins with the brewers, followed by defaults of court attendance, then citations regarding encroachments on the king's way (not cleaning a ditch, not cutting a hedge, making a pit, making a ditch, appropriating land by plowing, etc.) and notices of those outside the manor with licence. Then a new division, the bailiff's presentments, begins: *Ballivus presentat quod* (including *pro eodem* citations). This is followed by citations of villagers *pro transgressione* in the lord's meadow, interspersed with a few work defaults. A section headed *Wodewardus presentat quod* is followed by trespass "in the lord's wood" (*in bosco domini*). This is followed in its turn by work defaults under *Bedellus presentat*, and then cases of false claim, debt pleas, recognition of debt, and the like, that is, purely villager concerns; none of these citations employs the term transgression. Finally, the section made up of the jurors' presentments follows (*Iurati presentant quod)*, and includes citations for those who have withdrawn from the lord's mill, entries concerning those who have made waste in the marsh by "digging outside the bounds placed by the community" (*fodiendo extra bondas per communitatem positas*), and a final section that appears as a kind of unit by the predominance of women cited: six women and one man are cited for gleaning badly, a heriot payment (that is, a payment due to the lord from a tenement upon the death of the head of household) by Etheldred, widow of Robert Flemyng (*relicta Roberti Flemyng*), is recorded, and two women are cited for sexual misconduct (*leyrwite*).

The 1339/1340 court roll begins with villagers' business, that is, presentments by the ale tasters, then those by the *Iurati*, totaling together about sixty-five entries, in which *transgressio* figures only once (in connection with a charge of false claim). In the section beginning *Ballivus presentat quod* there are some sixty citations, starting with the notice that Sarah le Reue trespassed in the lord's meadow with four horses (*Sarra le Reue fecit transgressionem in pratis domini cum quatuor equis*), with numerous *pro eodem* citations following. The listing of those trespassing in the grain begins with Agnes le Reue, for trespass with pigs in le longWong, and is followed by notices of work poorly performed, tenants withdrawing from work, and the like, including some very specific activities: William Heryng trampled the lord's fallow at Duffhousdole with his cart (*quia calcauit Warett' domini cum carecta sua apud Duffhousdole*) and William Edward withdrew inopportunely (*recessit intempestiue*) from the lord's work, as did four others. The Woodward's section (*Attach' Wodeward*) lists some twenty-five people cited *pro transgressione in bosco domini* interspersed with a few work citations. Citations of trespass are almost entirely confined to the presentments of the bailiff and woodward. The record ends with a list of those outside the manor, thus completing the seigneurial portion of the record.

The 1344 roll shows the same basic divisions and the same tendency to reserve the *transgressio* label, with a growing exclusivity, for cases touching the lord's interests. Yet there are other related phenomena whose appearance may help us decipher these developments. Most striking is the increasing use of place names of fields and parts of fields in the narrative of the court roll, which had begun in the rolls of the earlier 1330s. There are some forty-five place names cited in three court rolls for Upwood (1340, 1344, 1347), including Hynewich, Fenfurlong, Halwod, Chichebury Feld, and Ryecroftdole. Such place names become standard in the court rolls from this time on into the fifteenth-century series and (as we will see in more detail in Chapter Five) they are joined by new names and changes in naming conventions. Thus, in the same decade when trespass is increasing in frequency, is more often committed with animals, and shows signs of being reserved for the lord's landed interests, these parcels of meadow, arable, and wood are also being named and noted, entering more overtly into the conduct of public business in the court.

The next surviving record, for 1344, is presented entirely by the jurors, except for brewing citations, so the brief experimentation with separate sections for the bailiff, beadle, and woodward seems to have ended with the court of 1339/40. With one exception,[27] all items concerning the brewers, default of attendance, watercourses, the hue and cry, gleaning badly, making waste in the marsh, and outsiders taking their wagons into the marsh (*carectas extraneorum in marisco*) are cited without use of the *transgressio* label, while matters that more nearly concern seigneurial interest are so labeled.

In the court roll for 1347, more place names are cited in comparison with the period before the 1340s. Notably, the term *transgressio* occurs somewhat more freely throughout the court roll text and is not confined to trespass on the lord's land: a citation in this court roll records that John Wadilowe was fined 2d for receiving an outsider trespassing in the common fields (*extraneum trespantem bladum communitatis*); *transgressio* is also used in four cases for inter-villager trespass, for example, Thomas Peny trespassed against Thomas de Thornhawe (*Convictum est per Iuratos quod Thomas Peny fecit transgressionem Thome de Thornhawe*). These citations are mixed in with entries regarding false claim, unjust detention, and other matters of purely villager interest. At the same time, notices about appropriating the commons are also increasing in frequency: John ate Welle by plowing took a portion of common land eight feet by six feet in size (*arando appropriauit de communa*), as did Robert Edward, Agnes Newman, and Cristina widow of Richard son of Simon, while John Galioun dug into a common boundary marker between the fields of Upwood and the hamlet of Raveley. These data suggest that the interests of lord and tenant, which had always been similar, are beginning to be perceived as overlapping or merging. This 1347 court also contains the earliest entry regarding the leasing of *terra dominicata*, the lord's demesne land.[28]

27 Under the section beginning *Conuictum est per Iuratos quod*, that is, villagers' business, there is a single entry that records that John de Nedham trespassed against John Bonde and his wife Amabil to their damages 40d (*John de Nedham fecit transgressionem Iohanni Bonde et Amabil' uxori eius ad dampna 40d*). The reason for associating trespass with this entry is not known.

28 "John Henry gives the lord 3d for the judgment of the Court concerning demesne land at As—Weye which he and Nicholaus Cowhirde took [held] by a shared lease" (*Iohannes Henry dat domino iiid pro consideratione Curie de terra dominicata apud As—Weye quam ipse et Nicholaus Cowhirde cepit ad firmam diuidend'*).

In 1349, the year plague struck Upwood, sixty-two citations of landed trespass are given, forty of which have the *transgressio* label. Seventeen of the forty continue to occur in connection with the lord's landed interests: *in prato domini, in blado domini* ("in the lord's meadow," "in the lord's grain"). Even the rector of the village church is cited "for trespass with animals in the lord's garden" (*De Rectore ecclesie pro transgressione cum bestiis in gardino domini*). The remaining trespass cases concern trespass in the common fields and woods (for example, in Estweye, in Westweye, in Uppenalecroft).

Predictably, change grows even more marked after 1350: both the activity of trespass and the label *transgressio* increase in incidence and also undergo a change in nature. Before 1350, trespass was most frequently in the form of commission, as in the 1278 entry in Ellington's roll that Thomas Bolle "placed metes and bound unjustly on William Aldyth's meadow," or the 1311 entry recording that Walter le Noble must answer for an unlawful encroachment (*purprestura*) he made in digging a ditch between himself and Ranulph Grym. Other citations, in addition to those already discussed, indicate the variety of trespass in this period: in 1340 Richard Plouwrghte, Nicholas Miller, and Agnes Buk were each fined for placing a dungheap on the king's street; in Upwood's 1295 court, Agnes the widow of John le Vacher (Cowherd) was cited for digging a ditch that impinged upon the king's way to the nuisance of passers-by, and also in plowing cut into a mere between herself and Simon le Vacher. In Ellington in 1325 John Brymbel appropriated common land at le Madheued six perches in width and five perches in length. In 1332 William son of Radulph made a purpresture by placing a dungheap at Foxholes, and he planted thorns (*spinas*) and willows across from his meadow in the common (*in communa*). In Upwood in that same year, Thomas Aspelon impinged by plowing on the land of Thomas Bigg at Cambokhegs.

After 1350, in spite of continuing population loss and a relative abundance of land released onto the local land market, landed trespass continues to have a high profile in the minutes of the court. Indeed, by the early 1400s most court roll entries are concerned with presentments of trespass in the fields and woods. However, the offences involve acts of omission as much as, or more than, commission. Villagers named each other, in large numbers, for not cleaning ditches, not mending hedges, and not closing gates that open onto the common fields, forms of trespass that suggest the faltering of local conventions regarding boundaries. A grouping of seven such entries is found in Ellington's court of January 1426 and indicates the varied nature of the new spirit of trespass in the early fifteenth century: not cleaning his ditch at le Bakno, not cleaning a ditch below his garden, not cleaning Rousdyche in Sybthorp, not cleaning his ditch in the same place and at Totehill, not removing a portion of a house standing on the common way (*parcellam cuiusdam domus stantis*), and not cleaning his ditch at Lynlond, and having (that is, not moving) a straw pile standing on a common path (*unum tassum straminis stantem in commun' semita ad nocumentum*). The lord Abbot is also cited for acts of omission: in 1438 he (*dominus Abbas*) and John Hendesson are fined for not cleaning a ditch at Snapende; in 1441 for not cleaning a ditch at the bridge near the pigsty (*apud Pontem iuxta porc*[*eria*]) and not repairing the (consequently) flooded roadway (*submersam viam*); and in 1448 for not cleaning a ditch at Frythdiche and damaging another at [Nest?]halediche.[29] The crowded landscape of the pre-1350 village gave way to a relative dearth of people; and when people disregarded their neighbors' rights following the sudden assault on traditional tenurial structures, that disregard often took the form of a failure to act.

The post-1350 rolls are filled with entries that exemplify a new spirit of violation by inaction and also find new language to deal with it. In Upwood's 1395 court record tenants are cited for not coming to shear the lord's sheep, badly mowing, not coming to plow, not trimming hedges, and "making waste on the lord's bondland with ruinous houses" (*fecit wastum super bond' domini de domibus ruinosis*). In 1409 William Bracer made waste on a half virgate of land "which he holds but does not plow" (*quam tenet sed non arat*). The 1406 record cites the following ruinous properties: two rooms, a house, two cottages, a room, and a barn. In the court of (8?) October 1425 it is noted that a local bridge, Howbrige, is extremely broken down, *est valde defectiuus*. In 1402 John Albyn left a gate open, possibly where a lane leads to the fields (*super campum ubi venellam* [illegible] *terram ad dampna communitatis*). The 1453 court roll includes two entries that target group inaction: all the tenants of Upwood and

29 No form of the word *transgressio* is used in any of these cases. That usage is reserved for a group of three villagers who "are trespassers" (*transgressores sunt*) in the grain, and two outsiders (from nearby Spaldewyck) who "are trespassers" in the common fields and pasture.

Raveley are to properly clean the ditches around the entire town (*circa totam villatam*), and each Brewster is to brew the entire year once she has begun, under a fine of 3s 4d to the lord and 3s 4d to the church (*pena cuilibet Brasiatrici quod postquam incipiet bras' quod brasiabit per totum annum*). In 1424 it is proclaimed that a penalty of 12d is attached to animals bound *solute* (loosely, negligently) in the grain fields (*Ponitur in pena quod nulle bestis capientur solute in bladis sub pena 12d*). The sense of limits not being maintained was furthered by the depredations of outsiders and transients (often indicated by their occupational surnames), such as Simon Schepherd, Umfrid Taillour, and others who, in 1378, took turves outside the marsh "with the wagons of outsiders, against the usage of the vill" (*cum carectis extraneis contra usagium ville*).

Beginning in the second half of the fourteenth century, the substance and language provided by the court roll narrative suggest a fairly rapid alteration of the structure of land-use rights, and a corresponding though slower modification of the understanding that lay behind it. A single 1350 Upwood entry summarizes many of these elements: "And that Hosloc Wauk is a common trespasser with his animals in the neighbors' grain" (*Et quod Hosloc Wauk est communis transgressor in blado vicinorum cum bestiis*), where we see an explicit emphasis both on neighbors' rights and on the presence of animals in the act of trespass. Most relevant for our discussion here, we also see an extension of the use of the term *transgressio* itself, a change that had begun in the court rolls of the mid-1340s. In the post-plague era, *transgressio* enters into regular use for trespass against neighbors, individuals, and the lord. In the same 1350 court roll that cited Hosloc Wauk, interspersed with notices of gleaning badly, theft of wood, adultery, false claim, unjust detention, pledges who failed to have their pledgees to answer, and work default, we find citations "for trespass with horses in the neighbors' grains" (*pro transgressione cum equis in bladis vicinorum*), "for trespass against Richard Wardebusk to his damages" (*pro transgressione facta Ricardo Wardebusk ad dampna*), and "for trespass with pigs in the lord's grain" (*pro transgressione cum porcis in blado domini*), followed by numerous *pro eodem* citations.[30] This use of *transgressio* prevails in the court rolls from this point onward.

30 Indeed, the fact that large numbers of people were committing the same type of trespass in the same place, possibly even engaging in forms of

Upwood's court roll for 1390, more concise than those of the pre-plague era, is one in which the sense of too few people and of things not done continues, and in which trespass overshadows every other activity, with further variations on entry types appearing; for example, John Aubes junior enclosed some of the common of the "whole community" to its harm (*Et quod Iohannes Aubes junior includit communam totius communitatis ad nocumentum*). The record for Upwood's court of 28 October 1421 shows the changes to the village landscape that make it abundantly clear why the lord abbot wanted out of direct demesne management. The entries about uncleaned ditches, unrepaired bridges, tenements, and bakehouses, unclosed gates, surcharged pastureland, and illegally dug turves, matters that were once of seigneurial as well as tenant interest, were now tenant matters alone because the abbot of Ramsey, like most early fifteenth-century estate holders, had leased his demesne to the tenants.[31]

The New Aggression of the Fifteenth Century

The histories of individuals are instructive in mapping out and analyzing these changes. Nicholas Aubyn (1405–1443), from a prominent

---

group trespass, led the scribe for the court roll of 1360 to experiment with abbreviating its format: instead of a running text stating a particular instance of trespass followed by the *pro eodem* citations, he lists names in columns, joins them with a line and enters a single notice: "for trespass in le Snape with horses," "because they made sheaves badly," "because they did not come to cart the lord's grain to Dounham well" (*pro transgressione in le Snape cum equis, quia male fecerunt ligamina, quia non venerunt ad carect' bladum domini apud Dounham well*). Villager entries, such as hue and cry, assault, and rescue, are given in the traditional running, narrative-type form in this court roll. With respect to group trespass, J.A. Raftis in *Peasant Economic Development within the English Manorial System* (Montreal, 1996), 61–62, 26–27, suggests that group refusals to perform work services should be seen as a "category of group action" similar to "large-scale trespasses" committed by tenants pasturing their beasts and selling turves to outsiders.

31 The abbot's remaining landed concerns were presented briefly near the beginning of the roll by the woodward (four outsiders taking wood from the lord's wood, four Upwood villagers taking underbrush), then the bailiff presented two men for trespassing with animals in the lord's wheat.

and long-lived village family, is a useful representative of trespassing activity in fifteenth-century Upwood:[32] of the forty-nine entries that survive for his forty-year career in the village, half involve some form of trespass or failure to repair his tenement. Aubyn is cited for trespass with horses in the lord's barley (1405), with a cow and calf in Rokesgrove (1411), with a mare (or mares) in the peas (1418), with pigs in Uppenhalecroft and geese in Estwey (1424), with horses in the barley (1425), with pigs in the grass (1428), with pigs in le Snape (1429), and with a mare (or mares) in the grain in Bentymadole (1438). We can integrate his individual history with the phenomenon of group trespass, since this 1438 entry also names thirteen other people who trespassed in the same place with pigs, horses, mares, and foals, and in turn is followed by two similar entries. In the first, seven people from both Upwood and the neighboring vill of Raveley are named for trespass in Duffhousedole with geese, mares, and common herds, and in the second, three men are fined for trespassing with horses and pigs in the lord's grain in Estwey. Indeed, the frequency of trespass with animals everywhere in the fifteenth-century village suggests that the streets that seemed so empty of people now teemed with animals, and that the atmosphere of lawlessness in the village arose in some measure from emptiness. The study of village trespass must consider the ways in which the presence of animals extended the range, varied the forms, and contributed to a more aggressive version of that activity.[33]

Notably, there is also a considerable increase in the number of strays appearing in the village, a type of entry that occurred only rarely in the court rolls before the plague. In the courts of 1297, 1334, and

32 For a discussion of him and his family in another context, see Olson, *A Chronicle*, 224–227.

33 An interesting variation of the extension of trespass and the increased mobility of villagers can be seen in a 1454 bylaw in Upwood's court roll, which fixes a penalty on anyone of (the hamlet of) Raveley who allows anyone, native or outsider, to go beyond their gardens (and thus into the fields), whether a walker or a rider (*quod non permittant aliquem ire ultra ortos suos neque pedestrem neque equestrem*). And see the court of 1450 where it is noted that (Richard) Benyle of Walton broke through a hedge, rode beyond the lord's grain (*ultra bladum domini*), and left a hole where animals were able to get through and do damage (*Et per quam fracionem animalia fecerunt Dampna*).

1339/40, a total of three strays are cited (one of which is a piglet "found wandering," *invenientem vagantem*, so probably not from outside Upwood). After 1350, strays are noted in fifteen courts between 1353 and 1452 (indeed this becomes almost a standard entry type, with a notation *Extrahura*, "Strays," in the margin). The 1350 court roll itself has approximately ten entries (the text is partly illegible in this spot) dealing with strays and accounting for them: foals, young oxen, and sheep are mentioned, as are two foals worth 13s 4d which an outsider from Ramsey had appropriated (*appropriauit sibi*, the same language used for stealing land by plowing or infringing on the common or the king's way) without licence of the bailiffs and which he had not yet proved were his own (*quos non dum probauit esse suos*). Other villagers are named for holding strays formerly someone else's for which they are to answer, and one villager is cited for receiving two fillies and four mares "from the chattels of Andrew Flemyng" in payment of a debt owed him by Flemyng (who presumably has died). Another entry notes that twenty sheep died *in defectu prepositi*, "for lack of a reeve" (that is, they were not watched properly).[34]

Trespass with animals is the dominant form of trespass by the early fifteenth century, overshadowing though not completely eclipsing the earlier, more varied, more localized profile of trespass by individuals. Indeed, the reality of animals straying and animals in trespass in large numbers are all part of a continuum of fewer people, more animals, and ambiguity about the management of flocks and herds. The division of land and livestock, the proper allocation of land and animals, the circulation of resources, and the traditional understanding attached to these arrangements upon which the common field regime depended, all had been disturbed. Recidivist trespassers like Nicholas Aubyn come to share the stage with trespassers en masse with animals – this is the new aggression of the fifteenth century, and the efforts to control it become accordingly the new policing, in contrast to the collective policing measures that had flourished earlier (hue and cry, suretyship, tithing groups), and whose supervision had occupied much of the business of the pre-plague courts.

34 For a fuller description of Ellington and Upwood in the post-plague era, see Olson, *A Chronicle*, Chapter Four. For the *Extrahura* marginal note, see courts for the years 1353, 1391(2), 1406, 1409, 1420, 1425 (1 and 2), 1427, 1430, 1443, and 1452. The remaining four courts are 1365, 1421, 1422, and 1428(2).

The New Policing

As the incidence of trespass continued to escalate, trespass with animals became all the more destructive. An array of instruments was devised, and old practices modified, to contain this destruction, such as the dismantling of the hue and cry, which had now become too confusing.[35] (We shall see in Chapter Five that changes were also occurring in the naming of the village landscape, chiefly in the attaching of family names to land.) Post-plague efforts to contain disorder in the village tended to use traditional mechanisms in new ways. This new policing included an effort to marshal the associations attached to the vocabulary of *transgressio* to discourage trespass against each other. We have seen that over the first third of the fourteenth century, as use of the term increased it was gradually reserved for the lord's interests, and thus played a part in maintaining distinctions between two different kinds of land, seigneurial and customary. Creating such distinctions was an ongoing phenomenon in the village: we recall, for example, the ease with which land passed from individual to collective use in the course of normal common field operations. In a farming community, the capacity and need to devise highly nuanced words for many different kinds of land, to name and rename land, created a rich and vast vocabulary.[36] Modernizing old practices and uses of vocabulary to preserve old, still potent associations was a typical mechanism of social regulation in the late medieval village. Something of the earlier power of *transgressio*, both in protecting the demesne and in protecting personal honor, is suggested to us by the use to which it was put in the post-plague era of demesne leasing: an increased employment of the term and an extension of its "vernacular usage" were deployed in the fifteenth-century village in the hopes they could still be effective deterrents.

Thus, the connection that has been made between the close monitoring of trespass on the demesne and trespass with animals to an

35 These points are also fully developed in Olson, *A Chronicle*, Chapter Four.

36 Plowland, mondaymanland, akermanland, cotland, forland, inlond, intakes, yardland, etc. See *A Medieval Farming Glossary of Latin and English Words*, ed. John L. Fisher (London, 1968), for numerous examples. A powerful sense of the regional diversity of this vocabulary is provided in Baker and Butlin, *Studies of Field Systems*.

"active guardianship of the lord's interests" is accurate.[37] However, to argue from this for a one-dimensional view of the court, concerned primarily with the protection of seigneurial interests, shortchanges the power of both change and symbolic thought that were fundamental to medieval village culture. Rather, the power that came to be attached to the trespass charge, by an emphasis on protecting the demesne and on defending individuals against personal violation, later entered the flow of cultural capital so characteristic of village economy and society and was harnessed to deter trespass on the same land when it was held by villagers. In a way, then, the attachment of "trespass" to specific land in the village resembles the tendency for rent, services, renderings, etc., to attach to land ("the tenement answers for"). The term once used to defend the lord's demesne and landed interests as the largest single shareholder in the village was, by c. 1400, being used to defend the same physical space (the old demesne) that was now leased out to tenants: in short, the same land is being defended against the same threats and encroachments using the same terminology. Now villagers were relying on those old associations in a post-plague setting to defend land they were leasing. In addition, customary land, which had previously been considered separate from demesne land, was now being defended in the same way. The careful protection of the lord's rights as a landholder in the village before 1350 became the model for protection for all after 1350, in an age of rapid change. If villagers could "think with women" and "think with men," they could also "think with the land" and "think with lords."

We may summarize much of the material for the pre-plague era as suggesting that lord and villager had a common outlook, a common interest, and saw themselves as beneficiaries of a regime based on common rights. The presence of demesne land and thus of immediate seigneurial interests, alongside the tenant smallholder interest, were essential parts of the diversification of landed "shares" in the village and were also counterparts creating a tension that made the system work. However, by the end of the fourteenth century, with the withdrawal of the lord from demesne farming, that tension dissipated, though the language remained. Also, land began to be concentrated among a smaller body of tenants, whose average tenements were larger than they had been before 1350. Many of these

37 See note 5 above.

changes become permanent features, indeed, become in the course of time the new common center around which future development occurs ("concentricity").

Increased tenant mortality and mobility, large-scale demesne leasing, an acceleration in the rate of the taking up and abandoning of tenements, and the beginnings of land-engrossing on the part of some families: these were the forces that were undermining the old partibility and fungibility of the common field system. The body of interests and people who enjoyed land-use rights in the village was increasingly simplified over our period, in a number of ways: the integrity of the common was repeatedly violated by increasingly transient tenants, and the variety of tenants and tenement sizes was reduced. In addition, the seigneurial demesne no longer survived as a counterweight to tenants' identity in an environment dominated by a shareholder's logic: tenants could only trespass against each other by the end of the fourteenth century.

We have noted Kerridge's observation that "the supersession of small occupiers by a small number of large ones, sounded the death-knell of the common fields."[38] This "supersession" of many smallholders by a small number of largeholders was a profound shift in the late medieval village. Common field use and stewardship lost ground to rights of land held in severalty, that is, held separately, individually, as private instead of common property. The less varied stock of characters, the smaller pool of personalities, the shrinking spectrum of tenement size that had once included smallholder and the abbot of Ramsey alike, were all components of a changing local landscape. We will consider in the final chapter how the villager of the fifteenth century continued to "think with the land" in ingenious ways to adjust to these and other changes.

38 Kerridge, *The Common Fields of England*, 4.

CHAPTER FIVE

The Loss of Memory and the Memory of Loss: Naming the Landscape in the Late Medieval Village

In 1349 the Arab historian Ibn Khaldun, who lost most of his family to the epidemic, recorded his reaction to the "great mortality," observing that "it was as if the voice of existence in the world had called out for oblivion and restriction, and the world responded to its call."[1] Examining the ravages of plague and the associated ravaging of memory is the focus of the present chapter. Historians have always been interested in gauging the plague's impact, an interest that has moved in recent years in the direction of uncovering and explaining a more detailed chronology of reaction and adjustment.[2] Because plague recurred periodically, an unpredictable common killer became a normal feature of the landscape: the "Great Pestilence" of the mid-fourteenth century was an event whose memory was not allowed to fade. These circumstances invite the study of local response. Indeed a recent synthesis, which provides a blow-by-blow account of the epidemic in the period 1346–1353, argues in particular that the "mechanisms and processes of adjustment and societal change triggered by the Black Death should be put more at the centre of manorial studies in the future."[3]

1 Cited in Robert S. Gottfried, *The Black Death: Natural and Human Disaster in Medieval Europe* (New York; London, 1983), 41–42.

2 Samuel K. Cohn's comparative study of six Italian cities using testamentary evidence has shown that the first recrudescence of plague in 1362–1363 introduced a new level of fear that radically altered patterns of bequeathal, patterns which had not been affected by the initial outbreak nearly fifteen years earlier. Now people understood for the first time that the deadly menace was permanently among them and might strike at any moment. See Samuel K. Cohn, Jr, *The Cult of Remembrance and the Black Death: Six Renaissance Cities in Central Italy* (Baltimore, 1992).

3 Ole J. Benedictow, *The Black Death, 1346–1353: The Complete History* (Woodbridge, 2004), 379.

As we have seen frequently in the above chapters, court rolls and related documents were well-placed witnesses to a period in which Europe's population may have declined by as much as two-thirds or more.[4] By the 1370s and 1380s English rural populations had had more than a generation's worth of experience making adjustments, in particular to the reversal of the land-to-people ratio that had existed in the typical medieval village before 1350: relatively speaking, where land had been scarce and people plentiful, now people were scarce and land was plentiful. In a time of rapid turnover of individuals and families caused by death and migration, post-plague village society experienced a marked increase in violence among villagers and in the vandalism of tenements and dilapidation of properties. Traditional methods of policing the village declined and were accompanied by a shift in the court's fining practice from collective to individual liability, suggesting a "privatization" of villagers' understanding of social control and conflict. The lowering and simplification of women's profile in the village court are also marked features of the rolls in this period.[5]

How did the people of Upwood and Ellington adjust to such a catastrophic winnowing of their numbers, and to what one contemporary called the "stupefaction" of "seeing the pain"?[6] Again, we take advantage of the abundance of names in the court rolls, reasoning that since names possess the power to identify and to "fix" reality for those who devise and use them, changes in naming

4 David Herlihy, *The Black Death and the Transformation of the West*, ed. Samuel K. Cohn, Jr (Cambridge, MA, 1997), 19: "Europe about 1420 could have counted barely more than a third of the people it contained one hundred years before." Benedictow, in *The Black Death, 1346–1353*, on the other hand, puts the mortality rate of the first epidemic alone at between 50% and 60% of the people of Europe.

5 See J.A. Raftis, "The Concentration of Responsibility in Five Villages," *Mediaeval Studies* 28 (1966): 92–118, for a detailed study of post-plague village life. A more recent discussion and relevant bibliography are in Sherri Olson, *A Chronicle of All That Happens: Voices from the Village Court in Medieval England* (Toronto, 1996), especially Chapter Four, where changes in village population, officeholding structures, and methods of social control are fully discussed.

6 This was the observation of Agnolo di Tura, a Sienese chronicler (cited in Gottfried, *The Black Death: Natural and Human Disaster*, 45).

practices are meaningful. Disaggregation of surname and topographical name formation will show that naming practices were involved in the response both to population pressure in the late thirteenth and early fourteenth centuries and to the relative emptiness of the village in the years around 1400.

How were people and land named over our period, and how did those practices change in the face of the demographic catastrophes of the fourteenth century? As we saw in Chapter Four, trespass, a constant feature of rural life, underwent a change in its nature and its vocabulary: acts of omission (as opposed to commission) assumed a higher profile, as did trespass with animals, and the terminology of trespass was used in an attempt to bring pre-plague associations to its post-1350 applications. The epidemic also impinged upon the mechanisms of social memory, fostering responses that represent some of the lesser-known rituals by which the living "tamed" death in late medieval Europe.[7]

The Work of Memory

Following recent scholarship, "memorial activity" is interpreted broadly here to mean "making present the voices of what is past, not to entomb either the past or the present, but to give them life together in a place common to both in memory."[8]

7 The notion of "taming death" has been described by Philippe Ariès, *The Hour of Our Death*, trans. Helen Weaver (New York, 1981). The cultural shifts induced throughout European society in the post-plague era represent a story often told in the historiography of the last century, much of it once inspired by the thesis of the "waning Middle Ages," and focused on developments within elite circles as representative. Current scholarship rejects older notions of decadence, seeing instead an extremely fertile response to mass mortality in the outpouring of resources for memorial services and prayers for the dead after 1350. See, for example, Eamon Duffy, *The Stripping of the Altars: Traditional Religion in England, c. 1400–c. 1580* (New Haven, 1992).

8 Mary Carruthers, *The Book of Memory: A Study of Memory in Medieval Culture* (Cambridge, 1990), 260. Carruthers describes medieval civilization as "fundamentally memorial" (p. 8). Also see James Fentress and Chris Wickham, *Social Memory* (Oxford, 1992), for another influential study of memory.

If "we are what we remember," and "the way we present ourselves in our memories" is a "study of the way we are," then village memory was a crucial anchor of the community, providing it with "material for conscious reflection" in an "active search for meaning."[9] Memory plays a central role in the continuum of behavior and belief, action and thought, in the gathering and sifting of ideas and in their application, a continuum which we have envisioned as highly integrated in medieval agrarian society.[10] Thus, memory involves the remembering and reworking of the past in connection with living in the present. The working hypothesis of the present chapter is that the peasant "arts of memory" became more self-conscious in late medieval Europe, when the people, places, and images that had been traditional receptacles of memory were under siege. The court roll, a document based on the self-reporting of a community's affairs, is therefore implicitly embedded in local memory. From its vantage point inside village culture, the court required its suitors to consult their memories of the time that had elapsed, whether weeks or months, since the last court. Jurors were formally charged with the task of reporting the affairs of the community, but every villager had the same standing charge to report what he or she knew or had heard. As we have seen, officials, complainants, victims, and bystanders all brought their information and their stories to the court for public discussion and action. As we shall see, thinking of the court as a kind of "memory theatre"[11] allows us to extend our understanding of the

9 The quotations are from Fentress and Wickham, *Social Memory*, 7, 26, 73. Carruthers calls this process "retrieval and reflection," "recollection and reminiscence." *The Book of Memory*, 16.

10 This notion of a continuum of action, understanding, and belief was decribed years ago by Robert Redfield in *The Folk Culture of Yucatan* (Chicago, 1941), and more recently by Robert B. Goheen, "Peasant Politics? Village Community and the Crown in Fifteenth-Century England," *American Historical Review* 96 (1991): 42–62. Links between changing values and behavior in the village in connection with election to village office have been explored in Olson, "Jurors of the Village Court: Local Leadership Before and After the Plague in Ellington, Huntingdonshire," *Journal of British Studies* 30 (1991): 237–256; and in Olson, *A Chronicle*, Chapters Three and Four.

11 Fentress and Wickham cite several examples where geography itself has acted as a "sort of memory theatre ... a direct aid for the recall of the

performance dimensions of the court, as discussed in Chapter One, and to consider the role of the European village in the formation of late medieval "memorial culture."[12]

First, we must recall how the rolls functioned in the village before the Black Death, as discussed above, particularly in Chapter Three. By 1350, English villagers had a long history of using the court rolls in a variety of ways, as a permanent record for numerous types of arrangements, indeed as a kind of aide-mémoire. The terms of leases, debt and credit transactions, land exchanges, and licences of agreement were routinely entered into the court roll, as were the results of inquests that individual villagers had called for in previous courts. Such entries attest to some of the conventions that underpinned villagers' use of the court rolls, and the links between the records, the demands of daily life, and local memory.[13]

The later court rolls suggest that in the fifteenth-century village there developed a more conscious desire to retrieve and preserve past practice, and to consult memory. For example, the scribe on several occasions enrolled rediscovered (yet usually superseded) charters, wills, and bylaws, some dating back to the late thirteenth century. At the end of the 1454 Upwood court there is a memorandum recording the provisions of a testament of one Alice Stain for her husband and children, dating to the year 1388 (*millensimo trecentensimo octogensimo octavo*), with no apparent connection to any of the entries in that court roll. An entry in the 1430 record reveals a truly archaizing strain: John Miles "made his law four-handed" (an example of oath-helping, as described in the Introduction) that he was not bound to William Dobyn (*perfecit legem iiii manu quod non tenetur Willelmo Dobyn in* [illegible]).[14] In 1441 it was announced that no one hence-

past." Fentress and Wickham, *Social Memory*, 93; their discussion centers around instances where the lapse between event and memory is much greater than those being studied here. Also see Raphael Samuel, *Theatres of Memory* (London, 1994), for a discussion of this term with respect to recent British popular culture.

12 See note 8 above.

13 The issue of peasant memory in Ellington and Upwood is briefly touched upon in Olson, *A Chronicle*, 230 with n2.

14 This is the 22 July 1430 court roll, and this notation is followed by a series of entries revealing charges of debt and trespass between Dobyn and Miles.

forth was to plow le havedom' except the lord, "according to custom from ancient time" (*secundum consuetudinem ex antique* [*sic*] *tempore*),[15] and in 1448 all capital pledges were reminded, under penalty of a fine, to collect *capitagium* (the chevage, or head tax) to be paid annually to the Steward as was anciently done, before he has his say (*coram Seneschallo antique* [*sic*] *tempore fuerit ante veredictum suum dicendum*). At the end of the Upwood courts for 1427 and 1428 there is a memorandum regarding how many bundles of turves tenants could dig, depending on tenement size. This was an item of acute contemporary concern in the 1420s, given the level of trespass through illegal digging of turves by resident tenants and even more elusive outsiders, yet the entry specifically states that these turf allowances were a concession of Abbot John, whose abbacy covered the period 1286–1316.[16] Both entries conclude with the note that "This letter was found in an old book of the steward" (*Ista litera inuenta fuit in antiquo libro senescalli*). Finally, it was in the court held in Upwood on 18 October 1428 that an eighty-four-year-old villager, John Hicson, was sworn in as a special juror to give information regarding possession of a parcel of woodland in the village.

These distinctive fifteenth-century entries are lineal descendants of the conventions surrounding the use of the court roll in earlier periods, and suggest an intensification of long-standing practices that relied in part upon the village's social memory. Whether the principal agent was the abbey administration, the major tenants, the whole body of customaries, or all of these, the minds at work agreed that the antiquity of the practice or of the authority enhanced its applicability

15 Compare this phrasing with the simpler phrasing used in earlier court rolls: *secundum consuetudinem, secundum consuetudinem prehabitam* ("according to custom," "according to established custom"). Another variant also found in the 1448 record concerns someone enclosing land who thus "made his private [land] where it ought to be common. And it has been [common land] from a time when memory does not exist of the contrary" (*Et fecit inde separalem suum ubi debet esse communem. Et solebat esse a tempore cuius contrarii non existit* [*memoria*]).

16 *Memorandum quod Abbas Iohannes unus predecessor istius abbatis concessit quod*, etc. There is a slight difference in the entry between the courts; the text for the court of 18 October 1428 is given here. The entry for the court of 27 October 1427 simply reads *Memorandum quod Johannes Abbas concessit quod*, etc.

and desirability. Evident too is the traditional idea, shared by the monastic administration and the tenantry alike, that important information should be posted in the court roll.

Occasionally, the court rolls even provide direct evidence of memory faltering, in spite of assistance by a written record: in Upwood, for example, Walter Fraunce was cited as outside the manor in more than thirty courts from 1386 down to the year 1430, where it is noted that he is dead (*mortuus*). His name then reappears, a quarter of a century later, in the 1456 court roll with the information that the villagers do not know where he and four others are now staying (*ubi modo trahunt moram ignorant*). In short, twenty-six years after Fraunce was reported as deceased, the current generation seems to have forgotten that he was dead.[17] The only memory left of him is that no one knows where he is.[18]

17 There are numerous other examples of villagers listed, year after year, for being outside the fee, such as Alice and Agnes Heryng, daughters of Edmund Heryng, who are listed in almost every court roll from 1403 to 1456 as outside the village at Bury St Edmunds. Agnes is listed again in 1473 and 1483. In the court of 1405 it is noted that one and a half virgates of land once held by William Robyn are now in the lord's hand (*in manu domini*), and that he and his brother John are outside the vill. This William is also listed as absent in nearly every court down to 1456. In Ellington, Nicholas and Thomas Foot are cited in court and account records from 1373 down to the 1450s, and John Foot from 1432 to 1460. The account rolls of the 1440s and 1450s continue to record the nonpayment of Nicholas's fee to be outside the vill, even though it is noted that he was dead in the record of 1443 (*nichil quia mortuus*).

18 The Fraunce family appeared in Upwood in the 1350s and maintained a very low profile, being noted mostly for trespass, failure to repair tenements, and being outside the manor without licence. A William Fraunce was cited as a *famulus* (a servant of the lord, usually performing agricultural service) in the account roll of 1402, and as a *porcarius* (pig-herder) in 1412–1413. The last active citation for the family is for a Thomas Fraunce who cut wood in 1430. In a document recording division of the waste at Upwood in 1448–1449, one cottage of Richard Fraunceys was in the lord's hand (cited in J.A. Raftis, *Tenure and Mobility* [Toronto, 1964], 30, 214). By 1456, when villagers "didn't know" where Walter Fraunce was, his family may well have been gone from Upwood for more than a generation. As note 15 above also makes clear, the record could be quite tenacious in conserving such information. The same spirit is also evident in account rolls, tenant lists, and other estate management records.

The evidence concerning names of land and people also suggests the presence of a mentality that appeals to past practice to secure adjustment and, specifically, to curb the sense of instability with respect to the land and its use.[19] James Fentress and Chris Wickham have described what they call the "cross-cultural markers" that distinguish peasant memory, in particular the "constantly recurring importance of local geography as a structure for remembrance: hills, caves, farmhouses, and fields all carry their memories for peasants to talk about." The geography of the community is thus "socialized," through a process which uses the land's "past associations" to give it a "meaning that makes sense for its inhabitants ... both space and time thus locking together to construct community identity."[20] Indeed, the importance of place in peasant culture is suggested by the very word *paysan*, whose primary reference is "to those who live in our area or patch, our fellow countrymen."[21] George Homans described the practical effect of this socialization of the landscape for the village in this way: "Fixed in the minds and sentiments of men, and related both to their economic interests and to their ways of conceiving the world, was an arrangement of houses and holdings to which, men felt, all proper villages should approach."[22]

This concrete attachment of memory and local history to specific sites in the village topography has other historical analogues, notably in Richard Gough's *History of Myddle*, written around 1700, in which this early local historian used the disposition of church pews and their corresponding tenements in the fields to tell family histories for a period that stretched back into the early sixteenth century. In addition to consulting local records and communal memory,

19 The desire to resuscitate past practice is evident in other ways: in Upwood, for example, the practice of attaching automatic juror service to the tenure of certain major tenements seems to be evolving in the years after 1400. This phenomenon can be interpreted as a mechanism to anchor a family in the village, and to reproduce the traditional bonds between landholding and service. For a fuller discussion, see Olson, *A Chronicle*, 161, 232, and Chapter Four, generally.

20 Fentress and Wickham, *Social Memory*, 113.

21 Noted in Paul R. Hyams, *Rancor and Reconciliation in Medieval England* (Ithaca, 2003), 29 n109.

22 Homans, *English Villagers of the Thirteenth Century* (1941; repr., New York, 1975), 86.

Gough's method was to move in his own mind, pew by pew, tenement by tenement, "retrieving" family by family in his reconstruction. Even the floor plans of the parish church which he drew up to accompany his history bear a striking resemblance to "memory theaters."[23]

Similarly, the court itself, as a public performance arena exhibiting great stability over many years, functioned as a kind of "memory theater" where the current contents of social memory were made public, following a traditional script. The document produced by that meeting not only recorded the proceedings but survive as a verbal "floor plan" of the meeting, in the names it preserved (as we will explore further below), and in the actual layout of the document itself: jurors grouped together at the head of the court roll, followed in turn by the presentments of other officials and villagers who came forward to speak.[24]

23 See Richard Gough, *The History of Myddle*, ed. David Hey (Harmondsworth, 1981). For Gough's brief description of his methodology, see pp. 77–78. Gough made two plans (pp. 80–84) of the church layout and its pews, as it was "anciently" and at the time of his writing (1701). For a discussion of "memory theaters" of the Renaissance, see Frances Yates, *The Art of Memory* (Chicago, 1966), especially Chapter Six and the accompanying plan between pp. 144 and 145; and see Eamon Duffy, *Stripping of the Altars*, 332, where he notes that, as more churches were fitted out with pews, sixteenth-century testators often asked to be buried at their pew, "indicating a desire to retain their place in the community quite literally." The same sensibility must be at work in the more typical requests to be buried in the churchyard as, for example, in a will dated 13 January 1529 in which Thomas Brydder, a major landholder in Ellington, asked to be buried in the churchyard of All Hallows in Ellington, and left a ewe to the sepulcher light there as well as 2s for the torches and bells. See *Wills and Administrations of the Archdeaconry of Huntingdon*, vol. 3, fol. 115 (held in the County Record Office, Huntingdon).

24 Indeed, scholars have seen a new kind of performance consciousness in some of the apparent cultural changes in Europe in the plague era: David Herlihy describes the elaborate funerals of the wealthy as "veritable 'theatres of death,'" and the public performances of the flagellants as "dramatic theatre." Herlihy, *The Black Death and the Transformation of the West*, 61, 68. David Nirenberg, *Communities of Violence: Persecution of Minorities in the Middle Ages* (Princeton, 1996), 217–218, describes Holy Week violence against Jewish communities in Southern Europe as a "theatre of conquest" that "reenacted the defeat and humiliation of the Jews." The phenomena he describes occurred before the plague as well as after.

In the public arena of a court whose very records extended the chronological range for a "village voice," the peasant tendency to "socialize the landscape" appears in villagers' talking about people and land. People and land had always spurred the liveliest discussion in the village, but that discussion must have sharpened over time as the painful contrast between people and land intensified after 1350: evident to all was the terrible transience of people amid the timeless fixity of the land. At such a time, when the desire to remember and preserve was as much under siege as the human population that made remembrance possible, how did villagers name themselves and each other in their court, and how did they name the land? These naming systems responded to, and therefore can illuminate, the changes that were occurring in the relationship between people and land in the village.

Surnames Before the Black Death

As we saw in Chapter Two, in the period before the Black Death, indeed before 1330, while most surnames in these two villages were tolerably fixed, there was still an ongoing formative process for a significant number of names. This surname formation typically drew upon occupation, as in the surnames Carpenter, Cissor, Fleichhewer, Whittawyer, Mattemaken, and Couper; on women's and men's given names, as in Cassandra, Catelyn, Dulcessone, Denys, Edessone, Helewys, Hildegar, Mariota, Matilda, Hugh, Leonard, and Martin; on nicknames, as in Twyt[25] and Dryngallday; and on local topography, as in Atte Dam, Atte Gate, and Lynlond (Inlond). Among these different methods of forming surnames, and their possible combinations and recombinations, it is the variant in which people take their name from the land, or are so named by the community, that is most important for our present purposes. In an

25 According to the *Oxford English Dictionary* (hereafter *OED*), s.v. "twit," this noun can mean a taunt, a fit of ill humor, a person given to fault-finding, or the imitation of the cry of an owl or small bird, among other substantive meanings. See P.H. Reaney, *A Dictionary of British Surnames* (London, 1958; hereafter *DBS*), especially pp. xxxvii–xxxviii, for a discussion of the variety of sources, many of them fortuitous, from which surnames arose in medieval England.

era when the ratio of people to land was undergoing a massive transformation, changes in the use of topographical features in surname formation can be interpreted as collective modifications that were highly purposeful.

In the period when fluctuation in surnames is readily apparent (that is, up to the 1330s), about fifteen percent of the surnames that appeared in these two villages were topographical names (approximately 40 out of a total of some 260 surnames).[26] From Upwood, the names are as follows: Abovestrate, Attebarre,[27] *Ad Capud Ville*,[28] Attebrok, Attechirche/*Ad Ecclesiam*, Attecross, Atte Dam, Attefryth,[29] Attegrene/*Supergrenam*, Attehalle, Attehill/Othehill, Atte Peretree, Attesnape,[30] Atestile, Attewell, Attewold/del Wold/Othe-Wold/Osszewold,[31] Copping,[32] Cotes,[33] de Elm, de Grascroft/de Garscroft, de Hirst,[34] Ilheyl/Illyl/Hilweyl/Hilhayl (hill?), Levere,[35] and Wodestrate. In Ellington: Abouebrok, *Ad Montem*/Atehyl, *Ad Pontem, in Angulo*/in the Hirne/Hirne,[36] AtteGrene, Beaumeys/Beu-

26 All surnames that first appeared in the court records of 1332 or before that year are included in this tabulation. The year 1332 was chosen as the terminal date because all topographical surnames had appeared by that year, and 1332 is a very full court record for Ellington, after which there are no rolls until 1340.

27 Attebarre: dweller by the barrier, gateway, weir. *DBS*, 22.

28 An *Edwardus Ad Capud Ville* is cited only in the lay subsidy rolls for 1290, where he was noted as paying 9s 2d. This name, either in its Latin or English form, does not appear in the court rolls for Upwood. A William atte Townsende appears in Upwood much later, in the account roll of 1408–1409, and therefore is not relevant to the discussion here. For the 1290 subsidy records, see *Early Huntingdonshire Lay Subsidy Rolls*, ed. J.A. Raftis and M. Patricia Hogan (Toronto, 1976).

29 Dweller by the frith, woodland. *DBS*, 120.

30 Snape: spring, boggy place in a field. *OED*, 2889.

31 Wold: forest, woodland. *DBS*, 340.

32 Copping: top, summit. *DBS*, 77.

33 Cote: cottage, hut. *DBS*, 79. (See discussion of this name in Chapter Two above).

34 Hurst: an eminence, hillock, knoll, or bank. *OED*, 1352.

35 Lever: rush, reed, iris. *DBS*, 199.

36 Hern (hirn, hirne): corner, nook, hiding-place. *OED*, 1296. A later variant of this name may be Attenok/Atte Nook/Atte Noke which appears in the 1370s through the early 1400s.

meys,[37] Bythebrok,[38] de Coten/Coten,[39] Delhe,[40] *in Estrate*, Hale,[41] de Holcote,[42] in Lynlond/de Lynlond/in Inlond/de Inlond,[43] *in Marisco*/Mersch/Marsh, and Unterhyl.[44]

Many of these names did not survive, though the process of their disappearance is largely hidden from us.[45] One possible family grouping in Upwood that may demonstrate that process includes three of the four variants for surname formation, all in apparent competition with each other over a period of some fifty years: *filius Olyuer* and Olyver (father's personal name), Ate Dam (topographical), and le Wayte (nickname meaning "the wise"). The nickname form seems to prevail, losing its article by 1325, and making its last appearance with a Matilda Weyte in 1340. If this is indeed a family grouping, the high levels of mobility

37 This surname first appears with the article "de" for Agnes de Beaumeys, in 1278, as it does for Richard de Beaumeys, a prominent villager from 1286 to 1311, and alternates with the article "le" down to c. 1310 when the name appears without any article. If it is a topographical surname, "meys" is "meadow." C. L'Estrange Ewen, *A History of Surnames of the British Isles; A Concise Account of Their Origin, Evolution, Etymology, and Legal Status* (1931; repr., Baltimore, 1968), 379.

38 The many variant spellings for this name include *Per Ripam*, Bethbrok, Bethebrok, Attebrok, and Bythe Brok'.

39 Coten: dweller at the cottages. *DBS*, 79.

40 Hay: enclosure. *DBS*, 99.

41 Hale: nook, recess. *DBS*, 151.

42 Holcote: cottage in the hollow. *DBS*, 167.

43 Inland: the inner part of an estate. *OED*, 1440. Inlandes: pieces of demesne rented to villeins. *A Medieval Farming Glossary of Latin and English Words*, ed. John L. Fisher (London, 1968), 19. See Chapter Two in Rosamond Faith, *The English Peasantry and the Growth of Lordship* (London, 1997), for a detailed discussion of this term and its early history. This name also appears in the court roll of 1425 where Thomas Moke senior is fined 2d for obstructing a water course between himself and "lynland" (*inter ipsum et lynland*).

44 Variant spellings include *Sub Monte*, Undrehill, Underhill, Undyrhill, Underthehyl, and Vnderthehill'.

45 Piecing together family histories sometimes enables us to view the disappearance of families as well as other forms of mobility in the village. See Olson, " 'Families Have Their Fate and Periods': Varieties of Family Experience in the Pre-Industrial Village," in *The Salt of Common Life: Individuality and Choice in the Medieval Town, Countryside, and Church*, ed. Edwin B. DeWindt (Kalamazoo, 1995), 409–448.

demonstrated by its menfolk over the 1280s and 1290s may be one explanation for the shifting of this surname in Upwood.[46]

Among the sixteen people who bear the name "Coten" and who appear by 1332, all have the article "de" associated with their name, thus the public voice that named them continued to emphasize their location. The surname disappears after 1332, and when it reappears briefly with Peter, Alice, and Richard Cotene in the early 1370s, the article is gone. As discussed in Chapter Two, this surname has a complicated history, since "Coten" appears to represent a defined neighborhood in Ellington by the end of the thirteenth and first part of the fourteenth centuries. As the name of a neighborhood, it was incorporated in the identifiable surnames of several families, including *Faber*, Edithson/Edesson, and *in Estrate* ("in East Street").

These examples suggest that people whose names are in transition tend to be people who are somewhat peripheral to the dominant village culture, a group that would include women because of the ambivalence that could attend their public role, men known primarily through their womenfolk, outsiders, transients, newcomers, and emigrants: people whose families are becoming more – or less – mainstream. The names of such people are shifting, because the people themselves are; one way in which they can be identified in public discourse, one source for the new names that evolve around them, is the local topography, the place where they choose to live, however briefly.

Place Names After the Black Death

The formation of surnames based on village topography is as lively as any other naming practice before c. 1350. In looking at post-plague name formation, one might reasonably expect to find continuity with pre-plague naming practice: people still come and go frequently in

46 Oliuer le Wayte is cited twice in the Huntingdonshire assize of 1287 for not coming, Roger le Wayte is fined for being outside tithing in 1294 and 1299, and *Rogerus filius Olyueri* is so fined in 1294, 1297, 1299, and 1301. For Oliuer le Wayte see *Royal Justice and the Medieval English Countryside*, ed. and trans. Anne R. DeWindt and Edwin B. DeWindt (Toronto, 1981), entries 804 and 818.

the village, indeed there is an increase in mobility by the end of the fourteenth century; surnames and place names still have a practical link in public discourse; and village discussion still anchors itself by referring to the local topography. However, the most striking changes in naming activity in the later village are apparent in place names, not surnames. In fact, after 1350, there has been a significant reversal in naming practices: instead of villagers, "peripheral" or otherwise, taking their names from the landscape, they now gave their names to the landscape. That is, villagers endowed the landscape with the names of local families, socializing the landscape in a way that integrated it into current realities.

In Ellington, for example, the following place names (given in chronological order of appearance) occur in the court rolls over the period 1373–1465:[47] Molcousyerd and Aldith (1373),[48] Baknonsyerd (1400), Hewmancest and Eyresholm (1405), le Bakno (1426), Holcotes (*iuxta holcotes*, "next to holcotes," 1429), Caytelane and Cayte-

47 The following list includes all place names that can be specifically tied to a known village family. Not included are place names that appear in the rolls prior to the family surname from which it is derived; "Briddishous," for example, appears in the 1350 court roll, but the surname Brydd does not appear until 1425, and then only for a single individual, Elena Brydd. By contrast, "Gernounscroft," cited in the 1350 court, can be linked to the Upwood family name Gernoun that first appeared in an account roll for 1268/9 (B.L. 39669), and that is also found in the earliest court roll. The last entry for a person with this surname is Richard Gernoun, one in a group of seven men and women listed as *nativi domini* in 1350 who have left the vill without licence. Another one of the late entries for this surname occurs in the 1347 roll, where a William Gernoun (undoubtedly elderly since he first appeared in 1311) surrendered his land to the use of his son Thomas. With one adult male representative having left the village, and only one son inheriting the family tenement from an elderly parent in 1347, it seems likely that this family was one of the many casualties of the first plague. The place name "Gernounscroft," then, appearing when it does, might either be marking the acquisition of the tenement by Thomas, or memorializing the extinction of the family.

48 In this entry, where Walter Burgeis is fined for leaving a gap open onto the field "at Aldith" (*apud Aldith*), the abbreviation *plac'* (*placea*) is written in as an interlinear addition above the word "Aldith." Note that the Aldith family was still active in Ellington in this period: Agnes Aldyth is cited twice, several lines below this entry, in connection with a plea of debt.

land (1443), Baknoo (1446), Backenco (1447), Eyryslane (1446, 1447, and 1455), Tayllloursland[49] and Walkelynyswode (1453), and Molkusyate (1465). In Upwood, the following place names occur over the period 1318–1456: Elyshauelond (1318), Aybescroft (1339), Eliushauelong and Gowlersdole (1347), Smythishous and Gernounscroft (1350), Cranesplace (1365), Nadeham place (1373), Buckeworthes tounisende (1375), Asplondesdole (1390 and 1391), Wadlowes place, Wadylofs place, and Flemynge (*iuxta Flemynge*, 1411), Jerkensplace, Gilesplace, and Bondesplace (1413), Grymesplace and Asplondole (1421), Cranesyerde (1422), Asplondole (c. 1424), Carterdyche (1424), Craneswell, Cranesyerde, Moynegrove, and Moynescroft (1425), Frauncescroft (1428), Hurres (*apud Hurres*), Newmans place, and Bracerstounesend (1430), Bracerstounseende and Carys tounesend (1435), Denys (*tenementum Denys*, 1438), Sadelersyerd and Herrysone (*apud herrysone*, 1439), Vernonsyate, Newmanscroft, Houghtonysplace, Spenserisplace, Grymested, Albyn Croft, Heryngcroft, and Henresson (*inter henresson*, 1448),[50] Albyncroftesende (1454), and Vernons (*versus Vernons*, 1456).

If we call to mind the actual meeting of the court as an arena where place names and people's names intermingled in the *narrationes*, that is, the facts stated and the stories told on that day, we get a sense of a public voice that connected people and place: in Upwood's court of 28 October 1430, for example, Joan Newman, the place name Hurres, Newman's place, John Hore (Hurre), Bracerstounsend, and John Bracer are all cited, for various reasons, within a space of ten lines.

Such developments are particularly striking when these fifteenth-century place names are compared with those of the earlier period. In Upwood's records between 1279 and 1370, that is, in the era before

49 In Ellington's court roll of 1446, John Fawkes is fined for not cleaning a ditch in a lane formerly held by John Tayllour (*in venella quondam Iohannis Tayllour*). The 1453 entry also concerns an uncleaned ditch at Tayllloursland. Here we may see something of the transition from a place cited in Latin connected with a person who used to hold it, to a new English place name.

50 This citation makes the connection between a person and his land very clear: Gilbert Hore was fined 20d for enclosing a certain croft at Rauele between henresson and his [own] tenement (*Et quod Gilbertus Hore inclusuit quamdam croftum apud Rauele inter henresson et tenementum suum*).

the new family place names described above begin to appear in significant numbers, there are some 215 place names mentioned in the court rolls which incorporate natural features of the landscape. For example, in one year alone (1339/40), the following place names are given in Upwood's court roll, usually in connection with trespass: le Slade, Hynewich, Fenfurlong, Halwod, Chicheburyfled, Hermyteseyt, Chiselepet, Le Longwong, le Benedole, Uppennale, le Bene, Westhirne, le Brache, Lamokehegge, Duffhousdole, and Stubbydole.[51] Such descriptive, even informative, place names occur throughout the Upwood rolls, such as le Heyerode-Weye (1295), Wistowebrok, le Byrcholt, le Holt (1307), Kylnehousdole (1322), Ashedole, Henemede, Lytelhul, and Westhale (1325). Places are also named in another way, in connection with people, as in *iuxta domum Hugonis Lauerok* (1295), *ad domum Iohannis Gleu* (1297), *Rivulum Agnetis Relicte Willelmi prepositi* (1320), *mesuagium Ricardi le Man* and *terram vicinorum suorum* (1339/40), *hayam domini apud Donnham Well* (1347), *tenementum Willelmi filii Henrici* (1350), and *tenementum quondam Thome Couhirde* (1365).[52] In short, in village court discourse before the Black Death, there is a great deal of talk about places, and places in connection with people, just as there is in the later period, but these earlier place names took a different form: as composites of pieces of land (Fenfurlong, Stubbydole), field corners (Westhirne), vegetation and woods (Halwod), landmarks such as dovehouses and kilns (Duffhousdole), and gravel pits (Chiselepet). Where family names occurred in connection with the land, the earlier construction rarely took a compound form, as in "Smythishous," but was given instead as "next to the house of Hugh Lauerok."[53]

51 Dola: a strip in an open field or meadow. See Fisher, *A Medieval Farming Glossary*, 11.

52 That is, "next to the house of Hugh Lauerok," "at the house of John Gleu," "the Rivulet of Agnes Widow of William reeve," "the messuage of Richard le Man" and "the land of their neighbors," "the lord's hedge at Donnham Well," "the tenement of William son of Henry," and "the tenement formerly of Thomas Couhirde."

53 Three apparent exceptions have been noted in Upwood's list above, Elyshauelond, Aybescroft, and Gowlersdole. Elys, Aubes and Gowler are all family surnames current in the village in 1318, 1339, and 1347, respectively. Note, however, that the 1347 court roll contains twenty-three other place names that fall into the other categories being dis-

In Ellington, place names which incorporate family names do not appear until 1373 (Molcousyerd), and become more numerous by the 1440s and 1450s. Again, as in Upwood, place names do occur in the rolls earlier, even in association with people, but the forms employed are not compound forms: for example, *parcum domini* (1292), *grangiam Simonis de Elyngton* (1294), *terra Iohannis Olyuer* (1308), *virgata terre que quondam fuit Thome Godman* (1322).[54] (Straightforward topographical features are also named, such as Wanbrige, Wellenschiremersh, and Estonemers in 1278, and le Groue, Chalkwell, and Foxholdes in 1332/3). Again, these earlier names of places differ qualitatively from the later compound place names being discussed in detail here, where family names are attached to topographical features in the local landscape to create new compound place names that are frequently used, indeed, may even outlive the families from which they originated. Since colloquial speech interweaves with Latin in the court rolls, as noted in Chapter Three, we may conjecture that if compound place names were being used in the court regularly before 1350, they would undoubtedly have entered into its written record more frequently, particularly in Upwood's fuller series. Yet, as we have seen, there are only four such instances in that village's rolls before the court of 1350: Elyshauelong in 1318, Aybescroft in 1339, and Eliushauelong and Gowlersdole in 1347. In a body of evidence that is full of topographical names, these compound place names,

---

cussed here: for example, Longeforland, le Rodedole, Snapmede, Brachedole, and Ryecroftdole. The 1318 roll, where Elyshauelond occurs, also lists Uppenhale, *in manerio domini, terram domini apud Doffhousdole, terras Agnetis le Reues, Roberti Coci, et Iohannis Crane, apud Schlade* and le Whyteston (that is, "on the lord's manor," "the lord's land (demesne) at Doffhousdole," "the lands of Agnes le Reues, Robert Cook, and John Crane," "at Schlade"). In other words, various place name forms are in circulation over this period. The compound place name in which a family surname appears is clearly concentrated in the later period in both Upwood and Ellington, especially after c. 1420. It is also worth noting that Elyshauelond and Gowlersdole both refer to strips of land in the arable (-lond, -dole), as opposed to areas of human habitation (-yard, -holm, -lane, -gate, -croft, -house, -place, -well, -stead, etc.).

54 That is, "the lord's park," "the grange of Simon de Elyngton," "the land of John Olyuer," "a virgate of land that formerly belonged to Thomas Godman."

formed with the names of local families, scarcely occur before 1350 but become a fairly regular feature of the court rolls by the early fifteenth century.

A few of the new compound place names seem to be formed with the names of families that have disappeared (Molkusyate, Backenho, Wadlowes place).[55] In these instances, the naming practice may point to the desire to memorialize the landscape, and therefore might be an act of remembrance.[56] Usually, however, the families whose names appear in these compound place names are still present in the village, so we must seek another explanation. Among the various methods of socializing the landscape (such as the ritual of "beating the bounds" discussed in Chapter One) that were current in the village over the fourteenth century (and possibly quite active, given the dramatic fluctuations in the numbers of people relative to available land), it may be that attaching family names to the land was among the more desirable options, which could explain why this was done to a degree not seen before in the community.

If true, this would suggest a new emphasis in villagers' understanding of themselves in relation to the land: before 1350, the villager tends to take his name from the land, while after 1400, he tends to give his name to it. In both periods the land functions as a marker of permanence which villagers use in different ways. Such a shift in emphasis might have been prompted by many events, indeed by grim new rituals that arose in connection with sudden and mass mortality at mid-century and recurrence of plague thereafter. A mass grave may have been hastily dug in the parish churchyard for the initial wave of victims from 1348 to 1351, followed by repeated burials of those who died in subsequent decades in a continual opening and reopening of the land to receive the newly dead.[57]

55 The family name Gernoun discussed above in note 47 may be an early instance of this.

56 It would, of course, be impossible to prove this point with court roll data, even with an unbroken series, since these documents do not necessarily record place names at the moment when they are first formulated.

57 One wonders whether (and if so, how) the great increase in numbers of burials and of deaths that characterized the fourteenth-century village affected the tendency for people to become attached to the places where their dead were buried.

Archeological excavations have uncovered some medieval cemeteries associated with the plague era, particularly in urban centers,[58] but for information regarding burial practice we are still heavily reliant on chronicles, such as that of the cathedral priory of Rochester which covers the period 1314–1350 and includes a reference to mass graves under the year 1348:

> Alas this mortality devoured such a multitude of both sexes that no one could be found to carry the bodies of the dead to burial, but men and women carried the bodies of their own little ones to church on their shoulders and threw them into mass graves, from which arose such a stink that it was barely possible for anyone to go past a churchyard.[59]

In his *Historia de Morbo*, Gabriele de' Mussis (d. 1356) of Piacenza noted that whole families, households, and their neighbors were often buried together, and that this had occurred in other "towns, villages, cities and settlements."[60] As one scholar has recently noted, "contemporary sensibilities must have been bruised by conveyor-line burials."[61]

The changes in village naming practices described here, from the use of topographical elements in surname formation before 1350 to the use of surnames in place name formation, especially by the early fifteenth century, occurred over a period of unprecedented upheaval in village history. The explanation offered here is that the social memory of the village intensified its traditional tendency to socialize and memorialize the landscape, in large part because the land provided a point of stability in the service of memory. In other words, it was there to fill a need in village life unlike any that had occurred previously in its history. Perhaps other village structures traditionally involved in remembering the dead, such as saying prayers and masses, or telling stories about people who had passed away, were

58 See Duncan Hawkins, "The Black Death and the new London Cemeteries of 1348," *Antiquity* 64 (1990): 637–642. According to Christopher Daniell, *Death and Burial in Medieval England, 1066–1550* (London, 1997), 143, "only about thirty excavations have taken place in English medieval cemeteries, of which about ten have more than a hundred bodies. Fewer still have been comprehensively published."

59 *The Black Death*, ed. and trans. Rosemary Horrox (Manchester, 1994), 70.

60 Ibid., 21.

61 Ibid., 245. Other references to mass burials are found ibid., 52, 74, 267.

approaching their limits as the effects of demographic cataclysm accumulated by the years around 1400. Perhaps it therefore became increasingly difficult and painful to memorialize so many dead in the conventional manner, or even to remember so large a number of dead people and the earlier incarnations of the village with which they were associated in the survivors' memories.

There is considerable explanatory power in the cultural mechanism being suggested here: a link between post-plague adjustment and changes in naming practice. To begin with, this naming of the landscape might have eased whatever burden of fear or guilt survivors felt in occupying lands whose former tenants they, the living, could still vividly recall. This problem must have been particularly acute after the revisitations of plague in the later fourteenth and fifteenth centuries, as the beneficiaries of the new opportunities in landholding, wage labor, and official service moved into the positions vacated just a little while before by people whom they, the survivors, could easily remember as individual men and women. John Hicson, a child of five or six when the plague reached Upwood in 1349, had repeated opportunities to witness the effects of epidemic, aftermath, and recurrence. Given that he was most active as an office-holder over the period 1370–1410, he was also in an excellent position to benefit from the opportunities created by depopulation – and to remember the men who had served before him as juror or reeve, and the families whose lands he and others now took up.[62] Perhaps endowing the land with family names helped psychologically to repopulate lanes, fields, paths, yards, places, crofts, and woods that had recently teemed with people. Villagers might also have hoped that attaching their name to the land might help fix their claim to it, to assert their rights to land when the "web of land-use rights" itself was being undermined.

Recent cultural history studies provide further clues to aid in interpreting these developments. According to one study, medieval

62 The Hicson family first appears in Upwood's records in the account roll of c. 1358 when John (senior) is cited as a former reeve owing arrears of £10 17s. He and his son John (b. 1344) acquire extensive holdings as reflected in the account rolls from c. 1371 to 1423. In 1371 alone, these two together held two and three/quarters virgates, that is, over sixty acres. See Appendix Four, the tenurial spread at three Ramsey manors (including Upwood), in J.A. Raftis, *Peasant Economic Development within the English Manorial System* (Montreal, 1996), 179.

people certainly wanted to remember their dead, but they also wanted to forget them; but "some of those dead ... apparently rebelled against the will of the living to forget and thus rekindled their memories, invaded their dreams, and haunted their homes."[63] This impulse to forget may have been one source for phenomena that have been noted in association with agrarian cults in early modern Europe. Carlo Ginzburg describes several medieval legends, which circulated in Italy in the sixteenth and seventeenth centuries, of "nocturnal cavalcades of the dead," which took the form of "ranks of those who had died prematurely," that "passed through the village streets at night, unrelenting and terrible, while the inhabitants barricaded their doors for protection." In another legend, a pagan goddess "was followed in her nocturnal wanderings by a band of the dead for whom there was no peace: people taken by death before their time, children snatched away at an early age, victims of a violent end."[64] The dead, silently moving in serried ranks, were still intensely present to the people – and the places – that had known them in life. Jean-Claude Schmitt points out that while ghost stories are universal in human society, and medieval ghost stories are therefore part of the "folkloric culture" of the Middle Ages, they are also anchored in specific times and places and therefore possess a powerful contemporaneity. "'Mentalities' consist not only of the ancient layers that survive from earlier thoughts and behaviors but also of the beliefs and the images, the words and the gestures, that fully find their meaning in the contemporary social relations and ideology of a given age."[65]

The collective mind at work behind these and other uses of the landscape displayed great vitality. Alongside the cross-cultural mechanism characteristic of peasant memory to use local geography as a "structure for remembering," conceptualizing the land as a kind of map to prompt the village's memory (with the court roll as another

63 See Jean-Claude Schmitt, *Ghosts in the Middle Ages: The Living and the Dead in Medieval Society*, trans. Teresa Lavender Fagan (Chicago, 1998), 6–7. Raphael Samuel, *Theatres of Memory*, x, remarks that "what [memory] contrives symptomatically to forget is as important as what it remembers."

64 Carlo Ginzburg, *The Night Battles: Witchcraft and Agrarian Cults in the Sixteenth and Seventeenth Centuries*, trans. John Tedeschi and Anne Tedeschi (New York, 1985), 40.

65 Schmitt, *Ghosts in the Middle Ages*, 3.

prompt to that memory), men and women also blanketed some of that land with a new gridwork, a labyrinth of names, to accommodate the pressing claims of the living alongside the inexorable memory of the dead. In the same way that a book was a mnemonic for the educated, one among several ways to "remember a text," or that a Gothic cathedral was a "Bible for the unlettered, full of pictures,"[66] so too the landscape was a mnemonic for the peasantry to remember a village "text": the land, the village, was a mute gospel. Socializing the landscape enabled villagers to be mindful of that "arrangement of houses and holdings to which ... all proper villages should approach." In the post-plague era specifically, it also helped survivors to re-invent that "arrangement" so that it might continue to work after the devastation wrought by the great mortality, a catastrophe of such proportions that it altered the contents of the "text" itself.[67] The ability of villagers to fashion ideas and strategies that could transcend individuals and their ceaseless comings and goings is suggestive of peasant practicality. It also suggests how their traditional collective culture, so much a product of the demographic and agricultural expansion of the High Middle Ages, was remade in an age of declining population and under-inhabited villages.

The cultural mechanisms described here place the peasantry at center stage in confronting the greatest challenge to European society in the later Middle Ages. Those who survived the plague and carried on despite their grief and loss had been dealt a terrible blow – but they were not without cultural resources to meet it. Indeed, in the "formidable task of maintaining and repairing its cultural heritage,"[68] Europe's peasants had a vital role to play. Understanding peasant strategies for seeking permanence, for "making present the voices of

66 See Carruthers, *The Book of Memory*, 8, 222.

67 Carruthers's definition of a "text" allows us to develop the correspondence offered here between book, cathedral, and village landscape. A text was not so much a definitive "statement" of fact or experience, but rather an "occasion for rumination and meditation, for the engagement of *memoria*." See *Book of Memory*, 256. We recall Richard Southern's observation that peasant inspiration underlay medieval civilization: "village life is the basis of every activity, and scholars and artists carry into the world of the spirit the qualities learnt in the stubborn struggle with the land." *The Making of the Middle Ages* (1953; repr., New Haven, 1992), 76.

68 Herlihy, *The Black Death and the Transformation of the West*, 69.

what is past," has a contribution to make to current research on the mentality of the "ordinary" people of medieval and early modern Europe. Such strategies hint at the villager's sense of how much and who had been lost. To put it somewhat differently, the desire to reinvent and refashion what had been lost to memory was largely driven by the memory that a great deal had been lost indeed: the loss of memory and the memory of loss.

In the rehabilitation of their culture, names and systems of naming had a significant role to play for villagers because those systems could draw upon the land, a traditional peasant point of reference. The tasks confronting the powers of peasant culture in the later Middle Ages were formidable: to lay the dead to rest, literally and figuratively, and to allay the sufferings invoked by their memory and the memories invoked by people's continued suffering in the revisitations of plague. Those cultural resources were needed by the survivors, who remembered all those people "taken by death before their time," and who then occupied their lands, living and working where the dead had once lived and worked, and where now they lay at rest. Indeed, villagers must have been conscious that the topographical names they invented and used might survive them, and that the place names which preserved their own family names might be prolonged by being spoken in court and written down – *bene irrotulare*, to be "properly enrolled" – in the court record, the collective aide-mémoire with which they had long been familiar. These responses represent new uses of old practices, and are consonant with other methods employed by late medieval people to be remembered, to defeat "oblivion and restriction."

Court roll evidence of the developments in naming practices illuminates the links between memory and agency in the medieval village. If in the earlier period people had sometimes sought stability of tenure and residence – and perhaps identity – by incorporating topographical elements into their evolving surnames, it may be that after the Black Death, they sought stability of tenure, defence against trespass, and formation of identity by endowing the land with their surnames. In naming themselves and the land, they also "shared words with each other" and "grasped" each other "in community and communication" in the late medieval village.[69]

69 David Warren Sabean, *Power in the Blood: Popular Culture and Village Discourse in Early Modern Germany* (Cambridge, 1984), 209–210.

Conclusion

What belongs to everybody belongs to nobody.

Spanish proverb

In a previous book, the author stated that thought and act were closer for peasants than for others because of their life of work,[1] an existential condition that may have given them a different notion of themselves from the one developed by conventional scholarship: peasants as subalterns who somehow internalized that status. That the medieval aristocracy thought peasants were animalistic, stupid, or inferior is not proof that peasants shared those ideas. In the harsh and arduous life of work in the village, what would have been valued more: ascribed status or achieved status? Would villagers necessarily have rated the opinions of others more highly than their own? Among themselves, peasants may have thought that aristocrats were inferior since they did not know how to do farm work, or could not have done it easily if called upon. A wainwright of ordinary abilities could make a cart or wagon that might, with repairs, outlast him in the village for a hundred years. How much did this matter?

Evidence from the antebellum South demonstrates that many African American slaves thought of themselves as "productive members of society"[2] and that their masters were inferior because the latter did not know how to work. "Plantation economies were famous for the extent of this dependence" of the power-holders upon the enslaved, and for the "languor and helplessness of the master class." The slaveholders' "monopoly of power" was constrained by, among other things, the "slaves' clear recognition of the masters' *dependence* upon

1 Sherri Olson, *A Chronicle of All That Happens: Voices from the Village Court in Medieval England* (Toronto, 1996), 133.

2 Eugene Genovese, *Roll, Jordan, Roll: The World the Slaves Made* (New York, 1974), 306.

them."[3] As a result of his master's indolence and incompetence, Josiah Henson essentially managed the plantation where he lived under slavery; and in his autobiography, published in 1849, he reports the belief he had at the time that his master was "absolutely dependent" upon him (indeed, he "frequently carried his drunken master home 'with the pride of conscious superiority'").[4] What were medieval villagers' opinions about themselves, their work, and their lords? Each longitudinal study of village behavior will provide the historian with more materials to address such complex issues.

This book has explored these questions by searching for some of the basic working ideas that informed peasant mentality, using documents rich in the recording of practice. What were the premises that informed their sense of the world and how best to make their way in it? The thought modes explored here include instrumentality, analogizing, and symbolic thinking. When a villager argued by proverb, participated in court ritual by finding a pledge, experienced some apprehension when a woman stood up in court to receive a tenement, or referred to a neighbor's land by his or her surname, he or she entered into those modes of thought. Underlying these were other, more fundamental ideas that we have characterized by such terms as partibility (the principle that everything can be divided into parts) and fungibility (the principle that everything can be exchanged or replaced, "in whole or in part, for another of like nature or kind").[5] The village, then, was a setting characterized by great fluidity of meaning and identity, and a corresponding readiness – a readiness that signals peasant confidence, and not a sort of *mauvaise honte* – to consider, decide, and assign meaning, thinking with people, thinking with things, and thinking with land.

It seems no more far-fetched to argue that we can retrieve and understand peasants' thoughts from court roll evidence, than to credit the confident assertions historians routinely make about the thoughts, feelings, and aspirations of the aristocracy that abound in the accounts

3 Sidney W. Mintz and Richard Price, *The Birth of African-American Culture: An Anthropological Perspective* (Boston, 1992), 27, 28; see discussion on pp. 25–28.

4 Quoted in John W. Blassingame, *The Slave Community: Plantation Life in the Antebellum South* (rev. ed., New York, 1979), 203.

5 *Random House Webster's Unabridged Dictionary*, 2nd edition (2001), s.v. "fungible."

of medieval chroniclers. Thus, we learn from the *Chronicle of Battle Abbey* not merely that King William founded that institution on the very battlefield where he felled his opponent and won his kingdom, but indeed that his conscience "was urging him from within" not to forget his vow to found a monastery "for the salvation of all."[6] Narrating and accounting for the personal urges of the elite, and linking those urges with the making of history, dominated mainstream historical analysis through the nineteenth and most of the twentieth centuries. The private ruminations of princes (which were, apparently, known to the typical medieval chronicler) have been made to stand for a great deal of history.

How are we to read the narrations that survive in the court rolls in order to discover and understand the thoughts of peasant farmers, and to link those thoughts with their actions and with the making of local history ? Is it possible to find our way to the reasoning of Agnes le Hopper, cited in Ellington's court of 1311 for taking green wood (*virid*[*as*?]) from the lord's wood, as were Walter in Marisco, William Pelliparius (Skynner), and Richard son of Teobalt, all cited *pro eodem* ("for the same thing")? What of the fathers who broke the lord's park many times, put their sons over the lord's walls, and urged them onto the best fruit trees, the widowed mothers who with their sons' aid felled oak trees at night and sold turves to outsiders? Can we reconstruct the reasoning of Thomas Brokenhorn and Ralph Shepherd who, according to the jurors' presentment in the 1319 court of Littleport, took hay from the lord's rick and "set it before their impounded beasts" without the lord's permission, an incident so common that the procedural manuals for holding a manorial court provide model language to deal with such cases?

The cultural history that has been assembled here, primarily from court roll evidence, suggests that analysis that favors any single causal explanation (for example, the conflict model of relations between lord and tenant) may be particularly shortsighted for study of the medieval village, a place of great complexity and nuance. In the incident in Littleport, as we saw above, the men did not attempt to free their animals from the pound, nor did they challenge the accuracy of whatever charge resulted in distraint of their animals, although such

6 See *The Chronicle of Battle Abbey*, ed. and trans. Eleanor Searle (Oxford; New York, 1980), 37, 43.

things occurred as well. If we set aside the grid of assumptions about lord-tenant conflict, we are then at liberty to consider what else might be at work behind this fairly unremarkable incident.

For example, we may imagine the village pound as a concrete, stable element of village geopolitics. Its immovable walls must have stood in sharp contrast to the moveable hurdles and temporary fencing that were so essential a feature of common field husbandry. The pound may be said to symbolize distraint (*distrinctio*), the practice (discussed in the Introduction) in which an object is taken and held temporarily in order to compel someone to meet an obligation, answer a charge, etc. Holding things aside, under consideration, as a charge (*sub latura*), all point to the principle of taking a "good" out of common circulation or use, where it will be palpably missed, where the pressure of its being missed as an item in the village store of "goods" will help to elicit a particular response. The practice of distraint has numerous analogues in other village institutions, such as essoining, putting matters in respect (*in respectu*), licence agreements (*licencia concordie*), and love days (*dies amoris*), where two or more disputants are given a day (*et datur dies*; or "have a day," *habent diem*) to come to an agreement, an action housed by the court because all parties agree to have it so. (Indeed, the procedural treatise *La Court de Baron* contains examples of the steward's role in monitoring such arrangements.)[7] Every tenant's claim to village wealth and resources ("what belongs to everybody belongs to nobody"), an understanding that formed the core of the common field regime, provided the fertile soil in which all such arrangements were grounded.

In effect, it seems that the heterogeneity and velocity of circulation of village resources paradoxically created a collective impression of individual wealth that was highly plastic, and that led individuals and groups to strategize, to maneuver, to cut deals, to bargain. The medieval village, like the classical Athenian city-state, was poor in technology (by modern standards) but rich in people and ideas, and accustomed to relying on both: surely this was a

7 *The Court Baron, Being Precedents For Use in Seignorial and Other Local Courts, Together with Select Pleas From the Bishop of Ely's Court of Littleport*, ed. F.W. Maitland and W.P. Baildon (London, 1891), 58.

source for much of the seeming randomness, heterogeneity, and idiosyncratic quality of its way of life.[8]

It has been said of modern Mexican peasants that the villager "spends his life learning to know a few things deeply."[9] This is a useful characterization for the medieval peasant as well (even if it discounts the great range of things that a farmer must know), but only if we understand that for the modern Mexican peasant, as for the medieval English one, the depth of such learning can be very deep indeed, and that depth of thought readily sends out lateral shoots that make connections, that is, that depth of thought lends itself to complexity of thought and even to contemplation. We recall Pieper's observation that the act of marvelling arises from a kind of immersion in the everyday and its objects, not in withdrawal from them.[10] The village supplied a fertile context for such thinking: the farm itself was a book, a mute gospel.

The medieval peasant lived within a tradition of freedom in the sense of daily self-government. That self-government, recorded in court rolls and other documents, helped make the peasant visible to his and her contemporaries, as well as to modern historians in search of a "usable past" to enrich our sense of place on the historical continuum. Peasant culture within a seigneurial framework provided the very foundation for medieval society. Yet much of this began to change in the fifteenth century. As Nellie Neilson observed years ago, the "building up of the royal power at the expense of all these private jurisdictions and functions was necessarily slow and painful. It forms a study of great interest and importance, and is valuable also for the

8 Ellen Meiksins Wood reminds us that the Athenian farmer-citizen "with a technology base easily matched and often surpassed by other civilizations ... left a cultural legacy whose richness has seldom been equaled." Wood, *Peasant-Citizen and Slave: The Foundations of Athenian Democracy* (London, 1988), 162. A thirty-nine-year-old gardener, interviewed in 1967 by Ronald Blythe, commented that "[l]ife now is much less elaborate and, consequently, much less interesting." Blythe, *Akenfield: Portrait of an English Village* (New York, 1969), 117.

9 Erich Fromm and Michael Maccoby, *Social Character in a Mexican Village: A Sociopsychoanalytic Study* (Englewood Cliffs, NJ, 1970), 40.

10 Josef Pieper, *Leisure, the Basis of Culture*, trans. Alexander Dru (1952; repr., New York, 1963), 98–99.

light it throws backward on the conditions it changes and destroys."[11] Early modern village England would gradually be drawn into a type of rural theater that differed from the medieval village court, a theater better suited to the exercises of deference and accommodation to a distant power broker than to holding and defending one's rights to gather, harvest, and graze animals in the common.

11 Nellie Neilson, *Medieval Agrarian Economy* (New York, 1936), 83.

Bibliography

Manuscript Sources

1 *Court Rolls*

Public Record Office, Special Collections 2 (SC 2 179/); British Library Additional Charters and Rolls (e.g. 34911)

UPWOOD

1279/80 Monday, 3 November: 34911; **1280** August/September: 179/4; **1294** Saturday, 4 December: 34769; **1295** Wednesday, 7 December: 179/9; **1297** Monday, 4 November: 34798; **1299** Thursday, 3 December: 179/10

1301 Thursday, 23 November: 179/12; **1306** [heading missing]: 34361; **1307** Tuesday, 31 January: 34799; **1307** Monday, 4 December: 179/15; **1308** Monday, 4 November: 34801; **1311** Wednesday, 3 November: 34802; **1313** [heading missing]: 34917; **1318** Saturday, 7 January: 34803; **1320** Monday, 14 January: 34804; **1322** Monday, 18 October: 34805; **1325(1)** January: 34806; **1325(2)** Tuesday, 5 November: 39851; **1326** Wednesday, 17 December: 34807; **1328/9** Saturday, 1 January: 39852; **1331** Monday, 16 December: 34321; **1332** Friday, 18 December: 39582; **1333** Monday, 6 December: 34810; **1334** Monday, 28 November: 34809; **1339** Thursday, 7 January: 34808; **1339/40** [heading damaged]: 34811; **1344** Tuesday, ? January: 39854; **1347** Wednesday, 28 November: 34849; **1349** Thursday, 12 November: 34850

1350 Friday, 29 October: 179/34; **1353** [Tuesday, 29 October?]: 39855; **1360** Saturday, 24 October: 34812; **1365(1)** Saturday, 26 July: 39860; **1365(2)** Saturday, 18 October: 179/37; **1369(1)** Friday, 13 July: 39473; **1369(2)** Saturday, 21 July: 39765; **1372** Thursday, 28 October: 39766; **1373** Thursday, 3 November: 179/39; **1375** Monday, 5 November: 179/40; **1378** Tuesday, 14 December: 179/41; **1382** Thursday, 14 November 4: 34306; **1386** Monday, 1 October: 34813; **1387** Friday, ? March: 179/42; **1390** Tuesday, 4 October: 34814; **1391(1)** Tuesday, [18?] July: 34815; **1391(2)** Saturday, 28 October: 34816; **1395** Saturday, 30 October: 179/44; **1398** Monday, [8 July?]: 34817

1402 Thursday, 20 July: 179/47; **1403(?)** [heading missing]: 179/48; **1405** [heading damaged]: 34818; **1406** Friday, 19 November: 39478; **1409** Thursday, 14 November: 179/52; **1411(1)** Friday, 12 June: 34819; **1411(2)** Tuesday, 22 December: 39863; **1413** Monday, 30 October: 34820; **1418** Saturday, 5 November: 179/55; **1420** Thursday, 11 April: 34821; **1421** Tuesday, 28 October: 34368; **1422** Saturday, 3 October: 34369; **c.1424** Saturday, ? August: 34800; **1424** Tuesday, 17 July: 179/57; **1425(1)** Monday, [8 October?]: 39645; **1425(2)** Saturday, 27 October: 39745; **1427** Monday, 27 October: 34370; **1428(1)** Monday, 2 August: 34370; **1428(2)** Monday, 18 October: 179/59; **1429** Saturday, 25 June: 179/59; **c.1430** Saturday, after 18 October: 39859; **1430** Saturday, 22 July: 39646; **1430** Saturday, 28 October: 34822; **1435** Monday, 24 January: 34371; **1438** Thursday, 9 January: 34823; **1439** Wednesday, 16 December: 34824; **1441** Saturday, 28 October: 39866; **1443** Thursday, 10 October: 34825; **1448** Saturday, 2 November: 34826; **1450** Saturday, 31 October: 39746; **1452** Thursday, 2 November: 34827; **1453** Monday, 29 October: 34828; **1454** Saturday, 23 November: 34829; **1456** Saturday, 6 November: 34830

Later rolls **1473** Thursday, 25 November: 39656; **1483** Thursday, 23 October: 39775; **1487** Monday, 5 November: 39871; **1488** Monday, 3 November: 39776

ELLINGTON

1280 Monday, 25 November: 179/4; **1290** Wednesday, 29 November: 179/7; **1292** Friday, 7 November: 34336(1); **1294** Tuesday, 19 January: 39597(5); **1299** Thursday, 17 December: 179/10

1306 Thursday, 10 February: 179/12; **1308** c. 25 November: 179/15; **1308/9** Friday, after December: 39739; **c.1310** [heading missing]: 34320; **1311** [heading missing]: 179/16; **1316** Tuesday, 7 December: 179/18; **1321** [heading missing]: 179/19; **1322** Wednesday, 3 November: 179/21; **1325** Tuesday, [?]: 179/22; **1329** Tuesday, 17 January: 39468; **1332/3** Friday, [?]: 179/26; **1340** Wednesday, 8 February: 179/30; **1350** c. 28 October: 179/34; **1356** Tuesday, 18 October: 179/36; **1360/66** Tuesday, before 28 October: 39738; **1373** Thursday, 20 October: 179/39; **1375** Wednesday, 31 October: 179/40; **1391** Thursday, 19 October: 179/43

1400 18 October: 179/45; **1402** Tuesday, before 24 June: 179/47; **1405** Wednesday, 28 July: 179/49; **1405** Thursday, 22 October: 179/50; **1407** Thursday, 20 October: 179/51; **1425(?)** Thursday, 5 April: 179/57; **1426**

Tuesday, 8 January: 179/58; **1428** Thursday, January: 34370; **1429(1)** Tuesday, 4 January: 179/59; **1429(2)** Thursday, [October?]: 179/60; **1432** Thursday, 6 November: 179/61; **1434** Thursday, 9 December: 179/62; **1440** Thursday, 13 January: 179/63; **1443** Thursday, 7 November: 34825; **1446** Thursday, November: 39867; **1447** Wednesday, 7 November: 179/65; **1450** Monday, 26 October: 179/66; **1452** Thursday, 5 October: 179/66; **1453** Friday, 19 October: 179/66; **1454** Saturday, 19 October: 34322; **1455** Monday, 20 October: 179/67; **1459** Monday, 25 June: 179/68; **1460** Thursday, 2 October: 179/68

Later rolls **1465** Friday, 18 October: 179/70; **1469** Monday, [?]: 179/71; **1473** Saturday, 30 October: 39656; **1486** Saturday, [October? June?]: 179/73; **1500(1)** Thursday, [12 March?]: 179/77; **1500(2)** Reconvened court, same: 179/78; **1500(3)** Thursday, 30 April: 179/77; **1508** Thursday, 12 October: 179/80; **1513** "Curia autumpnalis": 34310; **1516** Thursday, 2 October: 179/84; **1520** Thursday, 4 October: 179/86; **1527** Thursday, 10 October: 179/86; **1531** Thursday, 5 October: 179/87; **1534/5** ? April: 179/88; **1535** Thursday, 21 October: 179/89; **1536** Tuesday, 14 November: 179/89

Later Court Rolls for the Manor of Ellington Rectory, belonging to Peterhouse College, Cambridge
Ellington Rectory Court Rolls, Peterhouse College Library: 25 January 1544; 6 April 1576; 20 March 1577; 9 December 1583; 26 November 1588; 2 December 1589; 8 August 1594; 9 June 1596 (County Record Office, Huntingdon: file DDMS/1); 7 May 1600

2 *Account Rolls and Related Fiscal Records*

Public Record Office, Special Collections 6 (Ministers' and Receivers' Accounts); British Library Additional Charters and Rolls (dates given show the year in which the account was rendered).

UPWOOD

1268/9: 39669; **1288/9**: 39736; **1290**: 39672; **1293/4**: 34341; **1295**: 34761, 39716; **c.1298**: 885/11; **c.1299**: 885/12; **c.1304**: 885/13; **c.1300**: 885/14; **1307**: 34870; **1309/10**: 39693; **1313**: 34872; **1315**: 34883; **c.1316**: 34873; **1318**: 34883 (cont.); **1318**: 34516; **1318**: 34884; **c.1324**: 885/15; **c.1340**: 34851; **1343/4**: 34885; **c.1350**: 34875; **c.1351**: 34484; **c.1356**: 34485; **c.1357**: 34486; **c.1358**: 34487; **c.1359–63**: 34488; **c.1371**: 885/16; **c.1385**: 34852; **1385/6**: 34853; **1385/6**: 34888; **1386/7**: 34889; **1392/3**: 34854; **c.1396**: 34855; **1397/8**: 53687; **c.1398(?)**: 53688; **c.1398**: 39741

1401/2: 34856; **1402**: 39753; **1403**: 39744; **1405**, **1420/1**, **1439**, **1458**: 34608–34611; **1406/7**: 34857; **1408/9**: 34859; **1411/2**: 34858; **1411/2**: 34860; **1412/3**: 34861; **1417**: 34874; **1418/9**: 39742; **1420/1**: 34862; **1422/3**: 34863; **1446/7**: 34864; **1447/8**: 34865; **1448/9**: 34866; **1452/3**: 34867; **1455/6**: 34868; **1458/9, 1459/60**: 34869

ELLINGTON

1253/4: 39669; **1285/9** (Audits): 39736; **1312**: 876/26; **1313**: 876/27; **1315**: 876/28; **1316/17**: 876/30; **1396**: 875/22; **1397**: 875/23; **c.1401**: 876/8; **1407**: 875/24; **1411**: 875/25; **1415**: 875/26; **1416**: 875/27; **1443**: 875/28; **1444**: 876/1; **1449**: 876/2; **1450**: 876/3; **1451**: 876/4; **1453**: 876/5; **1454**: 876/6; **1458**: 876/7; **1473**: 876/9; **1474**: 876/10; **1475**: 876/11; **1478**: 876/12; **1481**: 876/13

3 *Terriers and Partial Listings of Holdings in Sixteenth-century Ellington*

8 September 1591: *Customs of the Manor of Ellington, County Huntingdon, Allowed and Approved at one Court there held on 8 September 1591, 33 E.R.* Lists the tenements of the thirty-two copyhold tenants of Robert Throckmorton, Esq. The original, now in extremely fragile condition, and a copy made in 1720, are both housed in the County Record Office, Huntingdon: File DDX 13/22/1.

28 February 1592: *Ellington Slade B. 2*, Peterhouse College, Cambridge. Indenture for the sale of 17 acres, 9 rods, 1 grove, and 1 pightil.

AD 1600: *Terrier of All Arable Lands, Leys and Meadows of Robert Throckmorton, Esq., within Ellington.* County Record Office, Huntingdon: File DDM 16G/.

4 *Grants of Land in Upwood and Ellington*

Ellington Parish Records, List 6 County Record Office, Huntingdon: 5 January 1399; 21 July 1420; 20 March 1457; 26 July 1466; 20 July 1496; 6 May 1566; 6 May 1566; 16 October 1593

British Library Additional Charters

UPWOOD

c.1285: 34106; **1285**: 34107, 34108; **c.1327**: 34109; **1332**: 34110; **1337(?)**: 34112; **1338**: 34111; **1342**: 33816; **1350**: 33829; **c.1350**: 33828; **1351**: 33832, 33835, 33836; **1351/2**: 33839; **1352**: 33841; **1354**: 34250; **1355**: 34113, 34114; **1360**: 34115, 34116; **1361**: 33422, 33860, 33861; **1364**: 34117; **1364/5**: 34118; **1369**: 33875; **1380**: 33902, 34119; **1383/4**: 33425; **1389**: 33916; **1393**: 33931; **1396**: 34120; **1397**: 34121;

1400/12: 34122; **1412**: 34219, 34123; **1433**: 34124; **1435**: 34125, 34126; **1448**: 34127, 34128; **1454/5**: 34129; **1455**: 34130; **1459**: 34131, 34132; **1465**: 34133

ELLINGTON

Tempus Edwardi I: 33252, 33294; **1417**: 33363: **1423**: 33379, 33380; **1433**: 33386; **1438**: 33390; **1445**: 33394, 33395, 33396; **1452**: 33397; **1453**: 33398; **1459**: 33255, 33256; **1467**: 333257, 33258, 33399; **1470**: 33259, 33400; **1540**: 39124; **1580**: 39375; **1581**: 33261, 39127; **1587**: 39128; **1599**: 39311; **1600**: 39310

Ellington Rectory Documents, 1563–1597:
Peterhouse College Library, Cambridge

A.1: 5 July 1563; A.2: 5 May 1565; A.4: 7 September 1567; A.6: 13 February 1576; A.7: 10 April 1580; A.9: 1 June 1575; A.10: 12 December 1588; A.11: 2 July 1597

Ellington Slade Documents, 1313–1598:
Peterhouse College Library, Cambridge

A.1: 25 November 1313; A.2: 15 March 1328; A.3: 4 May 1349; A.4: 25 December 1349; A.5: 1349; A.6: 1350, 18 September 1360 (French); A.7: 1373; A.8: 1380; A.9: 21 February 1381; A.10: 15 July 1389; A.11: 29 September 1389; A.12: 24 February 1402; A.13: 1 September 1402; A.14: 1407; A.16: 20 June 1423; A.17: 17 November 1426; A.18: 23 April 1429; A.19: 7 May 1453; No. 20: 11 May 1454; B.1: c.1580; B.3a: 1 November 1592; B.4: 16 February 1598; B.5: 14 February 1598; B.7: 1598; B.8: 11 December 1598

Ellington Manorial Records, Deed Collection, 1551–1600:
County Record Office, Huntingdon

4 July 1552: DDM 16/66; 11 July 1552: DDM 16/66; 10 February 1573: DDM 16/66; 23 September 1600: DDM 16/66

5 *Miscellaneous*

14 February 29 Edwardi I, inquest concerning forests: British Library Additional Charters and Rolls, 33141.

Tempus Edwardi I, inquest concerning value of churches in Leightonstone Hundred: BL 39591.

1384–85, Rents paid to Hinchinbroke Priory: BL 39589.

County Record Office, Huntingdon: Wills and Administrations of the Archdeaconry of Huntingdon, vol. 3, fol. 115.

Primary Sources in Print

Amelang, James S., ed. and trans. *A Journal of the Plague Year: The Diary of the Barcelona Tanner Miquel Parets, 1651*. New York: Oxford University Press, 1991.

Ault, Warren O., ed. *Court Rolls of the Abbey of Ramsey and of the Honor of Clare*. Yale historical publications. Manuscripts and edited texts 9. New Haven: Yale University Press, 1928.

Balestracci, Duccio, ed. *The Renaissance in the Fields: Family Memoirs of a Fifteenth-Century Tuscan Peasant*. Trans. Paolo Squatriti and Betsy Merideth. University Park: Pennsylvania State University Press, 1999.

Blassingame, John W., ed. *Slave Testimony: Two Centuries of Letters, Speeches, Interviews, and Autobiographies*. Baton Rouge: Louisiana State University Press, 1977.

Blythe, Ronald. *Akenfield: Portrait of an English Village*. New York: Pantheon, 1969.

Botkin, B.A., ed. *Lay My Burden Down: A Folk History of Slavery*. Chicago: University of Chicago Press, 1945.

Cartularium Monasterii de Rameseia. Ed. W.H. Hart and Ponsonby A. Lyons. 3 vols. Rerum Britannicarum medii aevi scriptores 79. London: Longman, 1884–1893.

Chronicon Abbatiae Rameseiensis. Ed. William Dunn Macray. Rerum Britannicarum medii aevi scriptores 83. London: Longman, 1886.

Cobbett, William. *Rural Rides*. New ed. 1853. Repr. London: Penguin, 1985.

Court Rolls of the Manor of Wakefield. Wakefield Court Rolls Series. Leeds: Yorkshire Archeological Society, 1977–.

DeWindt, Anne R., and Edwin B. DeWindt, eds. and trans. *Royal Justice and the Medieval English Countryside: The Huntingdonshire Eyre of 1286, the Ramsey Abbey Banlieu Court of 1287, and the Assizes of 1287–88*. 2 vols. Studies and Texts 57. Toronto: Pontifical Institute of Mediaeval Studies, 1981.

DeWindt, Edwin B., ed. and trans. *The Court Rolls of Ramsey, Hepmangrove and Bury, 1268–1600*. Subsidia Mediaevalia 17. Toronto: Pontifical Institute of Mediaeval Studies, 1990.

—, ed. *The Liber Gersumarum of Ramsey Abbey: A Calendar and Index of B.L. Harley Ms. 445*. Subsidia Mediaevalia 7. Toronto: Pontifical Institute of Mediaeval Studies, 1976.

—, ed. and trans. *A Slice of Life: Selected Documents of Medieval English Peasant Experience*. Document of Practice Series. Kalamazoo: Medieval Institute Publications, 1996.

Fisher, John L., ed. *A Medieval Farming Glossary of Latin and English Words, Taken Mainly from Essex Records.* London: The National Council of Social Service, 1968.

Gough, Richard. *The History of Myddle.* Ed. David Hey. Harmondsworth: Penguin, 1981.

Hazlitt, W. Carew. *English Proverbs and Proverbial Phrases.* London: Smith, 1869.

Hughes, Langston, and Arna Bontemps, eds. *The Book of Negro Folklore.* 1958. Repr. New York: Dodd, Mead and Co., 1983.

Humez, Jean McMahon, ed. *Gifts of Power: The Writings of Rebecca Jackson, Black Visionary, Shaker Eldress.* Amherst: University of Massachusetts Press, 1981.

Johnson, Clifton H., ed. *God Struck Me Dead: Religious Conversion Experiences and Autobiographies of Ex-Slaves.* Philadelphia: Pilgrim Press, 1969.

Langland, William. *Piers Plowman: The Prologue and Passus 1–7 of the B text as found in Bodleian MS. Laud Misc. 581.* Ed. J.A.W. Bennett. Clarendon Medieval and Tudor Series. 1972. Repr., Oxford: Clarendon Press, 1979.

Lewis, Oscar, ed. *Pedro Martínez: A Mexican Peasant and His Family.* New York: Random House, 1964.

Lock, Ray, ed. *The Court Rolls of Walsham le Willows, 1303–1350.* Suffolk Records Society 41. Woodbridge: Boydell, 1998.

Maitland, F.W., ed. *Select Pleas in Manorial and Other Seignorial Courts: Reigns of Henry III and Edward I.* Publications of the Selden Society 2. London: Quaritch, 1889.

—, and W.P. Baildon, eds. *The Court Baron, Being Precedents For Use in Seignorial and Other Local Courts, Together with Select Pleas from the Bishop of Ely's Court of Littleport.* Publications of the Selden Society 4. London: Quaritch, 1891.

Marcus Aurelius. *Meditations.* Trans. Maxwell Staniforth. Harmondsworth: Penguin, 1964.

Novae narrationes. Ed. E. Shanks and S.F.C. Milsom. Publications of the Selden Society 80. London: Quaritch, 1963.

Oschinsky, Dorothea, ed. *Walter of Henley and Other Treatises on Estate Management and Accounting.* Oxford: Clarendon Press, 1971.

Perdue, Charles L., Jr, Thomas E. Barden, and Robert K. Phillips, eds. *Weevils in the Wheat: Interviews with Virginia Ex-Slaves.* Charlottesville: University Press of Virginia, 1976.

Pickering, David, ed. *Cassell's Dictionary of Proverbs*. 1997. Rev. ed. London: Cassell; New York: Sterling, 2001.

Poos, Larry R., and L. Bonfield, eds. *Select Cases in Manorial Courts, 1250–1550: Property and Family Law*. Publications of the Selden Society 114. London: Selden Society, 1998.

Raftis, J.A., and M. Patricia Hogan, eds. *Early Huntingdonshire Lay Subsidy Rolls*. Subsidia Mediaevalia 8. Toronto: Pontifical Institute of Mediaeval Studies, 1976.

Rotuli Hundredorum tempore Henrici III et Edwardi I. Ed. W. Illingworth and J. Caley. 2 vols. London: Eyre and Strahan, 1812, 1818.

Searle, Eleanor, ed. and trans. *The Chronicle of Battle Abbey*. Oxford: Clarendon Press; New York: Oxford University Press, 1980.

Simpson, J.A., ed. *The Concise Oxford Dictionary of Proverbs*. Oxford Medieval Texts. Oxford: Oxford University Press, 1982.

Wenzel, Siegfried, ed. and trans. *Fasciculus Morum: A Fourteenth-Century Preacher's Handbook*. University Park: Pennsylvania State University Press, 1989.

Whiting, Bartlett, and Helen W. Whiting, eds. *Proverbs, Sentences, and Proverbial Phrases; from English Writings mainly before 1500*. Cambridge, MA: Belknap Press of Harvard University Press, 1968.

Secondary Sources

Algazi, Gadi. "Lords Ask, Peasants Answer: Making Traditions in Late-Medieval Village Assemblies." In *Between History and Histories: The Making of Silences and Commemorations*, ed. Gerald Sider and Gavin Smith, pp. 199–229. Anthropological Horizons. Toronto: University of Toronto Press, 1997.

Amelang, James S. *The Flight of Icarus: Artisan Autobiography in Early Modern Europe*. Stanford: Stanford University Press, 1998.

Archer, Margaret S. *Being Human: The Problem of Agency*. Cambridge: Cambridge University Press, 2000.

Ariès, Philippe. *The Hour of Our Death*. Trans. Helen Weaver. New York: Knopf, 1981.

Arnold, John H. *Inquisition and Power: Catharism and the Confessing Subject in Medieval Languedoc*. The Middle Ages Series. Philadelphia: University of Pennsylvania Press, 2001.

Ault, Warren O. "Manor Court and Parish Church in Fifteenth-Century England: A Study of Village By-laws." *Speculum* 42 (1967): 53–67.

—. *Open-Field Farming in Medieval England: A Study of Village By-Laws*. Historical Problems: Studies and Documents 16. London: Allen and Unwin; New York: Barnes and Noble, 1972.

—. *Open-Field Husbandry and the Village Community: A Study of Agrarian By-laws in Medieval England*. Transactions of the American Philological Society, n.s. 55.7. Philadelphia: American Philosophical Society, 1965.

—. *Private Jurisdiction in England*. Yale Historical Publications: Miscellany 10. New Haven: Yale University Press, 1923.

—. *The Self-Directing Activities of Village Communities in Medieval England*. [Boston University] University Lecture, Dec. 10, 1951. Boston: Boston University Press, 1952.

—. "The Village Church and the Village Community in Medieval England." *Speculum* 45 (1970): 197–215.

Ayton, Andrew, and Price, J.L. *The Medieval Military Revolution: State, Society and Military Change in Medieval and Early Modern Europe*. London; New York: I.B. Tauris, 1995.

Bak, János M., ed. *Coronations: Medieval and Early Modern Monarchic Ritual*. Berkeley: University of California Press, 1990.

Baker, Alan R.H., and Robin A. Butlin, eds. *Studies of Field Systems in the British Isles*. Cambridge: Cambridge University Press, 1973.

Bardsley, Charles. *English Surnames: Their Sources and Significations*. 4th ed., 1889. Repr. Rutland, VT: Charles E. Tuttle Co., 1968.

Bardsley, Sandy. *Venomous Tongues: Speech and Gender in Late Medieval England*. The Middle Ages Series. Philadelphia: University of Pennsylvania Press, 2006.

Barlow, Frank. *William Rufus*. English Monarchs. Berkeley: University of California Press, 1983.

Barnwell, P.S., and M. Mostert, eds. *Political Assemblies in the Earlier Middle Ages*. Studies in the Early Middle Ages 7. Turnhout: Brepols; Cheltenham: European Schoolbooks, 2003.

Bartlett, Robert. *The Hanged Man: A Story of Miracle, Memory, and Colonialism in the Middle Ages*. Princeton: Princeton University Press, 2004.

Beckerman, John S. "Adding Insult to *Iniuria*: Affronts to Honor and the Origins of Trespass." In *On the Laws and Customs of England: Essays in Honor of Samuel E. Thorne*, ed. Morris S. Arnold, Thomas

A. Green, Sally A. Scully, and Stephen D. White, pp. 159–181. Studies in Legal History. Chapel Hill: University of North Carolina Press, 1981.

Beckett, J.V. *A History of Laxton, England's Last Open-Field Village.* Oxford: Blackwell, 1989.

Benedictow, Ole J. *The Black Death, 1346–1353: The Complete History.* Woodbridge: Boydell, 2004.

Bennett, H.S. *Life on the English Manor: A Study of Peasant Conditions, 1150–1400.* Cambridge Studies in Medieval Life and Thought. Cambridge: Cambridge University Press, 1937.

Bennett, Judith. *History Matters: Patriarchy and the Challenge of Feminism.* Philadelphia: University of Pennsylvania Press, 2006.

—. *A Medieval Life: Cecilia Penifader of Brigstock, c. 1295–1344.* Boston: McGraw-Hill, 1999.

—. "Medieval Peasant Marriage: An Examination of Marriage Licence Fines in the *Liber Gersumarum.*" In Raftis, *Pathways to Medieval Peasants,* pp. 193–246.

—. "Spouses, Siblings and Surnames: Reconstructing Families from Medieval Village Court Rolls." *Journal of British Studies* 23 (1983): 26–46.

—. "The Tie that Binds: Peasant Marriages and Families in Late Medieval England." *Journal of Interdisciplinary History* 15 (1984): 111–129.

—. *Women in the Medieval English Countryside: Gender and Household in Brigstock Before the Plague.* New York: Oxford University Press, 1987.

Benson, C. David. "*Piers Plowman* and Parish Wall Paintings." *Yearbook of Langland Studies* 11 (1997): 1–38.

Bettelheim, Bruno. *The Uses of Enchantment: The Meaning and Importance of Fairy Tales.* New York: Knopf, 1977.

Bisson, Thomas N., ed. *Cultures of Power: Lordship, Status and Process in Twelfth-Century Europe.* The Middle Ages Series. Philadelphia: University of Pennsylvania Press, 1995.

—. *Tormented Voices: Power, Crisis, and Humanity in Rural Catalonia, 1140–1200.* Cambridge, MA: Harvard University Press, 1998.

Blassingame, John W. *The Slave Community: Plantation Life in the Antebellum South.* Rev. ed., New York: Oxford University Press, 1979.

Bloch, Marc. "From the Royal Court to the Court of Rome: The Suit of the Serfs of Rosny-sous-Bois." In *Change in Medieval Society: Europe North of the Alps, 1050–1500,* ed. Sylvia L. Thrupp, pp. 3–13. New York: Appleton-Century-Crofts, 1964.

Boswell, John. *The Kindness of Strangers: The Abandonment of Children in Western Europe from Late Antiquity to the Renaissance.* 1988. Repr., Chicago: University of Chicago Press, 1998.

Bourin, Monique. *Villages médiévaux en Bas-Languedoc: Genèse d'une sociabilité, Xe – XIVe siècles.* Collection Chemins de la mémoire. 2 vols. Paris: L'Harmattan, 1987.

Bouwsma, William J. *A Usable Past: Essays in European Cultural History.* Berkeley: University of California Press, 1990.

Bowden, Betsy. "A Modest Proposal, Relating Four Millennia of Proverb Collections to Chemistry within the Human Brain." *Journal of American Folklore* 109 (1996): 440–449.

Braet, Herman. " 'A Thing Most Brutish': The Image of the Rustic in Old French Literature." In Sweeney, *Agriculture in the Middle Ages*, pp. 191–204.

Briscoe, Marianne G., and John C. Coldewey, eds. *Contexts for Early English Drama.* Bloomington: Indiana University Press, 1989.

Britnell, Richard, ed. *Pragmatic Literacy, East and West, 1200–1330.* Woodbridge: Boydell, 1997.

—. "Pragmatic Literacy in Latin Christendom." In Britnell, *Pragmatic Literacy, East and West*, pp. 3–24.

Brooks, Christopher W., and Michael Lobban, eds. *Communities and Courts in Britain, 1150–1900.* London: Hambledon, 1997.

Burke, Peter. *Popular Culture in Early Modern Europe.* New York: New York University Press, 1978.

Cam, Helen M. *Magna Carta: Event or Document?* Selden Society Lecture 1965. London: Quaritch, 1965.

Campbell, Bruce M.S., and Ricardo A. Godoy. "Commonfield Agriculture: The Andes and Medieval England Compared." In *Making the Commons Work: Theory, Practice, and Policy*, ed. Daniel W. Bromley, pp. 99–127. San Francisco: ICS Press, 1992.

Carpenter, David A. "English Peasants in Politics, 1258–1267." *Past and Present* 136 (1992): 3–42.

Carruthers, Mary. *The Book of Memory: A Study of Memory in Medieval Culture.* Cambridge Studies in Medieval Literature 10. Cambridge: Cambridge University Press, 1990.

Chambers, E.K. *The English Folk-Play.* Oxford: Clarendon Press, 1933.

Clanchy, Michael T. *From Memory to Written Record: England, 1066–1307.* 2nd ed., Oxford: Blackwell, 1993.

Clark, Cecily. "English Personal Names ca. 650–1300: Some Prosopographical Bearings." *Medieval Prosopography* 8 (1987): 31–60.

—. "Women's Names in Post-Conquest England: Observations and Speculations." *Speculum* 53 (1978): 223–251.

Clark, Elaine. "Debt Litigation in a Late Medieval English Vill." In Raftis, *Pathways to Medieval Peasants*, pp. 247–279.

Coclanis, Peter A. "Agriculture as History." *Historically Speaking* 4.2 (November 2002): 3–4.

Cohn, Samuel K., Jr. *The Cult of Remembrance and the Black Death: Six Renaissance Cities in Central Italy*. Baltimore: Johns Hopkins University Press, 1992.

Coldewey, John C. "Some Economic Aspects of the Late Medieval Drama." In Briscoe and Coldewey, *Contexts for Early English Drama*, pp. 77–101.

Cook, G.H. *The English Mediaeval Parish Church*. 2nd ed., London: Phoenix House, 1955.

Dance, E.H. *History the Betrayer: A Study in Bias*. London: Hutchinson, 1960.

Daniell, Christopher. *Death and Burial in Medieval England, 1066–1550*. London: Routledge, 1997.

Darnton, Robert. *The Great Cat Massacre and Other Episodes in French Cultural History*. New York: Vintage Books, 1985.

Davies, Wendy. *Small Worlds: The Village Community in Early Medieval Brittany*. Berkeley: University of California Press, 1988.

Davis, Natalie Zemon. *Fiction in the Archives: Pardon Tales and Their Tellers in Sixteenth-Century France*. The Harry Camp Lectures at Stanford University. Stanford: Stanford University Press, 1987.

—. *Society and Culture in Early Modern France*. Stanford: Stanford University Press, 1975.

D'Avray, D.L. *Medieval Marriage Sermons: Mass Communication in a Culture without Print*. Oxford: Oxford University Press, 2001.

—. *The Preaching of the Friars: Sermons Diffused From Paris Before 1300*. Oxford: Clarendon Press, 1985.

Deetz, James. *In Small Things Forgotten: An Archaeology of Early American Life*. Rev. ed., New York: Anchor Books, 1996.

DeWindt, Edwin B. *Land and People in Holywell-cum-Needingworth: Structures of Tenure and Patterns of Social Organization in an East Midlands Village, 1252–1457*. Studies and Texts 22. Toronto: Pontifical Institute of Mediaeval Studies, 1972.

—, ed. *The Salt of Common Life: Individuality and Choice in the Medieval Town, Countryside, and Church: Essays Presented to J. Ambrose Raftis*. Studies in Medieval Culture 36. Kalamazoo: Medieval Institute Publications, 1995.

Dozer-Rabedeau, Jane B. "*Rusticus*: Folk Hero of Thirteenth-Century Picard Drama." In Sweeney, *Agriculture in the Middle Ages,* pp. 205–226.

Duby, Georges. *Rural Economy and Country Life in the Medieval West*. Trans. Cynthia Postan. Columbia: University of South Carolina Press, 1968.

Duffy, Eamon. *The Stripping of the Altars: Traditional Religion in England, c.1400–c.1580*. New Haven: Yale University Press, 1992.

Dutton, Paul Edward. "Thunder and Hail over the Carolingian Countryside." In Sweeney, *Agriculture in the Middle Ages*, pp. 111–137.

Dyer, Christopher. *Everyday Life in Medieval England*. 1994. Repr., London: Hambledon and London, 2000.

—. *Making a Living in the Middle Ages: The People of Britain, 850–1520*. The New Economic History of Britain. New Haven: Yale University Press, 2002.

—. *Standards of Living in the Later Middle Ages: Social Change in England, c. 1200–1520*. Cambridge Medieval Textbooks. Cambridge: Cambridge University Press, 1989.

Evans, Ralph. "Merton College's Control of its Tenants at Thorncroft, 1270–1349." In Razi and Smith, *Medieval Society and the Manor Court*, 199–259.

Ewen, C. L'Estrange. *A History of Surnames of the British Isles; A Concise Account of Their Origin, Evolution, Etymology, and Legal Status*. 1931. Repr., Baltimore: Genealogical Pub. Co., 1968.

Faith, Rosamond. *The English Peasantry and the Growth of Lordship*. Studies in the Early History of Britain. London: Leicester University Press, 1997.

Farmer, Sharon. *Surviving Poverty in Medieval Paris: Gender, Ideology and the Daily Lives of the Poor*. Conjunctions of Religion and Power in the Medieval Past. Ithaca: Cornell University Press, 2002.

Feierman, Steven. *Peasant Intellectuals: Anthropology and History in Tanzania*. Madison: University of Wisconsin Press, 1990.

Fentress, James, and Chris Wickham. *Social Memory*. New Perspectives on the Past. Oxford: Blackwell, 1992.

Fichtenau, Heinrich. *Living in the Tenth Century: Mentalities and Social Orders*. Trans. Patrick J. Geary. Chicago: University of Chicago Press, 1991.

Franklin, Peter. "Normans, Saints, and Politics: Forename-choice among Fourteenth-Century Gloucestershire Peasants." *Local Population Studies* 36 (1986): 19–26.

—. "Politics in Manorial Court Rolls: The Tactics, Social Composition, and Aims of a pre-1381 Peasant Movement." In Razi and Smith, *Medieval Society and the Manor Court*, pp. 162–198.

Freedman, Paul H. *Images of the Medieval Peasant*. Figurae. Stanford: Stanford University Press, 1999.

Fromm, Erich, and Michael Maccoby. *Social Character in a Mexican Village: A Sociopsychoanalytic Study*. Englewood Cliffs, NJ: Prentice-Hall, 1970.

Fussell, G.E., and K.R. Fussell. *The English Countrywoman: A Farmhouse Social History, A.D. 1500–1900*. London: Melrose, 1953.

Geertz, Clifford. *The Interpretation of Cultures*. New York: Basic Books, 1973.

—. *Local Knowledge: Further Essays in Interpretive Anthropology*. New York: Basic Books, 1983.

Genovese, Eugene. *Roll, Jordan, Roll: The World the Slaves Made*. New York: Pantheon Books, 1974.

Gies, Frances, and Joseph Gies. *Life in a Medieval Village*. New York: Harper and Row, 1990.

Giesey, Ralph E. "Inaugural Aspects of French Royal Ceremonials." In Bak, *Coronations*, pp. 35–45.

Ginzburg, Carlo. *The Cheese and the Worms: The Cosmos of a Sixteenth-Century Miller*. Trans. John Tedeschi and Anne Tedeschi. 1980. Repr., New York: Penguin Books, 1982.

—. *The Night Battles: Witchcraft and Agrarian Cults in the Sixteenth and Seventeenth Centuries*. Trans. John Tedeschi and Anne Tedeschi. New York: Penguin Books, 1985.

Given, James B. *Inquisition and Medieval Society: Power, Discipline and Resistance in Languedoc*. Ithaca: Cornell University Press, 1997.

—. *State and Society in Medieval Europe: Gwynedd and Languedoc under Outside Rule*. Wilder House Series in Politics, History, and Culture. Ithaca: Cornell University Press, 1990.

Goheen, Robert B. "Peasant Politics? Village Community and the Crown in Fifteenth-Century England." *American Historical Review* 96 (1991): 42–62.

Goldberg, P.J.P. *Women, Work and Life Cycle in a Medieval Economy: Women in York and Yorkshire, c. 1300–1520*. Oxford: Clarendon Press, 1992.

Goodich, Michael, ed. *Voices From the Bench: The Narratives of Lesser Folk in Medieval Trials*. The New Middle Ages. New York: Palgrave Macmillan, 2006.

Górecki, Piotr. *A Local Society in Transition: The Henryków Book and Related Documents*. Studies and Texts 155. Toronto: Pontifical Institute of Mediaeval Studies, 2007.

Gottfried, Robert S. *The Black Death: Natural and Human Disaster in Medieval Europe*. New York: Free Press; London: Collier Macmillan, 1983.

Guenée, Bernard. *States and Rulers in Later Medieval Europe*. Trans. Juliet Vale. Oxford: Basil Blackwell, 1985.

Gunn, Steven, and Antheun Janse, eds. *The Court as a Stage: England and the Low Countries in the Later Middle Ages*. Woodbridge: Boydell, 2006.

Gurevich, Aron. *Historical Anthropology of the Middle Ages*. Ed. Jana Howlett. Chicago: University of Chicago Press, 1992.

—. "Medieval Culture and *Mentalité* According to the New French Historiography." In Gurevich, *Historical Anthropology of the Middle Ages*, ed. Howlett, pp. 21–49.

—. *Medieval Popular Culture: Problems of Belief and Perception*. Trans. János M. Bak and Paul A. Hollingsworth. Cambridge Studies in Oral and Literate Culture 14. Cambridge: Cambridge University Press; Paris: Maison des sciences de l'homme, 1988.

Hanawalt, Barbara A. "Medieval English Women in Rural and Urban Domestic Space." *Dumbarton Oaks Papers* 52 (1998): 19–26.

—. *The Ties that Bound: Peasant Families in Medieval England*. New York: Oxford University Press, 1986.

Harrison, Christopher. "Manor Courts and the Governance of Tudor England." In Brooks and Lobban, *Communities and Courts in Britain*, pp. 43–59.

Harvey, P.D.A. "English Estate Records, 1250–1330." In Britnell, *Pragmatic Literacy, East and West*, pp. 107–118.

—. *Manorial Records*. Archives and the User 5. London: British Records Association, 1984.

—. *A Medieval Oxfordshire Village: Cuxham, 1240 to 1400*. Oxford Historical Series, 2nd Series. London: Oxford University Press, 1965.

Hawkins, Duncan. "The Black Death and the New London Cemeteries of 1348." *Antiquity* 64 (1990): 637–642.

Herlihy, David. *The Black Death and the Transformation of the West.* Ed. Samuel K. Cohn, Jr. Cambridge, MA: Harvard University Press, 1997.

—. *Medieval Households.* Studies in Cultural History. Cambridge, MA: Harvard University Press, 1985.

Hilton, Rodney. *Class Conflict and the Crisis of Feudalism: Essays in Medieval Social History.* History Series 28. London: Hambledon, 1985.

—. *The Economic Development of Some Leicestershire Estates in the 14th & 15th Centuries.* Oxford Historical Series 17. London: Oxford University Press, 1947.

—. *The English Peasantry in the Later Middle Ages: The Ford Lectures for 1973 and Related Studies.* Oxford: Clarendon Press, 1975.

Hogan, M. Patricia. "The Labor of Their Days: Work in the Medieval Village." *Studies in Medieval and Renaissance History,* n.s. 8 (1986): 75–186.

—. "The Slight to Honor: Slander and Wrongful Prosecution in Five Medieval Villages." *Studies in Medieval and Renaissance History,* n.s. 12 (1991): 3–42.

Homans, George. *English Villagers of the Thirteenth Century.* 1941. Repr., New York: Norton, 1975.

Horrox, Rosemary, ed. and trans. *The Black Death.* Manchester Medieval Sources Series. Manchester: Manchester University Press, 1994.

Howe, John, and Michael Wolfe, eds. *Inventing Medieval Landscapes: Senses of Place in Western Europe.* Gainesville: University Press of Florida, 2002.

Howell, Cicely. *Land, Family and Inheritance in Transition: Kibworth Harcourt, 1280–1700.* Cambridge: Cambridge University Press, 1983.

Hudson, John. *The Formation of the English Common Law: Law and Society in England from the Norman Conquest to Magna Carta.* Medieval World. London: Longman, 1996.

Hufton, Olwen. *The Prospect Before Her: A History of Women in Western Europe.* Vol. 1: *1500–1800.* New York: Knopf, 1996.

Hunnisett, R.F. *The Medieval Coroner.* Cambridge Studies in English Legal History. Cambridge: Cambridge University Press, 1961.

Hyams, Paul R. *Rancor and Reconciliation in Medieval England.* Conjunctions of Religion and Power in the Medieval Past. Ithaca: Cornell University Press, 2003.

—. "What Did Edwardian Villagers Understand by Law?" In Razi and Smith, *Medieval Society and the Manor Court*, pp. 69–102.

Ingram, Martin. "Juridical Folklore in England Illustrated by Rough Music." In Brooks and Lobban, *Communities and Courts in Britain*, pp. 61–82.

Jaritz, Gerhard. "The Material Culture of the Peasantry in the Late Middle Ages: 'Image' and 'Reality'." In Sweeney, *Agriculture in the Middle Ages*, pp. 163–188.

Jewell, Helen M. *English Local Administration in the Middle Ages*. New York: Barnes and Noble, 1972.

—. "Women at the Courts of the Manor of Wakefield, 1348–50." *Northern History* 26 (1990): 59–81.

Jones, Andrew. "Harvest Customs and Labourers' Perquisites in Southern England, 1150–1350: The Corn Harvest." *Agricultural History Review* 25 (1977): 14–22.

—. "Harvest Customs and Labourers' Perquisites in Southern England, 1150–1350: The Hay Harvest." *Agricultural History Review* 25 (1977): 98–107.

Kapferer, Bruce. "The Ritual Process and the Problem of Reflexivity in Sinhalese Demon Exorcisms." In MacAloon, *Rite, Drama, Festival, Spectacle*, pp. 179–207.

Kelly, Susan. "Anglo-Saxon Lay Society and the Written Word." In McKitterick, *The Uses of Literacy*, pp. 36–62.

Kerridge, Eric. *The Common Fields of England*. Manchester: Manchester University Press, 1992.

Kipling, Gordon. *Enter the King: Theatre, Liturgy, and Ritual in the Medieval Civic Triumph*. Oxford: Clarendon Press, 1998.

Kroll, Jerome, and Bernard S. Bachrach. *The Mystic Mind: The Psychology of Medieval Mystics and Ascetics*. New York: Routledge, 2005.

Kuper, Adam. *Culture: The Anthropologists' Account*. Cambridge, MA: Harvard University Press, 1999.

Kupperman, Joel. *Learning From Asian Philosophy*. New York: Oxford University Press, 1999.

Langdon, John. "Agriculture, Animal Husbandry, and Forestry." In Mantello and Rigg, *Medieval Latin*, pp. 459–464.

Lawrence, C.H. *Medieval Monasticism: Forms of Religious Life in Western Europe in the Middle Ages*. 3rd ed., New York: Longman, 2001.

Le Roy Ladurie, Emmanuel. *Montaillou: The Promised Land of Error*. Trans. Barbara Bray. New York: Braziller, 1978.

Levack, Brian, Edward Muir, Michael Maas, and Meredith Veldman. *The West: Encounters & Transformations*. 2 volumes. New York: Pearson Longman, 2004.

Lozovsky, Natalia. *"The Earth Is Our Book": Geographical Knowledge in the Latin West, ca. 400–1000*. Recentiores. Ann Arbor: University of Michigan Press, 2000.

Lynch, Joseph H. *The Medieval Church: A Brief History*. London: Longman, 1992.

MacAloon, John J., ed. *Rite, Drama, Festival, Spectacle: Rehearsals toward a Theory of Cultural Performance*. Philadelphia: Institute for the Study of Human Issues, 1984.

Mantello, F.A.C., and A.G. Rigg, eds. *Medieval Latin: An Introduction and Bibliographical Guide*. Washington, DC: Catholic University of America Press, 1996.

Marshall, Richard K. *The Local Merchants of Prato: Small Entrepreneurs in the Late Medieval Economy*. The Johns Hopkins University Studies in Historical and Political Science, 117th Ser. Baltimore: Johns Hopkins University Press, 1999.

Martin, G.H. *The Early Court Rolls of the Borough of Ipswich*. University College of Leicester, Department of English Local History, Occasional papers 5. Leicester: University College, 1954.

Martin, Jacqueline, and Willmar Sauter. *Understanding Theatre: Performance Analysis in Theory and Practice*. Acta Universitatis Stockholmiensis: Stockholm Theatre Studies 3. Stockholm: Almqvist and Wiksell, 1995.

Masschaele, James. *Peasants, Merchants, and Markets: Inland Trade in Medieval England, 1150–1350*. New York: St Martin's Press, 1997.

McCloskey, Donald N. "English Open Fields as Behavior Towards Risk." *Research in Economic History* 1 (1976): 124–170.

McIntosh, Marjorie K. *Autonomy and Community: The Royal Manor of Havering, 1200–1500*. Cambridge Studies in Medieval Life and Thought, 4th Ser., 5. Cambridge: Cambridge University Press, 1986.

—. *A Community Transformed: The Manor and Liberty of Havering, 1500–1620*. Cambridge Studies in Population, Economy, and Society in Past Time 16. Cambridge: Cambridge University Press, 1991.

—. *Controlling Misbehavior in England, 1370–1600*. Cambridge Studies in Population, Economy, and Society in Past Time 34. Cambridge: Cambridge University Press, 1998.

—. "The Diversity of Social Capital in English Communities, 1300–1640 (with a Glance at Modern Nigeria)." *Journal of Interdisciplinary History* 29.3 (1999): 459–490.

McKitterick, Rosamond, ed. *The Uses of Literacy in Early Mediaeval Europe.* 1990. Repr., Cambridge: Cambridge University Press, 1995.

Mieder, Wolfgang, and Alan Dundes, eds. *The Wisdom of Many: Essays on the Proverb.* Garland Folklore Casebooks 1. New York: Garland, 1981.

Miller, Edward, and John Hatcher. *Medieval England: Rural Society and Economic Change, 1086–1348.* Social and Economic History of England. London: Longman, 1978.

Mintz, Sidney W., and Richard Price. *The Birth of African-American Culture: An Anthropological Perspective.* Boston: Beacon Press, 1992.

Moore, Ellen Wedemeyer. *The Fairs of Medieval England: An Introductory Study.* Studies and Texts 72. Toronto: Pontifical Institute of Mediaeval Studies, 1985.

Muchembled, Robert. *Popular Culture and Elite Culture in France, 1400–1750.* Trans. Lydia Cochrane. Baton Rouge: Louisiana State University Press, 1985.

Muir, Edward. Introduction. In *The Renaissance in the Fields: Family Memoirs of a Fifteenth-Century Tuscan Peasant,* ed. Duccio Balestracci, trans. Paolo Squatriti and Betsy Merideth, pp. ix–xv. University Park: Pennsylvania State University Press, 1999.

—, and Guido Ruggiero, eds. *Microhistory and the Lost Peoples of Europe.* Trans. Eren Branch. Selections from Quaderni storici. Baltimore: Johns Hopkins University Press, 1991.

Neilson, Nellie. *Customary Rents.* Oxford: Studies in Social and Legal History, 1910.

—. *Medieval Agrarian Economy.* Berkshire Studies in European History. New York: H. Holt and Co., 1936.

Nirenberg, David. *Communities of Violence: Persecution of Minorities in the Middle Ages.* Princeton: Princeton University Press, 1996.

Oexle, Otto Gerhard. "Peace Through Conspiracy." In *Ordering Medieval Society: Perspectives on Intellectual and Practical Modes of Shaping Social Relations,* ed. Bernhard Jussen, trans. Pamela Selwyn, pp. 285–322. The Middle Ages Series. Philadelphia: University of Pennsylvania Press, 2001.

Olson, Sherri. *A Chronicle of All That Happens: Voices from the Village Court in Medieval England.* Studies and Texts 124. Toronto: Pontifical Institute of Mediaeval Studies, 1996.

—. " 'Families Have Their Fate and Periods': Varieties of Family Experience in the Pre-Industrial Village." In DeWindt, *The Salt of Common Life,* pp. 409–448.

—. "Family Linkages and the Structure of the Local Elite in the Medieval and Early Modern Village." *Medieval Prosopography* 13 (1992): 53–82.

—. "Jurors of the Village Court: Local Leadership Before and After the Plague in Ellington, Huntingdonshire." *Journal of British Studies* 30 (1991): 237–256.

Orwin, C.S., and C.S. Orwin. *The Open Fields*. 3rd ed., Oxford: Clarendon Press, 1967.

Palmer, Robert C. *Selling the Church: The English Parish in Law, Commerce, and Religion, 1350–1550*. Studies in Legal History. Chapel Hill: University of North Carolina Press, 2002.

Parkes, Malcolm B. "The Literacy of the Laity." In *The Mediaeval World*, ed. D. Daiches and A. Thorlby, pp. 555–577. Literature and Western Civilization 2. London: Aldus, 1973.

Pegg, Mark Gregory. *The Corruption of Angels: The Great Inquisition of 1245–1246*. Princeton: Princeton University Press, 2001.

Phythian-Adams, Charles. "Ceremony and the Citizen: The Communal Year at Coventry, 1450–1550." In *Crisis and Order in English Towns, 1500–1700: Essays in Urban History*, ed. Peter Clark and Paul Slack, pp. 57–85. Toronto: University of Toronto Press, 1972.

Pieper, Josef. *Leisure, the Basis of Culture*. Trans. Alexander Dru. 1952. Repr., New York: New American Library, 1963.

Platt, Colin. *The Parish Churches of Medieval England*. London: Secker and Warburg, 1981.

Pollock, Frederick, and Frederic William Maitland. *The History of English Law before the Time of Edward I*. 2 vols. 2nd ed., 1898. Repr., Cambridge: Cambridge University Press, 1968.

Poos, Larry R. "Peasant 'Biographies' from Medieval England." In *Medieval Lives and the Historian: Studies in Medieval Prosopography*, ed. Neithard Bulst and Jean-Philippe Genet, pp. 201–214. Kalamazoo: Medieval Institute Publications, 1986.

Postan, Michael M. *Essays on Medieval Agriculture and General Problems of the Medieval Economy*. Cambridge: Cambridge University Press, 1973.

—. *The Famulus: The Estate Labourer in the XIIth and XIIIth Centuries*. Economic History Review Supplement 2. London: Published for the Economic History Review at Cambridge University Press, 1954.

—. *The Medieval Economy and Society: An Economic History of Britain in the Middle Ages*. London: Weidenfeld and Nicolson, 1972.

Potter, Jack M., May N. Diaz, and George M. Foster. *Peasant Society: A Reader*. The Little, Brown Series in Anthropology. Boston: Little, Brown and Co., 1967.

Power, Eileen. "The Position of Women." In *The Legacy of the Middle Ages*, ed. C.G. Crump and E.F. Jacob, pp. 401–433. Oxford: Clarendon Press, 1926.

Raboteau, Albert J. *Slave Religion: The "Invisible Institution" in the Antebellum South*. 1978. Updated ed., New York: Oxford University Press, 2004.

Raftis, J.A. "The Concentration of Responsibility in Five Villages." *Mediaeval Studies* 28 (1966): 92–118.

—. *Early Tudor Godmanchester: Survivals and New Arrivals*. Studies and Texts 97. Toronto: Pontifical Institute of Mediaeval Studies, 1990.

—, ed. *Pathways to Medieval Peasants*. Papers in Mediaeval Studies 2. Toronto: Pontifical Institute of Mediaeval Studies, 1981.

—. *Peasant Economic Development within the English Manorial System*. Montreal: McGill-Queen's University Press, 1996.

—. *A Small Town in Late Mediaeval England: Godmanchester, 1278–1400*. Studies and Texts 53. Toronto: Pontifical Institute of Mediaeval Studies, 1982.

—. *Tenure and Mobility: Studies in the Social History of the Mediaeval English Village*. Studies and Texts 8. Toronto: Pontifical Institute of Mediaeval Studies, 1964.

—. *Warboys: Two Hundred Years in the Life of an English Mediaeval Village*. Studies and Texts 29. Toronto: Pontifical Institute of Mediaeval Studies, 1974.

Razi, Zvi. *Life, Marriage and Death in a Medieval Parish: Economy, Society and Demography in Halesowen, 1270–1400*. Past and Present Publications. Cambridge: Cambridge University Press, 1980.

—, and Richard M. Smith, eds. *Medieval Society and the Manor Court*. Oxford: Clarendon Press, 1996.

—, and Richard M. Smith. "The Origins of the English Manorial Court Rolls as a Written Record: A Puzzle." In Razi and Smith, *Medieval Society and the Manor Court*, pp. 36–68.

Reaney, P.H. *A Dictionary of British Surnames*. London: Routledge and Paul, 1958.

—. *The Origin of English Surnames*. New York: Barnes and Noble, 1967.

Redfield, Robert. *The Folk Culture of Yucatan*. The University of Chicago Publications in Anthropology: Social Anthropology Series. Chicago: University of Chicago Press, 1941.

Reynolds, Susan. *Ideas and Solidarities of the Medieval Laity: England and Western Europe*. Aldershot: Variorum, 1995.

—. *Kingdoms and Communities in Western Europe, 900–1300*. 2nd ed., Oxford: Clarendon Press; New York: Oxford University Press, 1997.

Riché, Pierre. *Daily Life in the World of Charlemagne*. With expanded footnotes. Trans. Jo Ann McNamara. The Middle Ages Series. Philadelphia: University of Pennsylvania Press, 1988.

Rosenthal, Joel T. *Telling Tales: Sources and Narration in Late Medieval England*. University Park: Pennsylvania State University Press, 2003.

Sabean, David Warren. *Power in the Blood: Popular Culture and Village Discourse in Early Modern Germany*. Cambridge: Cambridge University Press, 1984.

Samuel, Raphael. *Theatres of Memory*. Vol. 1: *Past and Present in Contemporary Culture*. London: Verso, 1994.

Schmitt, Jean-Claude. *Ghosts in the Middle Ages: The Living and the Dead in Medieval Society*. Trans. Teresa Lavender Fagan. Chicago: University of Chicago Press, 1998.

—. *The Holy Greyhound: Guinefort, Healer of Children since the Thirteenth Century*. Trans. Martin Thom. Cambridge Studies in Oral and Literate Culture 6. Cambridge: Cambridge University Press; Paris: Maison des sciences de l'homme, 1983.

Schofield, Phillipp. *Peasant and Community in Medieval England, 1200–1500*. Medieval Culture and Society. New York: Palgrave Macmillan, 2003.

Searle, Eleanor. "Seigneurial Control of Women's Marriage: The Antecedents and Function of Merchet in England." *Past and Present* 82 (1979): 3–43.

Shanin, Teodor, ed. *Peasants and Peasant Societies: Selected Readings*. 2nd ed., Oxford: Blackwell, 1987.

Sharpe, Richard. "Latin in Everyday Life." In Mantello and Rigg, *Medieval Latin*, pp. 315–341.

Shinners, John, ed. *Medieval Popular Religion, 1000–1500: A Reader*. Peterborough, ON: Broadview, 1997.

Smith, Richard M. " 'Modernization' and the Corporate Medieval Village Community in England: Some Sceptical Reflections." In *Explorations in Historical Geography: Interpretative Essays*, ed. Alan R.H. Baker and Derek Gregory, pp. 140–179. Cambridge Studies in Historical Geography 5. Cambridge: Cambridge University Press, 1984.

Smith-Bannister, Scott. *Names and Naming Patterns in England, 1538–1700*. Oxford Historical Monographs. Oxford: Clarendon Press; New York: Oxford University Press, 1997.

Smoller, Laura A. "Miracle, Memory, and Meaning in the Canonization of Vincent Ferrer, 1453–1454." *Speculum* 73 (1998): 429–454.

Southern, Richard. *The Making of the Middle Ages*. 1953. Repr., New Haven: Yale University Press, 1992.

Stern, Steve J. *The Secret History of Gender: Women, Men, and Power in Late Colonial Mexico*. Chapel Hill: University of North Carolina Press, 1995.

Stock, Brian. *The Implications of Literacy: Written Language and Models of Interpretation in the Eleventh and Twelfth Centuries*. Princeton: Princeton University Press, 1983.

Stone, David. *Decision-Making in Medieval Agriculture*. Oxford: Oxford University Press, 2005.

Strayer, Joseph R. "The Historical Experience of Nation-Building in Europe." In *Medieval Statecraft and the Perspectives of History: Essays by J.R. Strayer*, pp. 341–348. Princeton: Princeton University Press, 1971.

Sweeney, Del, ed. *Agriculture in the Middle Ages: Technology, Practice, and Representation*. The Middle Ages Series. Philadelphia: University of Pennsylvania Press, 1995.

Thirsk, Joan. *The Rural Economy of England*. History Series 25. London: Hambledon, 1984.

Vardi, Liana. "Imagining the Harvest in Early Modern Europe." *American Historical Review* 101 (1996): 1356–1397.

The Victoria History of the County of Huntingdon. Ed. W.W. Page, Granville Proby, and S. Inskip Ladds. The Victoria History of the Counties of England. 3 vols. London: St Catherine Press, 1926–1936.

Ward, Benedicta. *Miracles and the Medieval Mind: Theory, Record and Event, 1000–1215*. The Middle Ages Series. Rev. ed., Philadelphia: University of Pennsylvania Press, 1987.

Wenzel, Siegfried. *Macaronic Sermons: Bilingualism and Preaching in Late-Medieval England*. Recentiores. Ann Arbor: University of Michigan Press, 1994.

White, A.B. *Self-Government at the King's Command: A Study in the Beginnings of English Democracy*. Minneapolis: University of Minnesota Press, 1933.

White, Stephen D. "Proposing the Ordeal and Avoiding It: Strategy and Power in Western French Litigation, 1050–1100." In Bisson, *Cultures of Power*, pp. 89–123.

Wood, Ellen Meiksins. *Peasant-Citizen and Slave: The Foundations of Athenian Democracy*. London: Verso, 1988.

Yates, Frances. *The Art of Memory*. Chicago: University of Chicago Press, 1966.

Ziolkowski, Jan M. *Fairy Tales from Before Fairy Tales: The Medieval Latin Past of Wonderful Lies*. Ann Arbor: University of Michigan Press, 2007.

Index